Dear Harry, Love Bess

Dear Harry Love Bess

Bess Truman's Letters to Harry Truman 1919–1943

Clifton Truman Daniel

Truman State University Press

Cover images: Bess Wallace, ca. 1917 (TL 82-56), and excerpt from Bess Wallace to
Harry Truman, March 16, 1919 (TL 3-16-19 3).

Cover design: Teresa Wheeler

Library of Congress Cataloging-in-Publication Data

Daniel, Clifton Truman, 1957–
Dear Harry, love Bess : Bess Truman's letters to Harry Truman, 1919–1943 / Clifton
Truman Daniel.
  p. cm.
Includes index.
ISBN 978-1-935503-26-2 (hardback : alk. paper)
ISBN 978-1-935503-25-5 (pbk. : alk. paper)
ISBN 978-1-61248-009-1 (electronic)
1. Truman, Bess Wallace—Correspondence. 2. Presidents' spouses—United States—
Biography. 3. Truman, Harry S., 1884–1972—Family. 4. Presidents—United
States—Biography. 5. Truman family. I. Truman, Bess Wallace. II. Title.
E814.1.T68D36 2011
973.918092—dc22

                                                                    2011006063

For Polly, Aimee, Wesley, and Gates.

Contents

Illustrations

Preface

My grandparents, Harry and Bess Truman, had one of the great marriages in American politics, a rock-solid partnership based on shared values, mutual respect, and love. It was the foundation for one of the most successful, highly regarded presidencies in United States history. Of course, you'd never know that from my grandmother.

Grandpa was an open book. He'd tell you exactly what was on his mind. Often, he wrote it down. In addition to his public papers, he preserved scads of receipts, notes, diaries, and other private papers, including 1,316 letters that he wrote to my grandmother between 1910 and 1959. He firmly believed that the American public had the right to know and learn from the mind of their president.

My grandmother, on the other hand, had not been the American public's president. She thought her business was her own damn business and nobody else's.

She was naturally shy and hated having her picture taken. In most of the photos from the 1944 Democratic Convention, which put Grandpa on the ticket with President Franklin Delano Roosevelt, Grandpa and my mother, Margaret, are grinning from ear to ear, waving and shaking hands with everyone in sight. My grandmother is just sitting there, the expression on her face suggesting she has just smelled something horrendous.

Despite being born at the top of Independence, Missouri, society, she was modest and self-effacing. And her view on the role of the political wife ran contrary to that of her predecessor, the gregarious and outspoken Eleanor Roosevelt. "A woman's place in public," my grandmother said, "is to sit beside her husband, be silent, and be sure her hat is on straight."

As first lady, she discontinued the regular press conferences instituted by Mrs. Roosevelt and issued only a succinct biography. Her favorite interview method thereafter was through written questions. Her most frequent answer, in print or in person, was "No comment."

A good deal of this reticence was due to tragedy. Her father, David Willock Wallace, had committed suicide in 1903, when my grandmother was eighteen. She adored him, and his death was sudden, unexpected, heartbreaking, and in that day and age, shameful. She never spoke of him. What other thoughts and feelings she had were reserved for family and close friends, and she was determined to keep it that way.

During their courtship and marriage, my grandparents must have exchanged more than 2,600 letters. That's a guess because the Truman Library has only about half of the correspondence—Grandpa's half. Most of her half is gone.

One evening close to Christmas in 1955, Grandpa came home from his office in Kansas City and found my grandmother sitting in the living room burning stacks of her letters in the fireplace.

"Bess!" he said in alarm. "What are you doing? Think of history!"

"Oh, I have," she said and tossed in another stack.

Fortunately, she did not pitch them all into the fire. Thanks to what Ray Geselbracht, special assistant to the director of the Truman Library, called "poor housekeeping," we know that at 10:20 p.m. on the evening of July 15, 1923, while Grandpa was at his annual National Guard encampment, my thirty-eight-year-old grandmother was in bed, lonely and unprotected, waging war on the local insect population, species undetermined.

"There was a big black bug on my bed when I turned the sheet down and I had to kill it myself," she wrote indignantly. "But that wasn't the first time I had wished for you."

This and the other 184 letters my grandmother overlooked were not tied in neat bundles and squirreled away in a trunk or box. Most had been pushed to the backs of desk drawers or tucked between the pages of books as bookmarks. Truman Library archivists found them in the early 1980s while carrying out an inventory of the contents of my grandparent's home. Liz Safly, the library's recently retired research room supervisor, took them to the library in the trunk of her car. "Just think what would have happened if I'd had an accident," she said.

The letters span twenty years, from 1923, when my grandparents were newly married and my grandfather was beginning his political career as eastern judge of Jackson County, Missouri (county judges are actually county administrators in Missouri), to 1943, when he was a U.S. senator a year away from being nominated for vice president. There is also a single letter from March 1919, written by Grandma to Grandpa while he was still overseas following the end of World War I.

The Bess Truman I knew was a little old lady. She was kindly, as long as you didn't drop your marbles down her furnace grates or climb up on the roof of the house, but she didn't say much beyond, "How was your trip?" "Play with that outside!" or "Where's your mother?" The Bess

Truman I discovered in her letters was a talker. She could go on for pages reporting family and political news, making wry observations about people and events, or just recounting shopping, eating lunch, or the amount of ironing she had to do.

She was also a worrier, fretting endlessly about everyone's health, my mother's and grandfather's in particular. At the start of the July 1923 National Guard encampment, when Grandpa reported that he'd stood a perfect physical exam, she wrote back that she was glad to hear it but wanted to know just what the camp doctor said about his tonsils. "Bet he didn't even look at them," she grumbled.

Yet she could blithely ignore her own woes. During that same 1925 encampment, she sprained her foot. How, I don't know, but I'll bet you my mother had something to do with it. Despite the fact that it must have really hurt, she put off having it treated. "I am very sorry about your foot," Grandpa wrote to her in admonishment. "If you'd just be as anxious to take care of yourself as you are to doctor me and the young lady, you'd be all right nine times in ten. You should have had the doctor when your foot first hurt you."

About many things, good and bad, she had a sense of humor. While removing the wrapping from her foot, which she did herself, she reported using up "most of the benzine in the county." Two years earlier, when it took her dentist more than an hour to remove her infected tooth, she said it had worn him out worse than it had her. In 1937, when Grandpa was a U.S. senator, she wrote to him that she wished he'd organize a committee to investigate "the mucilage on the flaps of Gov't envelopes. I have got to get out my tube of glue every time I use one of those brown ones."

Along with her sense of humor came a sharp tongue. When the dentist, Dr. Berry, initially put off removing her tooth in July of 1923 because he said he wanted to consult a colleague, my grandmother figured he was just waiting for "some day when it rains, I reckon, and he can't play golf." In the same letter containing the mucilage committee crack, she reported that she was hoping to catch a cold that was running through the rest of the family so she wouldn't have to attend a luncheon given by "Nutty Mrs. Webb." Days later, when the luncheon had turned out well, she recanted, saying she had done "the poor old gal quite an injustice."

She loved politics and not only expressed her opinion, often negative, but took an active role. She read the papers daily and saved or sent Grandpa all relevant articles and editorials. While he was at camp in 1923, during his tenure as eastern judge of Jackson County, she reported that so many women were clamoring to have their dirt roads oiled that "they must have a league out there." In the summer of 1926, she directly intervened, with the help of Jackson County Democratic boss Tom Pendergast, to keep Grandpa from making an alliance that might have hurt his chances of being elected presiding judge that fall.

More than anything though, what comes through my grandmother's letters is love. When she and Grandpa were apart, they wrote to each other as often as twice a day, usually starting by exulting over a letter received or complaining about one that hadn't arrived.

"I just had your Thursday letter," she wrote on July 19, 1923. "Had been sitting at the front window waiting for the postman for <u>hours</u>."

He came right back with: "I sure raised sand with the adjutant yesterday morning when I didn't get a letter, but it came in the afternoon and boy! how nice it was."

They rose early and stayed up late to write. Letters even invaded my grandmother's dreams. "I was powerfully glad to get your special late last night," she wrote on July 22, 1923. "And then I <u>dreamed</u> that I got still another one, which was <u>very</u> nice as long as it lasted."

If she missed sending a letter, her excuse was thorough ...

"I was so delighted to get that 'special' this morning. It made me sick not to have sent yours that way yesterday— but there wasn't anybody here who could take it to the P.O. (Frank and Fred were both gone all day) and I just felt like I could <u>not</u> make it up town and back and I didn't have enough stamps at home. Sorry as I can be that you won't have even a piece of a letter today for I know how much I would have missed mine."

... or interesting:

"It was so blazing hot last night I didn't have the nerve to keep on enough clothes so I could have a light long enough to write a letter."

But there were few excuses. She couldn't go for very long without touching base and telling him how she felt. "Lots and lots of love," she ended her last letter to him near the finish of his July 1925 encampment,

"and please keep on loving me as hard as ever. You know I just feel as if a large part of me has been gone for the last ten days.
                                   Devotedly, Bess"

Acknowledgments

I'd like to thank my agent, Bob Diforio, for believing in this project and taking it on; Kate Morton Schuler, for transcribing my grandfather's letters while I was busy with my grandmother's; the Truman Library staff—Liz Safly, Randy Sowell, Sam Rushay, and particularly Ray Geselbracht—for encouraging me and doing everything they could to help; and my editor and publisher, Barbara Smith-Mandell and Truman State University Press, not only for publishing these letters but also for helping me present them in the best light.

Editor's Note

My grandparents were busy people. Like those of us today who use e-mail, Facebook, and Twitter, they wrote fast—grammar, spelling, and punctuation be damned. My grandfather could trot out nearly endless sentences that included lists of names, items, or activities without using a single comma. He changed the spelling of people's names, sometimes from one letter to the next. Both he and my grandmother used capital letters whenever it suited them—or not. My grandmother strung together thoughts with dashes and ampersands, often launching into a sentence without the help of the first-person pronoun. Every once in a while, inexplicably, one of them might throw in a semicolon somewhere.

I have left all of this intact. Rather, I should say that I have put it all back, because when I first began transcribing the letters, I could not resist the urge to clean them up. That, according to my editor, was not the best course of action and I agree with her. Like anyone, my grandparents had a unique way of corresponding.

Their handwriting was tough to decipher, Grandpa's especially. His *N*s looked like his *U*s, his *B*s like his *L*s, and his *I*s like his *R*s. If I absolutely could not read something, I put [illegible] after it. If either of my grandparents misspelled a word, I left it as is and followed it with [*sic*]. When they left out a word, I put it in for them with brackets. My grandmother sometimes noted the day and time, but rarely put dates on her letters, so I added these based on postmarks, although occasionally it seemed that the post office had not advanced the date on their postmark stamp.

If I took something out, say a laundry list of my grandfather's daily activities or meals, I put an ellipsis […] in its stead. I only did this with Grandpa's letters because they've been public for nearly thirty years. And I never removed something, be it laundry list or menu, when my grandmother responded to it. For example, in 1923, when he reported every item of a huge dinner he'd eaten on the road to camp, she wrote him back that he'd have to be "pretty strenuous to keep that <u>front down</u>."

⚙ Courtship

For the rest of his life, my grandfather would remember the day he first saw my grandmother. It was 1890 during Sunday school in Independence, Missouri. He was six. She was five. The meeting stirred him so much that he even included mention of it in his memoirs. He fell in love right then and there, and as far as anyone knows, he never looked at another woman.

My grandmother, on the other hand, paid him no attention whatsoever. They went all the way through grade school and high school together, my grandfather carrying a torch and my grandmother completely unaware of it. They were tutored in Latin together and may have occasionally wound up at the same social gatherings, but most often they moved in completely different circles. Grandpa's father, John Truman, was a farmer and livestock trader. My grandmother's father, David Willock Wallace, was a politician, son of a former Independence mayor, and son-in-law of George Porterfield Gates, co-founder of the highly successful Waggoner-Gates Milling Company.

Grandpa was shy and, because of farsightedness and thick glasses, not the least bit athletic. My grandmother was the equal of any boy on the schoolyard. She threw a ball hard and fast, whistled through her teeth, and excelled at tennis and golf. It was widely known that she could hold her own in a fight and possessed a wicked uppercut. In later years—in the White House, in fact—Grandpa gleefully let slip to Clark Clifford that she had been shot put champion at her ladies' finishing school.

In the classroom, however, he could only sit, his chin on his palm and a dreamy smile on his face, mooning at her. He counted it a banner day if she let him carry her books home from school. The only thing she felt in return was kindness and sometimes pity, because he had to work after school.

After graduating from high school in 1901, Grandpa spent two semesters at Spalding's Commercial College in Kansas City, and then when his father suffered serious financial losses speculating on grain futures, took a job as a timekeeper for a railroad construction contractor to help make

Bess at age four, above left, about a year before she met Harry
in Sunday school (TL 62-103), and in 1898, center (TL 62-109).
Harry in 1897, above right (TL 62-412).

Harry in the
first grade,
ca. 1891,
right (TL
62-768).
Harry and
Bess in the
1901 senior
class photo,
below (TL
66-9984).

ends meet. In 1903, he was hired as a clerk at the National Bank of Commerce in Kansas City. Two years later, he moved to the Union National Bank and took a position as a bookkeeper. He earned praise and promotions at both institutions and might have made a career of banking had John Truman not taken over the running of his mother-in-law's six hundred-acre farm in Grandview and called his two sons—Grandpa and his brother, Vivian—home to help.

My grandmother, meanwhile, had her world turned upside down. In many ways, David Wallace was an ideal father—outgoing, intelligent, and generally considered one of the nicest, most thoughtful, and most generous men in Independence. He was a handsome, dashing man with a thick, bushy moustache who rode his huge black horse at the head of every holiday parade. I suspect that were David alive today he might also be described as "being in touch with his inner child." It probably didn't take much for Bess and her three brothers to entice him into a game of tag. My grandmother adored him.

Unfortunately, when it came to his career and his marriage, David Wallace was in over his head. He had wooed and wed Margaret Elizabeth "Madge" Gates, daughter of one of the richest men in town, and for the rest of his life he fought a losing battle to keep her in the style to which she had become accustomed.

He won several solid political appointments, including Jackson County treasurer and deputy surveyor in the Kansas City office of the U.S. Bureau of Customs, but

David Willock Wallace in 1900, above (TL 67-6841). Madge Gates Wallace in 1890, left (TL 82-84).

he never attained higher rank. To keep up appearances, he borrowed heavily, particularly from his father-in-law, which must have been hugely embarrassing because George Gates never thought David to be an ample provider in the first place. And it was never quite enough. Although my grandmother wore the latest fashions and counted the children of the town's gentry among her friends, she could not go to college like many of them because her father simply could not afford to send her.

Bess in 1901 (TL 94-1).

As the debt worsened, David turned increasingly to drink. Never a temperate man, he was now more and more often carried home by friends and deposited, insensate, on his front porch. Madge never said a word to him about any of it. Like most of the women of her time and station, she kept her nose out of her husband's affairs. She even dutifully, and without reproach, nursed him through one hangover after another. She had no idea how far or fast he was sinking.

Early on the morning of June 18, 1903, David arose before dawn, dressed, and went into the bathroom on the second floor of their home at 608 North Delaware. There, he pressed a pistol to his head behind his left ear and pulled the trigger.

My grandmother was heartbroken and, I think, furious with him for the rest of her life. When her friend Mary Paxton ran to her side that morning, my grandmother was in the backyard, pacing in stony silence, dry-eyed, her hands balled into fists at her sides.

Bess and Mary Paxton in 1901 (TL 67-2303).

L to R: Fred, Bess, Frank, and George Wallace, ca. 1905 (TL 82-99).

Madge came apart at the seams. She retreated from society, forever shamed by the stigma. Her father rescued her and her four children, Bess, Frank, George, and Fred. They fled to Colorado Springs for a year, away from their neighbors' scrutiny, then moved into the Gates mansion at 219 North Delaware. My grandmother would call it home for the rest of her life.

Following their return from Colorado, Bess studied literature and history at Barstow, a young ladies' finishing school in Kansas City. At home, she renewed old friendships, played tennis, saw an occasional show, and went on picnics and to parties. She even entertained one or two suitors, but none of these relationships was serious. Not only was she deeply ambivalent about marriage after her father's suicide, but she also had become Madge's full-time companion and sole source of emotional support.

Grandpa, meanwhile, didn't have time for much of anything but plowing, sowing, reaping, tending animals, and repairing equipment. He had enjoyed life as a city bank clerk

Harry plowing a field in a dress shirt and boater (TL 64-100).

Harry's parents, John
and Martha Truman,
in their wedding photo,
right (TL 62-96).

and probably was disap-
pointed by the turn of
events. But as he did with
everything, he went at
farming head-on, deter-
mined to make the best
of it. The Grandview farm
was a whopper for its day,
a square mile of fields, and it took him, his parents, his sister, Mary, several
hired hands, and for a time, his brother, Vivian, to work it. When he did
get free time, he often spent it in Independence with his aunt, Ella Noland,
and his cousins, Nellie and Ethel. Although Grandview was only twenty
miles away, the trek involved varying combinations of buggies, streetcars,
foot travel, and trains that were frequently late, so Grandpa often stayed
overnight, sleeping on the living room couch.

It was during one of his visits that Aunt Ella announced she had a
cake plate that needed to go back to Mrs. Wallace. Grandpa snatched it up
and walked it over to the Wallace house; he rang the bell and my grandmother answered the door.

The Harry Truman she had known in high school had been a pale,
shy, skinny kid with glasses. This Harry Truman still had the glasses, but
he was more than twenty pounds heavier, all of it muscle. He was tanned
and wind-burned from years spent outdoors, and he fairly brimmed with
the self-confidence that comes from mastering a tough job day-in and day-
out. It didn't hurt that he also had been drilling regularly as a member of
the Missouri National Guard. Stunned, she invited him in. Later, when he
asked if he could write to her, maybe visit occasionally, she said yes.

Thus began a nearly nine-year formal courtship. They carried out
most of it by mail, owing to the unreliable mass transit system; although
in 1914, Grandpa bought a used car, which not only made it easier to travel

Harry (above right) with his Noland
cousins whom he was visiting when he
grabbed the chance to return a cake plate
to Bess and began their courtship
(TL 72-3559).

Harry in National Guard uniform in 1905,
the year he joined, right (TL 73-2596).

One of the outings that made up the backbone of my grandparents' face-to-face
courtship, Bess at right, Harry at front (TL 82-58-14).

back and forth but also allowed him to take my grandmother and their friends on outings. Knowing her love for sports, he also flattened part of one of his farm fields into a tennis court. Unfortunately, she never had the chance to play on it.

Nonetheless, she grew very fond of him very quickly. Despite never having been close, they had known each other almost all their lives, had nearly identical educational backgrounds, and shared tastes in literature. (Thanks to learning from the same teachers, they had similar handwriting as well.) Both were bright, straightforward, no-nonsense people with strong opinions and no qualms about expressing them. One of the things my grandmother liked best about my grandfather, in fact, was that he shared everything. While her father had kept her mother in the dark, Grandpa held nothing back. She could have used his letters as an operations manual, just by referencing the details he provided on farm life. So deep was her regard for him that when he jumped the gun six months into the courtship and asked her to marry him, she let him down gently so as not to discourage him.

He also was not a quitter, which I think is how she saw her father. During their courtship, Grandpa suffered a series of reversals. The family farm lost money thanks to falling produce prices, bad weather, and a family lawsuit. Martha Truman's mother had left the farm to Martha and her brother, Harrison Young. Their siblings sued, forcing Martha and Uncle Harrison to pour much of their earnings into their defense. Prices for lead and zinc plummeted right after Grandpa invested in a lead and zinc mine. An oil well failed to produce—until he sold it to someone else. Despite all of it, Grandpa bounced back, time after time, vowing to work harder than ever.

Harry with the oil rig illustrates his never-say-die attitude (TL 82-58-79).

Finally, in mid-1913, my grandmother told Grandpa that if she married anyone, it would be him. Apparently, this caught him completely off guard. The man who had poured out his heart, in person and on paper, who had shared every facet of his life, no matter how small, was now utterly speechless. At the sight of him with his mouth hanging open, gawping at her, my grandmother burst out laughing.

"Harry Truman," she said. "You're an enigma."

In 1917, Harry Truman was thirty-three, the head of a household, and a farmer. These things would have exempted him from the draft, but my grandfather felt it was his duty to fight.

"I was stirred in heart and soul by the war messages of Woodrow Wilson and [...] I thought I ought to go [to war]," he wrote in 1931. "I believe that the great majority of the country [was] stirred by the same flame that stirred me in those great days. I felt that I was a Galahad after the Grail and I'll never forget how my love cried on my shoulder when I told her I was going. That was worth a lifetime on this earth."

Despite this romanticism, Galahad was in a lot of trouble with the future Mrs. Galahad. It didn't help that he refused to marry her before shipping out, saying he wouldn't have her tied to a "cripple" or a "sentiment" if things went badly. After her outburst, he apologized profusely, writing that he had "felt like a dog all week." From then on, to comfort my grandmother, he recounted every facet of basic training at Fort Sill, Oklahoma, and adopted the tactic of assuring her that the Germans were not capable of making shells or bullets that could hit him.

Arriving in France in the spring of 1918, he was given command of an artillery battery, Battery D of the 129th Field Artillery. The two hundred men, most of them college-educated Kansas City Irishmen, loved to drink and fight and had a healthy disdain for military authority. They had already been through a handful

Grandpa in uniform in 1917 (TL 62-94).

of captains—mostly because none of the captains stood up to them—and they thought the little man in glasses and a tin hat would be no different. They greeted Grandpa on his first day with a Bronx cheer. That night, they got drunk and stampeded the camp's horses.

Grandpa busted the miscreants. The next day, the rest "were so anxious to please me and fire good that one of my gunners got the ague and simply blew up," he wrote. In short order, they were out-firing every other battery in the regiment.

"I think of Battery D as the most mischievous, unpredictable, and difficult-to-handle unit in the whole Allied Expeditionary Force," battery member Harry Murphy said years later. "But when the chips were down, to the man, they were a fine bunch of soldiers. I am proud to have been one of them. Captain Truman, who did successfully handle this outfit, deserved to be president of the United States."

They fought in the Vosges Mountains in northeastern France, in the Battle of Saint-Mihiel, and in the Meuse-Argonne Offensive that lasted from late September of 1918 until the armistice was signed on November 11. They slogged through mud, slept in trenches, and fought on fields where exploding shells unearthed corpses from earlier battles. Grandpa wrote to my grandmother that one German shell missed him by only fifteen feet and that another landed where he had been sleeping only minutes earlier. During their first engagement, the Germans drew a bead on them and a sergeant and several of the men bolted. Grandpa rallied the rest, rescued the horses and guns, and referred to the incident ever after as the Battle of Who Run.

My grandmother did her duty as well, serving as what was known as a Liberty Soldier. By war's end, her committee had sold $1.78 million in government bonds.

Grandpa brought himself and all of his men through the war in one piece, and when the fighting was over, he wanted nothing more

Bess in the oft-used photo that Harry took with him to war (TL 82-56).

than to get home. His yearning was compounded by the fact that both Bess and Mary, his sister, had come down with influenza. This was not "flu season." This was the pandemic of 1918/19 that killed approximately fifty million people worldwide and, statistically, shortened the average lifespan in the United States by ten years. My grandmother's brother George contracted the flu as well. But while he and Mary recovered quickly, my grandmother was feverish and delirious for weeks. Several times, her family thought she might die. When she finally came out of it, she found that the illness had cost her much of the hearing in her left ear.

Madge in 1920 (TL 2009-1539).

During late January and early February of 1919, the top brass began canceling leaves and ordering the men to turn in their guns and horses. In Grandpa's letter of February 18 and my grandmother's response dated March 16, their mutual relief and anticipation are palpable.

Grandpa also reports that he mouthed off to his commanding officer, Colonel Arthur Elliott, for whom he'd never had very high regard. He had even less regard for the regular army officers he mentions, principally because they suggested things like feeding the horses cooked oatmeal instead of oats. My grandmother agreed wholeheartedly. She had no patience with buffoons. In her letter, she compares war to her picnics, which often involved marathon hikes around the countryside. Participants who threw their weight around, complained, or made asinine suggestions quickly fell by the wayside.

My grandmother also mentions that her mother, Madge, sent Grandpa her love and said the young couple could have either floor of the house. This was a surprise to me at first, since family lore has always held that Madge was forever telling my grandmother that she could have married better, even when they were sitting in the White House. In fact, Madge's offer was calculated to keep her only daughter close to home.

[Rosières, near Bar-le-Duc]
February 18, 1919

Dear Bess:

I wrote you day before yesterday but I very much fear you won't get it. The mail orderly doesn't know whether he got it or not and can't find it. I had just gotten some letters from you and naturally told you how glad I was. Also I told you that we are coming home right away. I know it officially now because General Pershing shook hands with me— and told me so. I also met the Prince of Wales, as did every other company and battery commander in the 35th Division. [...] My battery got to stand in front of the whole regiment. I don't know if it was luck or if they looked the best. They looked pretty fine if I do say it as I shouldn't. [...] We went over in trucks and of course one of 'em got smashed and part of the men had to walk some distance and the same thing coming back but no one was hurt in any way. I was in charge of the Battalion going over and coming back. The new Colonel gave me a good calling down because I gave Colonel Elliott a public sassing and I guess I deserved it but so did Elliott. The new Colonel is a Regular and he can't see this National Guard lack of cringing when a Colonel or a Lieutenant Colonel comes around. I have an awful bad habit of using a very sharp tongue when one of 'em says something he has no business to me. It doesn't work in play soldiering. You have to say yes sir and no sir and alright sir even when you should punch his head. Hence my urgent desire to get back to the farm. There's one or two whom I want to meet when I get on my overalls and they'd better have on their armor. [...] Please get ready to march down the aisle with me just as soon as you decently can when I get back. I haven't any place to go but home and I'm busted financially but I love you as madly as a man can and I'll find all the other things. We'll be married anywhere you say at any time you mention and if you want only one person or the whole town I don't care as long as you make it quickly after my arrival. I have some army friends I'd like to ask and my own family and that's all I care about, and the army friends can go hang if you don't want 'em. I have enough money to buy a Ford and we can set sail in that and arrive in Happyland at once and quickly.

Don't fail to write just 'cause I'm starting home.

Yours always,
Harry

[Independence, Mo.]
Sunday, March 16, 1919

Dear Harry,

According to the *Star*'s latest information you are on your way to Le Mans and I'm wondering if any of these <u>last</u> letters will ever be delivered. It seems to take them <u>long enough</u> to get to you even when postal authorities know where you are exactly— and if you begin to move again, what <u>will</u> happen to the letters?

Was mighty glad to get your letter of Feb. 18. Hadn't heard for such an age was afraid you were sick! Mary [Jane Truman] was worrying too, so I wrote her a card at once telling her I had had my letter in case she didn't get one in the same mail.

You may invite the entire 35th Division to our wedding if you want to. I guess it's going to be <u>yours</u> as well as <u>mine</u>. I guess we might as well have the church <u>full</u> while we are at it. I rather think it <u>will</u> be anyway whether we invite them or not, judging from a few <u>remarks</u> I've heard. What an experience the review etc. must have been. I'll bet D Battery looked grand and no wonder they led the Division. I couldn't help spilling that little bit of "info" to C. C. I hope you don't mind. Were you at all overcome at greeting the Prince of Wales? He doesn't mean any more to me than the <u>orneriest</u> doughboy but I know I'd choke if I had to address him. It was splendid you got to shake hands with Pershing.

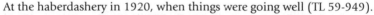

At the haberdashery in 1920, when things were going well (TL 59-949).

I'll be just about ready alrighty when you come and then we can settle the last details. Mary said Mr. Morgan had a job waiting for you and if you should decide to put in part of your time there, you'll have another home waiting for you in Indep. for nothing would please Mother any better. She said we could have either floor we wanted.

I wore my new spring bonnet out to Helen's last week and she said she hoped I wouldn't wear all the newness off it before you got here and I told her I hoped I wouldn't have the time to.

Polly and Ben and the kiddies are coming tomorrow. I don't know why in the world they are coming right now before Miss Jessie gets out of school. She won't enjoy them much, I'm afraid. Wish they could stay 'til after <u>the</u> wedding.

Hold on to the money for the car! We'll surely need one. Most anything that will run on four wheels. I've been looking at used car bargains today. I'll frankly confess I'm scared to death of Fords. I've seen and heard of so many turning turtle this winter— but we can see about that later. Just get yourself home and we won't worry about anything.

Did you hear that Mr. Morgan said he was going to give you a suit! Pretty fine— eh? Are you longing to get back into cits [civilian clothes]? Eugene says they sure feel fine.

Am glad you gave Colonel Elliot the calling down— in spite of Colonel Smith. I bet he needed it. It's strange that such widely different things as <u>war</u> and <u>picnics</u> will so surely show a man up. I've liked lots of people 'til I went on a picnic jaunt with them and you can say the same thing about several men 'til you went on a war "jaunt" with them— eh? The dear ex-Colonel landed Friday.

I must quit. Hope you have the chance to cable as you said.

Loads of love,
Devotedly,
Bess

Mother sends her love.

This certainly is some scratching but I'm sitting in the big chair under the light and it isn't easy to write.

1923

Grandpa came home from the war and went into business with his former canteen sergeant, Eddie Jacobson. During basic training at Fort Sill in Oklahoma from 1917 to 1918, he and Eddie had run the camp's only successful regimental canteen—successful largely because they knew what they were doing. Eddie had been in retail before the war and did the purchasing. Grandpa, the one-time bank clerk, kept the books. They were earning at the rate of 621 percent a year, Grandpa said, "like Standard Oil." Reasoning that they could translate that success to the private sector, they opened Truman and Jacobson, a men's cloth-

The wedding photo (TL 73-1668).

ing store, in downtown Kansas City in the fall of 1919, shortly after my grandparents were married, in June of that year.

At about the same time, Jim Pendergast, another army buddy, approached Grandpa about running for eastern judge of Jackson County, an elected administrative position. Jim's uncle, Tom Pendergast, and his father, Mike Pendergast, ran the Kansas City Democratic machine. Grandpa turned them down. Business was too good. That first year, he and Eddie made the equivalent of $750,000.

By 1922, however, a postwar recession had ruined the business and when Jim came back with the same offer, Grandpa said yes. He made a good candidate. He was a war hero—an officer whose men "didn't want to shoot him," as the joke went—and a businessman who understood the suffering of other businessmen. He'd also had a lifelong interest in politics, even musing to my grandmother during the war that he might like to run for eastern judge some day.

With the Pendergasts' backing, he won the 1922 election and spent the next two years learning about and trying to fix Jackson County's shaky finances, deplorable roads, and outdated or nonexistent public buildings.

My grandmother, meanwhile, ran the whopping Gates and Wallace household. Since her father's suicide, it had been her duty to take care of her mother and younger brothers. Residents of the main house included her grandmother, Elizabeth Emery Gates, her mother, Madge Gates Wallace, herself and Grandpa, and her youngest brother, Fred Wallace. Next door, in nearly identical cottages, lived brothers Frank and George Wallace and their wives, Natalie and May.

Boss Tom Pendergast in 1925, about the time Grandpa met him face-to-face for the first time (TL 58-795).

In July of 1923, Grandpa took off for the annual Missouri National Guard encampment at Fort Leavenworth, Kansas. He had reenlisted in the Guard despite declaring at the end of the war that peacetime soldiering was an awful bore and "anybody who wants to do it is certainly off in his upper works." In fact, he enjoyed the camaraderie. And he and my grandmother both viewed the two-week encampment as a welcome break from the stress of the judgeship. It was the longest they had been separated since being married.

In addition to news of the day and Grandpa's rather detailed accounts of life at Fort Leavenworth, the major thread running through these letters is that my grandmother had to have several teeth removed. The operation, when it happened, exhausted both patient and doctor. My grandmother also reports that a bunch of women in Jackson County were clamoring to have their roads oiled. At the time, most roads were dirt and oiling them kept down the dust. The "Eddie" my grandmother refers to is Eddie Jacobson, who occasionally drove her to Fort Leavenworth for visits. Why he wanted to stop by the fort's prison on each trip is a mystery, even to his family.

One letter refers to a badger fight perpetrated by Grandpa and his cronies. This was generally a prank played on the new men in camp. The veterans promised a fight between a badger and a dog and offered one of the new guys a chance to loose the badger. I've read of a Texas version in which the conspirators brought in a large barrel and placed it shoulder high on a table or shelf. The victim was then told to yank the barrel down to free the badger. When he did, he found the barrel was actually filled with kitchen slop or, in some cases, a full chamber pot. Grandpa and the other older Guardsmen may instead have rigged a box with a spring designed to fling a fake "badger" point-blank at the victim.

Despite being married for more than four years, my grandparents were still experimenting with nicknames for each other. My grandmother also teased Grandpa, an incurable clotheshorse, about the short time the men were given to shower and dress in the morning. The one thing glaringly omitted from these letters is any mention of my grandmother's impending motherhood. Mom was born February 17, 1924, so in late July of 1923, my grandmother was about two months pregnant. Superstition and heartbreak over two previous miscarriages kept my grandparents from writing about it.

[Independence, Mo.]
[July 15–16, 1923]

Dear Pettie,

I hope you didn't run into the rain <u>we</u> had about five-thirty— It didn't last long but it was good and wet while it did last.

It is now 10:20 and I am <u>in bed</u>— There was a <u>big</u> black bug on my bed when I turned the sheet down and I had to kill it myself— but that wasn't the first time I had wished for you.

I would love to know how you are settled for the night etc. Hope you didn't find either one of the two you mentioned in your tent.

Mrs. Mize and Mary spent the evening with us. They are quite enamored of army life.

How did you like playing around with another <u>lady</u> today? Did you and the fair Jean have a good time? Did you have a good dinner at Tonganoxie? I could see you weren't going to get out of going there first.

Lots and lots of good night kisses— I am going to read one story and hope I'll be <u>asleep</u> before I finish it.

Yours,
Bess

Monday a.m.

It's just 7:30 and I've had breakfast! Natalie and I are going to K.C. She saw a sweater ad yesterday that <u>intrigued</u> her. Am busy— will write tonight. (Not going to bake any cakes tho'.)

Loads of love,
Bess

[Ft. Leavenworth, Kans.]
[July 16, 1923]

My Dear Wife:

I hesitated somewhat on that word. I wanted to say honey, sweetheart, Miss Bessie. But the one I used is in the last analysis the finest and loveliest word in the world. When a man has a perfect one as I have, what in life is better?

Mr. Kirby refused to bring me up here until he'd delivered Miss Settle in Lawrence, so I got stuck for the dinner at Tonganoxie at a $1 per head. They were 25 cents higher than week day dinners. We had cold roast country ham, cold roast veal, old fashioned country fried potatoes, three kinds of salad, pickled beets, oranges, four kinds of preserves and jam with iced tea and angle [sic] food and orange cake with preserves or peaches for desert [sic]. It was a good dinner and worth twice the money. I was homesick for you all the way here and after I got here. It was 10:30 when we arrived and Kirby, I think, was sorry to leave me in the camp.

Colonel Clendening was in the office. He gave me a blanket, <u>two sheets</u>, two <u>pillow cases</u>, (think of that) and took me to a tent where I found an iron spring cot with a pillow and mattress and a mosquito bar to cover it. The tent has an electric light and I have my individual wash basin.

I got up at 5:30 went down to the end of the street in my pajamas and took a cold shower ran back dressed and was ready for breakfast at six thirty. We had a half grapefruit, cream of wheat, ham, two eggs, two hot cakes and coffee, <u>and I ate it all</u>.

After breakfast I went for a physical examination. Shut my mouth and said ah! Bent over, hopped on one foot and then the other, had my heart tested, my lungs tapped and my throat examined and the old Major who did it said that I sure am a healthy specimen. He looked me over and remarked that he guessed I'd always been healthy too. Aren't you glad to hear that.

I hope you slept better than I did last night. My bed was good, the air fine, but I wanted someone to keep me covered up and to hug.

[*Illegible*] has been here and given me a job so I'll have to go and attend to it. It is teaching 8 second Leu'ts how to read a map. I used to be a bear at it but I doubt my ability now.

Please come and see me. We have nothing to do after six. I just can't get over wanting to see you.

I am always yours,
Harry

[Independence, Mo.]
[July 17, 1923]
Tuesday— noon

Dear Old Sweetness,

My! but I was glad to get that letter this morning. And it sure was a <u>nice</u> one— about the nicest I ever had. I'm glad you are so beautifully settled and are getting such <u>excellent</u> food. That was some breakfast! You'll have to be pretty strenuous to keep that <u>front down</u>. You certainly had a grand dinner at Tonganoxie. I wished all evening I had gone on with you. You weren't a bit "home sicker" than I was, I can tell you that. Thank goodness two nights are gone.

Eddie called up this a.m. He was at Ted's and they wanted to go up to see you, and he wanted to know what you said about coming up and I told him to go on any day <u>after six</u> so, you may see them on Friday. I'd give my head to go— maybe he will ask me yet.

The Swifts got off to Colorado early yesterday morning. He started that old car right on the dot of five o'clock— and I lay there in bed and watched them get ready. I wouldn't have missed seeing Mrs. Swift in knickers for a hundred dollars.

Called Dr. Berry this morning— (the pictures came yesterday.) He said there were two he believed should come out— one back one and one <u>front</u>— (just on the side). He couldn't tell just how bad they were but that they <u>might</u> be secreting poison. I'm going up tomorrow and <u>maybe</u> have the big one and the wisdom one out. There's no use putting it off. My temp. hasn't run over 99 for the last four or five days. Ho!

Natalie and I spent all of yesterday morning in K.C. The sweater sale made a hit. We only bought <u>three</u>— one for her, one for Miss Rose and one for Mother.

How did the map-reading class come out?

Well, it's awfully darned lonesome but I know you are going to get lots of good out of the trip— and I'm glad too that you are taking it by yourself for I am sure you needed to get away from everything and everybody. Believe me I'll be up there if I can get there for you don't want to see me any worse than I want to you. I'm going to town to mail this so you will get it tomorrow.

> Loads of love,
> Devotedly,
> Bess

> Ft. Leavenworth, Kans.
> July 17, 1923

Dear Bess:

I am up at 5:15 again this a.m. 30 minutes before reveille so I can write this letter. We have a schedule now. Get up at 5:45, fifteen minutes for the bend overs, shave, bath and breakfast at 7:00. Then duty at 7:30.

Every day we have a problem of some kind about war which we must solve in some way and make a written report on. I have a war map of Leavenworth County and I suppose we'll have army all over the place before we get done. Every day at 11 a.m. there is a grand mount out in front of our place and every evening at 5:30 a parade and review by a whole battalion of infantry at the same place. You should come up some evening and see it and then have supper at the camp. You'll be surprised at what you get to eat.

We all have our proper places at the table and are now assigned to our permanent quarters in tents. Dinwiddie Groves, a major, and two St. Louis fellows are in my tent, a Major Notebloom and Captain Bliss. All nice fellows.

The horn's blowing and I've got to quit. I've not had a letter yet.

> Yours,
> Harry

> [Independence, Mo.]
> [July 18, 1923]
> Wednesday 11 o'clock

My Dear,

I was mighty glad to get your <u>before breakfast</u> letter this morning. It pretty nearly <u>got</u> here before breakfast, too— right around nine o'clock. I've been to the dentist and the doctor this morning. Dr. Berry wouldn't pull those teeth 'til Dr. K. had seen the pictures— a mere matter of courtesy! I was sort of peeved for I had made up my mind to have two of those out today. He says now he'll pull them the last of the week. Some day when it rains, I reckon, and he can't play golf— Three have to come out.

I am sure glad to hear you stood a perfect examination— Just what did he say about your tonsils? Bet he didn't even look at them. I was powerfully glad to hear your voice yesterday evening. We had wonderful connections didn't we?

I'm going to the city pretty soon to get some linen for the church— I'm going to have a Guild meeting tomorrow and we want some thing to work on.

Fred knows the Groves man. Went to school with all of his brothers and cousins— They are all Sig Alphs.

They certainly keep you busy don't they? How did you make it teaching the 2nd Lieuts how to read maps?

Don't you want your bath-slippers? I should think you'd need them traveling down the street to your bath every morning. I'd like a picture of you shaving, bathing, and dressing in fifteen minutes.

Loads of love. Will write tomorrow.

Yours,
Bess

[Ft. Leavenworth, Kans.]
July 18, 1923

Dear Bess:

Your letter came yesterday and I was so elated I just had to spend .35 to call you up.

We get up officially at 5:45 but I get up at 5:15. I shaved this morning then fell in for bend overs, and they are real ones, I want to tell you. I expect to be as sore as a mule in war time before I get hardened to it.

Yesterday we had to carry a small four-legged stool about a 1/4 of a mile and sit on it listening to lectures on map reading, combat orders, a speech by Gen. Smith, the Mayor of Leavenworth, Pres. of Chamber of Commerce, and a representative of Sec. of War. I got to see a battery drill and I'll tell you it made me crazy to do it. The Captain had just finished school at Ft. Sill with Peter Allen. There is nothing finer than a battery drilling.

They call us the milk maids brigade, the stool pigeons, and other vile and ribald names. By they I mean the medicos and others who don't have to carry the stools.

Today we go five miles west (in autos) and work a real problem. If you come up for supper soon come up about 4:30 and see the parade on our parade ground. There is a board with a clip on it in the bottom box outside the wooden box in the attic. Would you bring that to me if you come? (Am busy.) Breakfast's ready.

Lots of love,
Harry

[Independence, Mo.]
[July 19, 1923]
Thursday a.m.

Sweetie— (burn this in the kitchen stove)

I just had your Thursday* letter— had been sitting at the front window waiting for the postman for <u>hours</u>. Had to chuckle over the <u>kind</u> of <u>bend-overs</u> you are doing.

I've just been talking to Mrs. Jacobson. The baby is sick for a change but if she is OK tomorrow we are <u>all</u> driving up. Eddie wants to leave about noon so as to go through the prison (nice morbid trip) and we will try to turn up in time for Parade at the Camp no doubt. I'm very thrilled at the idea of going— we'll have supper in Leavenworth as long as there are so many of us coming— Can't you leave at six and go in? I think we'll want to visit a hotel anyway by that time and that will solve the question— See?

I found your <u>clip</u> but <u>not</u> in the bottom box.

If you happen to meet a Col. Allen at the Post, his wife is a good friend of Dicie and Jessie's. Also an Aunt of William Bland's. The Mac's only got as far as Marysville. Dicie gave out. Had a letter from her this morning. Don't worry if we don't show up tomorrow— it depends entirely upon the baby— she has a high fever and sore throat today.

Have you been enjoying these chilly nights? I've been sleeping under a spread— Am surely glad it hasn't been so hot while you've been there.

Lots of love,
Bess

[Ft. Leavenworth, Kans.]
July 19, 1923

Dear Bess:

I sure raised sand with the adjutant yesterday morning when I didn't get a letter, but it came in the afternoon and boy! how nice it was. I am so sorry about the teeth and I do hope you will have them out right away. You ought not to put it off because it might make you have something real at a <u>time</u> when you couldn't afford it, so please have them out.

Well we are in the middle of a great war between Kansas and Missouri and the mean part about it is that I am in the Kansas army and am helping to lick my own people and doing a good job of it. Say but this is fine for brain work and they keep us in such excellent physical shape that

---

* she is probably referring to his letter of Wednesday, July 18.

our brains really work. I'd give most anything to take the school of fire course and then take the year at Leavenworth. We were out again yesterday watching that battery work and I've cooked up a deal to put all the 2nd Lieuts here on horses and the guns and take that battery out once for a real go around. I guess it will go across and I'll have a real time.

If Jacobson doesn't ask you to come up here Friday I'll not have anything more to do with him, but I'm sure he'll ask you. He told me he would.

I am going to have to write orders for a whole Division today and believe me it's a real job. I won't have time to think of any politicians or jobs or roads either for the balance of the week.

Don't fail to write, because my day is ruined if I don't get that letter. All the love in the world.

Yours,
Harry

I'm still busy but still writing.

Ft. Leavenworth, Kans.
July 20, 1923

Dear Bess:

Your sweet letter came on time and I was looking for it. There'd have been war if I hadn't gotten it. We go out on another problem today. Yesterday we had lectures in the morning and watched a battalion of infantry put on a sham battle. It was very warm on those old infantrymen with their blouses and packs and guns, but they came out all right and won the war without any trouble.

Colonel Elliott's wife came up yesterday evening and he and the colonel across the way, Siegmund by name, went over [to] the golf club to dinner and a dance. Any one of us could have gone if we'd made reservations, but I went to bed at 10 p.m. and read about artillery and how to manage a battery. I've got to give a lecture on battery administration tomorrow morning to all the artillery, about 48 officers, including a couple of colonels and half [a] dozen majors.

I've been up since five-thirty, had a cold bath, fifteen minutes of bend overs, watched the battery pull out for K.C. to fire a salute for the French general tomorrow. Now I'm writing you and in five minutes I'll be at breakfast and then I'll have to read fifteen pages and go put an imaginary regiment of art. in the war between Mo. and Kas. I hope I see you today. Much and many love and kisses. (Am still busy.)

Yours always,
Harry

[Independence, Mo.]
[July 21, 1923]
Saturday 1 pm

Dear Harry,

Here it is, the morning after and yesterday seems just a happy dream. I sure did hate to leave last night. What became of you after we got in the car— I looked and looked to see you drive by—

We got home about 10:30. Ted brought me out in his wonderful new car. Have you seen it?

We had a mighty fine time visiting your summer home. ("Summer" is right, too— Golly! That's one hot place.)

And that dinner was a dandy. I couldn't help smiling inwardly when Col. E. was telling of all he had eaten for breakfast. But I believe he really had improved.

How is Capt. [*illegible*]'s wife? Where is Capt. Boatright from? The teeth are coming out Monday. Helen and Eugene came last night to take me driving in George's car. H. promised to come back some night next week if they could annex the car again. Thank Capt. or Major Groves for his car. It saved our lives. I don't believe I could have made it afoot. But I wasn't a bit tired when I got home and feel fine this morning. Major Bachelor seemed to be mighty nice. Is he married? We must have them out.

I suppose you will go to church tomorrow. I just talked to your mother— said she and Mary were feeling pretty good— she surely sounded like it. She was glad to know I had just seen you. They had a letter yesterday from you.

The last call for lunch has been shouted at me— and I'm hungry. Was mighty glad to get that letter this a.m. just the same.

                                        Loads of love,
                                        Bess

[Ft. Leavenworth, Kans.]
July 21, 1923

My Dear Wife:—

I am going to have a bum day today because I won't get any letter. It was a treat to see you certainly, but there were so many around I couldn't enjoy you[r] company as I could if we'd been alone. I sure hated to see you go back. Just for a small amount I'd have gone home with you.

You perhaps can see something of the pull there is on a man when he's had some military training to do it again. There is no explanation for it but it's there. He'll cuss the military and all that pertains to it and then he'll go right back and take more punishment. There is something about it that's not to be explained by reason or common sense, any more than why a man loves his wife. We are a bunch of nuts and can't help it I guess but we enjoy it. You can see that I'm not the only one affected.

I have to use my brain today sure enough because when you tell some[one] else something that you know yourself it's a real job.

You be a good girl and I'll be a good boy. I have been. I haven't had a thing to drink nor have I drawn a single card.

I love you an awful lot, can't help it and don't want to.

> Your
> Harry

> [Independence, Mo.]
> [July 22, 1923]
> Sunday 10:30 am

Friend Husband—

I can see already that this is going to be a <u>long hot day</u>. My conscience is bothering me considerably but I don't seem to be able to propel myself to church. George and May are coming to dinner and I wish they would suggest driving to Leavenworth but there is a golf tournament on so the chances are slim.

I was powerfully glad to get your special late last night. And then I <u>dreamed</u> that I got still another one, which was <u>very</u> nice as long as it lasted.

I saw in *Star* this morning that Col. E. had a dinner last night at KC Club for Colonels Siegmund and [*illegible*]. Is Colonel Siegmund a regular? He acted like it.

There is an article in the last *American* that you would subscribe to heartily. Its headlines say the more you fuss about it the [illegible] you'll be. I'm going to read it when I finish this. I hope you and Major Bachelor Enjoy the day working your Problem.

I hope your lecture was most successful— Will you have to do any more? I surely hope you get to take that Battery out this week. I guess Ted is busy packing up today, just as you were <u>last</u> Sunday. Well, see you Thursday, I hope. Do you want Fred and me to drive up for you next Sunday and Monday evening— whenever it is you can leave.

> All the love in the world,
> Bess

> Ft. Leavenworth, Kans.
> July 22, 1923

My Dear Honey:—

Your special delivery came as it should; it was a lifesaver. Yesterday

was awful without any letter. We had a lecture on the next problem at
7:30 yesterday and then went through the Disciplinary Barracks. It is quite
an institution. They drilled their special battalion for us, showed us the
kitchen, dining room, assembly hall, dairy, etc. There was a red-headed
quartermaster captain along to explain things and he was worth the price
of admission. With the usual Irish wit and brogue, he was unconsciously
very entertaining to Bachelor and myself.

I got up at 7 o'clock this a.m., took my usual cold shower and had
breakfast at 7:30 and then went back to my tent and slept the sleep of
the just until noon, got up for dinner of chicken and the trimmings with
watermelon for desert [*sic*] and then Bachelor and I went out on our
problem after walking through the National Cemetery. We solved our
problem to our satisfaction went over [to] the officers club and had a cold
<u>soft</u> drink with the Captain of this battery that's here and now I'm doing
what I ought to have done before I went to sleep. I'm sorry about that
railroad. It will cut the place squarely in two, and that will be a shame.

I am hoping you will come to see me Thursday.

Yours,

Harry

[Independence, Mo.]

[July 23, 1923]

Monday

Dear—

I didn't get my letter this morning and I sure am sick about it. I
guess they don't have regular mail hours on Sunday up there. I'm afraid
you didn't get an <u>early</u> letter today either as I didn't make the P.O. 'til
almost six yesterday evening.

It was so hot all day and Fred wasn't feeling very good, so I didn't
like to ask him to go 'til it got cooler.

I sure was homesick for you last night. It was the worst night yet.
I'm sure glad this is the <u>last</u> week.

There were burglars in the neighborhood early this morning. Stole
some money from Mr. Allen right over next to Dunn's and got $30 from
the people back of Allen's. I'm sure going to hide things to-night. Money
and jewelry seem to be all they want.

Honey, will it be alright if I come up with Fred Thursday instead
of Eddie? Fred is crazy to go— he begged and begged me to go yesterday
but I was afraid he couldn't make the trip. Besides, I just <u>don't</u> want to go
through that prison with Eddie. I just think it's awful to go gape at those
people like they were so many animals in cages. We may go to Platte

early Thursday a.m. and then on to Leavenworth by five o'clock to see the drills. Louise Duke is having a luncheon Thursday but I would rather see you by a long shot.

If I don't get a letter this afternoon I'm sure going to call up tonight. Another woman wanted her road oiled this morning. I referred her to Les [*illegible*]. She lives on Hodges Av. Said she has hay fever and the dust is just killing her.

Hope you are perfectly well. I didn't have any temperature yesterday & haven't any today so far (12 o'clock).

Lots of love,
Bess

Ft. Leavenworth, Kans.
July 24, 1923

My Dear Bess:

We are still fighting the war. I was up at 5:15 this a.m., had a bath and a shave and then some cream of wheat with blackberries and plums for breakfast. I decided to cut out the ham & eggs because my belt is getting rather tight.

You should see my eyebrow on my upper lip, or toothbrush, as someone called it. You won't be able to approach me very closely if I leave it on.

The gang in here is very energetic, shining shoes and leggings and mine look like the dickens and I'll have to go to work on them. The officers from our regiment put on a march to the colors that was not so very good and Col. Elliot almost had a hemorage [*sic*] (someone told him where the mistakes were). I had no part in it. Tomorrow I've got to drill the battery mounted. I think I can do a good job. I have done it many a time.

I'll have lot of green recruits and I'm not expecting to put on a very showy party.

Hope to see you Thursday. The whistle's blown.

Yours,
Harry

Sure was good to hear your sweet voice over the phone.

[Independence, Mo.]
[July 24, 1923]
Tuesday afternoon

My Dear—

Both of your letters came this a.m. The Sunday letter didn't leave Ft. L. until 2:30 yesterday. It was silly of me to get worried yesterday. I knew it, even when I called but I was so afraid maybe the heat had laid you up or something. Anyway I wanted to talk to you.

The tooth is out. And it's a good thing. Doctor B. said it was much worse than he expected— the x-ray doesn't even show the abscess in the middle of the tooth. He had a pretty bad time getting it out. It had to be cut and drilled out entirely. It took him an hour and five minutes to do it. He was as worn out as I was. But it isn't bothering me much now. He had to give me so many hypodermics, my head feels funny. I'm going back tomorrow to have it syringed out good, to get rid of that pus. I hope this cooler breeze keeps up over Thursday— the trip will be much more pleasant.

There've been a world of airplanes over since the R.O.'s [Reserve Officers] have been at Richard's Field.* They seem to keep them as busy as you are.

This is some scratching but I can't do it over.

Fred is going up to mail it for me.

Lots of love—

Bess

Ft. Leavenworth, Kans.

July 25, 1923

Dear Bess:—

It sounded mighty fine to hear your voice over the phone but I surely feel like busting a dentist I know of. It does seem to me that he could have extracted that tooth in a shorter time than that. I'm very glad it's out and I hope you'll get the rest of them fixed. Whenever you do I'll have my throat cut. I sure feel fine this morning. It's cool and the pep is in everyone. I have been eating too much and I cut my diet day before yesterday. The result has been marvelous. Then we've had a new physical instructor the last day or so and he's been putting us through some real stuff. I'll be able to lick all the rabbits [Shannon Democrats] and the *Kansas City Journal* too when I get home. I hope your old lady gets her road oiled. If she does not there won't be any harm done.

That battery drill today is going to be some exercise. I'll have about forty green men and you can guess what will happen. We are going to show the infantry how fast we can take up a position and start action. If someone doesn't fall off his horse and break his neck or point the gun north when we want to shoot south we'll be all right.

I've got a good executive and I guess everything will come out all

* Richard's Field was the first airport in the Kansas City area.

right. Hope to see you tomorrow. Lots of love. I hope your tooth extraction hasn't caused any aftermath.

Yours,
Harry

[Independence, Mo.]
[July 25, 1923]
Wednesday 8:15 a.m.

My Dear—

Had a good night and am feeling very much better. Am going up to let Dr. Berry wash out the cavity so as to be sure there is no infection. "Cavity" is right, too. It looks like a shell-hole.

I was <u>awful</u> glad you called up last night— Did me a lot of good.

I surely hope tomorrow is a decent day— We both want to go so badly.

Am glad your lecture went off alright. I surely would like to be there today to see you drill that Battery.

Did Ted get there Sunday? I've wondered several times— he was so wild to go.

Nick Phelps called up about day break yesterday. Said he'd been away and just wanted to talk to you a <u>little bit</u>. It wasn't anything important, etc.— Asked about every member of the family. You'd have thought he had been a life long friend. I couldn't help being rather amused, altho' I was ready to kill him for calling that time of the day.

I must get dressed in a hurry. Here's hoping I'm getting ready to go to Leavenworth by this time tomorrow. Don't look for us before five.

Loads of love—
Bess

Ft. Leavenworth, Kans.
July 26, 1923

Dear Bess:—

The Battery drill was a success. I had not forgotten entirely how to do it and the rest of the gang were very anxious to do it right and so we succeeded very nicely. They wouldn't let me have but one hour and a half to perform and get the battery from a mile away and then when I got the first maneuver over they called off the show with still 30 minutes to go, made us give up the battery and walk a mile and a half to see machine guns and automatic rifle work. The colonel in charge of the school and the major in charge of artillery were satisfied with the [artillery] exhibition so I guess it was all right.

It sure looks like rain this morning and a shower would be thankfully received, but I don't want it to rain enough to keep you home. I'll bet the CMTC boys get all the rain next month. Someone said our pictures were in the *Post* but I didn't see it. I sure hope I see you this evening. I hope the tooth is better. Lots of love from
Your Harry

[Independence, Mo.]
[July 26, 1923]
Thursday— AM
<u>Early</u>

Honey—

From the looks of the skies I think it very doubtful that we get off today. Fred and Mother both insist that it is going to clear off, but I'm not so sure— but here's hoping. My <u>face</u> feels pretty comfortable. Dr. B. said it looked fine yesterday. He's right proud of the job he did— but I'm <u>afraid</u> (?) it wore him out so he couldn't play golf Tuesday afternoon. Eddie called up yesterday and said he would like to have me get the Leavenworth road in perfect condition by today and I assured him it would be done.

Just <u>one</u> woman has <u>hollered</u> about roads this week. All of these women who have called up live out around Bristol and Maywood. I think they must have a league out there. It's downright chilly this morning. I had to grab for the spread <u>early</u> (4 a.m.).

I want to get this down in the box before the postman gets here.
Loads of love—
Bess

[Independence, Mo.]
[July 27, 1923]
Friday— A.M.

Honey—

Just a short note to let you know we arrived home safely. If I had known what kind of a driver your friend Bill Kirby is, I would have taken a longer breath before leaving Leavenworth, because I didn't get another one 'til we hit [*illegible*] Gladstone. I guess we really didn't make much better time than Fred and I made going up, but it seemed powerfully fast to me in the back seat.

I'm on my way to the dentist to have that place washed out.

Julia is having her tonsils out this morning. [*Name illegible*] is back in the hospital and in a very serious condition.

I surely enjoyed my trip yesterday and particularly my brief visit
with you. Did you get part of that terrific rain we had this morning?
Mother said it came from the northwest so I guess you did. I am glad it
didn't get here any sooner. Your ditches were dug just in time, weren't
they?

> Lots of love—
> Bess

> Ft. Leavenworth, Kans.
> July 27, 1923

Dear Bess:—

I wanted to go home with you so badly last night I could hardly
stand it. You just looked as if you needed a shoulder to put your head on
and I of course acted like a man brute usually does. I am dead sure you
didn't feel a bit good and that bumping did not make you any better.
Well it won't be but a couple of days more. I'll bet you'll feel fine though
when all those teeth are fixed as they should be.

Well yesterday you know was Turnip Day and the instructions are to
sow them wet or dry. If they'd been sown they'd have been up tomorrow.
We had a trash mover* about 12:30 last night and I got up and loosened
the ropes of our tent with the assistance of Groves & Bliss to keep it from
pulling the pegs out and falling down. There was more racket and chasing
around in Avenue A about that time than there is on the real one. (Our
street is A.) We had a game of leapfrog this morning across the lot and
back and it was a circus. All the short legged men got bumped or thrown
and it was almost a riot. Then double time and the usual light breakfast
of prunes, oatmeal, fried eggs, milk, and oranges. We go on a communication problem today. I hope you are feeling well. Lots of love.

> Yours,
> Harry

> [Independence, Mo.]
> [July 28, 1923]
> Saturday morning

My Dear—

If I [am] to get to the dentist's on time this will have to be brief—
I'm afraid to let that cavity go even one day without treatment for fear of
infection. As long as I am saturated with aspirin it feels fine, but as soon
as that wears off— goodnight! Dr. B. says the reason it hurts so much

---

* i.e., a heavy rain or downpour

more now is because it has started healing. I hope the process is "speedy."

I suspect you will see Eddie before today is over. Mrs. J. said yesterday he wanted to go up today, if he still felt alright. I know you are <u>almost</u> sorry your two weeks are up— but I can't say that <u>I</u> am. *The Examiner* last night said that you would be home Sat. so I guess there will be a million calls tomorrow.

Do you know that Mrs. Kirby didn't know where he was the other night? That man ought to be strung up. And then he wouldn't stop in K.C. & call her.

I <u>must</u> go or Dr. B. will be off to the golf club.

Lots of love—
Bess

Ft. Leavenworth, Kans.
July 28, 1923

Dear Bess:

I was sure glad to get your letter. If I hadn't there'd have been a call for you. The rain was very satisfactory and did no damage except to get your old man a little damp when he tightened the tent ropes.

We had a real problem this morning. Everyone had a horse and rode west about five miles along Sheridan Drive and then went to war. I was a major of F. A. [Field Artillery] with three batteries, each represented by a 2nd Lt. and a Battalion staff composed of a couple of captains and a first Lt. We received orders from the Colonel of F. A. (Elliott) by courier to report at a point about three miles from where we were at 8:30. It was then 8:25 and orders were not to trot the horses. I arrived at 8:45 which was time enough. Got a long string of orders about the enemy, the doughboys etc. and was instructed to get my batteries into a certain area, fire certain fire and support a regiment of infantry, the Col. of which I was introduced to. I put my batteries in, wrote my orders, and had every thing ready 30 minutes before zero hour, which was 11:30. The idea was to show the time required to get orders down from a Major General in command of a Division to a second Lt. in the front line. When you consider that a Division is 5,000 more people than the total population of Indp. and that it has enough vehicles to move rations [*illegible*] and ammunition for a three days supply besides all the artillery and wagon soldiers you see it's some job. How much trouble would it be to get out the whole population of Indp. and assemble them in three lines 3,000 yards wide and a mile apart, one behind the other? That's putting a Division into action. A two star general is some man.

Last night we had a party at the golf club, without extra charge. The mess fund paid for it. A right good meal and then stunts. A takeoff on Col. Sigmund [*sic*] that was a dandy. Initiated Col. Clendening into the F. A. to which he's been transferred, a mock court martial, and a badger fight which was a scream. The boys who were sold on it were nearly scared to death before it came off and when the badger was pulled one of them jump[ed] over the table and nearly broke his neck. I'll tell you what a badger fight is when I get home if you don't know.

I just got some sad news. I can't leave until after breakfast Monday A.M. I hope to be in Indp. at 8:30. Be a good girl until I arrive. I hope I'll never be away from you so long again. I love you.

Yours,
Harry

🌀1925

Grandpa was now out of a job politically. The Jackson County Democrats had split over who received the plum political appointments and a Republican had snuck through the gap. Having lost the 1924 election for eastern judge, Grandpa was reorganizing and selling memberships in the Kansas City Automobile Club. The fall of that year, he also would be running a savings and loan with two partners. He had to quit the law courses he had been taking, complaining to my grandmother that he couldn't get any work done with all the Battery D veterans coming to him for advice and favors.

The biggest change in their lives, however, had occurred earlier, on February 17, 1924, with the birth of their daughter, Mary Margaret Truman. Because of her two miscarriages and the heartbreak of coming home to a house filled with baby clothing and furniture, my grandmother had not prepared in advance, so she had nothing for my mother to wear and no place for her to sleep. So Mom spent her first couple of nights wrapped in a blanket and tucked into a dresser drawer. This was common practice at that time and, in our case, was passed on to the next generation. When I was born in 1957, my father had to run out at the last minute and buy a crib. He put it together under my grandmother's supervision. Dad was no mechanic, so he was banging his knuckles and pinching his fingers and, in deference to

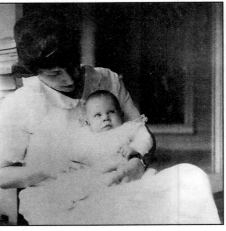

Gammy holding my mother, 1924
(TL 83-10).

my grandmother, swearing under his breath. "Oh, go ahead and say it out loud," she said finally. "It's not like I haven't heard it before."

Aside from my mother's antics and infected eyes and my grandmother's sprained ankle, the main thread running through these letters is my grandparents' scuffle over my grandmother's wish to cut her hair short. Grandpa resisted, unwilling to let her give up the "golden curls" she'd worn since the age of five, when he'd first seen and fallen in love with her. They had apparently had a face-to-face argument about it before he left, solved nothing, and continued the war on paper.

Another minor thread here has to do with swimming. Grandpa, who loved the water, was delighted to find that Fort Riley had a pool, albeit a cold one. My grandmother, who could not even dog paddle, was horrified and repeatedly warned him to be careful.

[Independence, Mo.]
[July 6, 1925]
Monday A.M.
Eight o'clock

Dear—

I'll steal a few minutes and send a short note— as Fred is going to the P.O. pretty soon.

We missed you like the mischief yesterday and your daughter kept asking all day for "da-da"— then— "bye?"

I'm afraid you had a hot trip— it was so awfully warm here all day.

I forgot your bathing suit after all the conversation about it. I'll send it at once if you have any use for it. Let me know.

If you <u>can</u> come back on Friday— why don't you come on the train— It will be so much easier on you. George says he thinks the U. P. [Union Pacific] goes through Junction City about every two hours. I can't have much luck writing with the youngster grabbing everything out of my hands. That Doc came [to] strap up my ankle yesterday— it hurt so badly all day. He said it is a sprain only. That's enough— I'll say.

Have to quit—

Hope you'll have a fine time and take care of yourself.

Lots of love from both of us—

Devotedly,
Bess

[Independence, Mo.]
[July 6, 1925]
Monday night— late

Honey—

I decided I wouldn't risk waiting 'til morning to write for I might not connect with spare time very well. I was surely glad to get your telegram and still gladder to get your letter this afternoon. I sent the ornament you wanted— also those white socks I found while looking for the ornament. I trust you have bought a tooth brush and a nail brush ere this! Hope those things get there early tomorrow— I got Frank to take me up to the P.O. as soon after your letter came as I could get ready— (That's one garbled sentence but you get me, no doubt!)

Frank & Natalie took Margaret for a long ride this evening then she came home, ate and went straight to sleep. She slept all night last night on the sleeping porch— and waked up the minute the sun struck her— about five o'clock! I brought her in at 5:30— she was up parading around her bed by that time. Her eye looks pretty badly tonight but Dr. K says it's just a bland infection— whatever that means— I'm using boric on it— hope it will be better in the morning. My ankle seems much better tonight— wish I'd had Doc adhesive it earlier.

Nellie Noland has had her hair cut and she looks perfectly fine. Ethel is going to do it this week. They say they can't afford to get in Miss Mary Atkins' and Miss Barhart's class— they are about the only old teachers left with long hair. I am crazier than ever to get mine off— Why won't you agree enthusiastically? My hair grows so fast, I could soon put it up again if it looked very badly— Please!— I'm much more conspicuous having long hair than I will be with it short.

I called the Prudential & got the check off— $37.90. It was due June 23rd.

Hope you are having good food. Am glad you found everything comfortable and am mighty glad you had a good trip out!

Every time M. has heard a step in the house today she has said "Da-da?"

It has been red hot here today— and I saw in the *Post* it had been so all over Kansas.

Loads of love—

Bess

Colonel Klemm told Fred he was going out to visit you all for a few days.

Ft. Riley, Kans.
July 7, 1925

Dear Sweethearts:—

Another day gone or nearly so and the pace has been just as strenuous. We had our call on the general and his lady. It consisted of going by
them on their front porch and off at the other end and away. He always
kids me about my political career and I tell him if there weren't politicians to run the gov't he would not be a B. Gen. [brigadier general]. That
usually stops the conversation— at least it [did] last evening.

We had a horseback ride this A.M. in addition to our other duties. It
was not very strenuous. I can use that swimming suit if it isn't too much
trouble to send it. This day has been much brighter because of your note.
I am very sorry about your foot. If you'd just be as anxious to take care
of yourself as you are to doctor me and the young lady, you'd be all right
nine times in ten. You should have had the doctor when your foot first
hurt you.

I wish I could take you and the baby "bye." I guess it was pretty
selfish in me to come off up here and leave you and take the car and I
shouldn't have done it. I need the work out though and it's doing me
good. Jay Lee is here. I've just had a bath and a fine breeze is blowing
from the southwest, but it was sure hot this A.M.

I hope I get that letter in the morning. Kiss the kid and remember I
love you.

Harry.

Ft. Riley, Kans.
July 8, 1925

My Dear Hon & Baby:—

I got your letter at noon today. Where did Miss M. get her bad eye?
It sure was a surprise to me to hear that she had a bad one. I do hope it's
nothing serious. I am glad your ankle is improving. The box came today
and I was very glad to get the stocks as I only had one. Laundry service is
not the best in the world here and I only had one white stock. We have to
dress up in the evening either in civies or full dress uniform. It's a good
thing I brought my civilian clothes. They are very handy when it's hot.

I think I told you I went swimming yesterday and it was the coldest pool I was ever in. Minnesota lakes has nothing on it. Our showers
are the same way. I can't understand what causes it. I got the Colonel to
let us ride to work in cars this morning and it has improved the moral[e]
considerably. We'd been walking a mile and a half to a lecture, then riding
some rough ponies for an hour and then walking another mile to another

lecture and then walking back a mile and a half to the noon meal and
then walking to the lecture room and back at 3:30. Some of these birds
looked like a picked chicken after two days of it and now we use the cars.
I saw a fellow just now who says he loves his wife as much as I do mine.
He writes her every day anyway. His name is Claud Sowers. I borrowed
stationary [*sic*] from him the first day. You kiss my baby and <u>write me</u>.

Harry.

[Independence, Mo.]
[July 8, 1925]
Wednesday night— 10:30

My Dear—

Today was a decided blank without a letter— but anyway I was not
worried— and that helped some. I was surely glad to hear your voice last
night— This has been the longest week I've ever spent— and it's only half
gone at that.

This has been another red-hot day but it's fairly decent tonight. The
baby is out on the porch— she spent all of last night there and didn't
wake up until a quarter of seven.

Am so glad you are having such good food— expect you will gain
back all you have lost. It's too bad you and Jay couldn't have bunked
together. Remember me to him.

I am glad too that you had the boots for the General's reception—
did you have a good time?

Hope your bathing suit <u>landed</u> alright. I didn't have time to wrap it
up any better— Ted was in such a hurry for it.

Ethel had her hair cut today and she looks great. When may I do it?
I never wanted to do anything as badly in my life. Come on, be a sport.
Ask all the married men in camp about their <u>wives' heads</u> & I'll bet any-
thing I have there isn't one under sixty who has long hair.

Your daughter seems well— but is powerfully cross— We took a
short drive this evening and she enjoyed that immensely.

Have you found out about Friday yet? Miss Railing (I've no idea in
the world how to spell it) called up yesterday and wanted your address.
She said things were going fine.

Lots of love—

Bess

Be careful of the pool— don't try any deep water swimming please!

Ft. Riley, Kans.
July 9, 1925

Dear Sweethearts:—

Today is fine and cool and a beautiful day, but for all that it's a dull one— there was no letter. I got the swimming suit by air and I am very glad you sent it. We have swimming parties every afternoon and while the pool is cold as the mischief it's very good for us. I'm as healthy as a farmhand.

Say, if you want your hair bobbed so badly go on and get it done. I want you to be happy regardless of what I think about it. I am very sure you'll be just as beautiful with it off and I'll not say anything to make you sorry for doing it. I can still see you as the finest on earth so go and have it done. I've never been right sure you weren't kidding me anyway. You usually do as you like about things and that's what I want you to do.

I hope that you and the baby are both well and not entirely roasted. We've never been uncomfortably hot although yesterday was a stinger. Be sure and let me hear from you. The days are awful dull without the letters. I don't know if I'm to come home Friday or not. If I can't I can't that's all. We had a fine ride this A.M. and we're going to pistol practice shortly.

Lots of love to you & kiss my baby.

Harry

P.S. Daughter, you be sure and have your mother write me <u>every day</u>.

Ft. Riley, Kans.
July 10, 1925

Dear Bess and Margaret:

[The first two-thirds of the letter is devoted to a detailed explanation of the camp mail system, apparently to mollify Bess when she didn't get a letter.]

I'm glad that you are feeling well and that the baby is all right. I'm so afraid she won't know me when I get home I don't know what to do. I've turned as brown as an Indian and am feeling fine. The swimming pool isn't deep or large and it's always full of the finest swimmers— So don't worry.

Be sure and write,

<u>Your</u> Sweetie,

Harry

P.S. Jay Lee wants to be remembered to you and our family. He told me that before I got your letter.

[Independence, Mo.]
[July 11, 1925]
Saturday a.m.

My Dear—

I didn't get a letter written last night— was too tired to think after a good warm day.

I'm trying to keep the child on the "chair-chair" while I do this, but it's one fine job— and 'most hopeless.

I was awfully glad you called last night— wish it didn't cost so much so we could do it every night— but one week is gone and the other can't last forever— <u>I hope</u>.

I called your mother and talked to Mary. She said they both [were] well but not enjoying the weather. They were over at Vivian's.

Gates Wells is coming tomorrow to spend the day— principally to play golf.

Margaret's eyes look really better this a.m. so will not go in to Dr. Berger's unless they seem worse by afternoon. She is pulling and slapping me and is on my back at present (I'm sitting on the floor) so if you can read this scrawl you are doing pretty well.

She hasn't forgotten you yet. I show her your picture & she says, "da-da bye." She is trying to swallow my dorine [?] now.

I can't write any more— she is yanking the paper out of my hands now.

Lots of love and kisses from us both.

Devotedly
Bess

What about the hair-cut?

Ft. Riley, Kans.
July 11, 1925

Dear Bess:—

It surely was fine to get a letter today— I am homesick to see you and my girl baby. I wish you could come out and spend the week end with me. I wouldn't care if I never saw Independence again but I surely would like to be close to you today. It's going to be a long old day tomorrow. [...] I didn't come home because it would cost 10^{\underline{00}}$ to make the round trip and I wouldn't have accomplished much only to get all the week's worries on my mind and I decided I'd get 'em next Saturday. Be sure and write me. I wish I could take you & Margaret "bye" this P.M. I am going to take a bath, a swim and a rest. Your letters did not double up. I

only had one today. I hope I get one every day. Let me know what Berger
says about her eyes. Take care of your foot. As always, your
                                    Harry

                                              [Independence, Mo.]
                                                  [July 12, 1925]
                                                      Sunday—
My Dear—
    Frank & Natalie have taken the youngster for a short "bye"— so
maybe I'll get a letter off in peace. I was so delighted to get that "special"
this morning. It made me sick not to have sent yours that way yesterday—
but there wasn't anybody here who could take it to the P.O. (Frank and
Fred were both gone all day) and I just felt like I could not make it up
town and back and I didn't have enough stamps at home. Sorry as I can
be that you won't have even a piece of a letter today for I know how much
I would have missed mine.
    M's eyes look much better so we haven't gone to Berger yet. I'm
going to try to go to K.C. tomorrow to take her proof back and try out
Katz's.
    That was a dear letter you wrote me about bobbing my hair— it
almost put a crimp in my wanting to do it. But if you knew the utter
discomfort of all this pile on top of my head— and the time I waste
every day getting it there you would insist upon me cutting it. I most
sincerely hope you'll never feel otherwise than you said you do in that
letter— for life would be a dreary outlook if you ever ceased to feel just
that way. Now, you don't have to exhort your daughter to have me write
you. I haven't missed but one day and I wouldn't have missed that one if I
hadn't talked to you.
    Today is one of those days you called a stinger. The heat is really ter-
rific but if I can just keep the baby well I don't care otherwise.
    Do you really mean you will be home next Saturday? Are you trying
for the cup Gen'l [Col.] Klemm has offered? Don't work yourself to death
for it— this is your vacation. I wouldn't mind that ice cold dip myself this
afternoon. You really are situated better than at Leavenworth, aren't you?
    Tom Bourke called up last night and was mighty glad to hear from
you.
    I think you did the right thing in staying. The trip wouldn't have
done you half the good if it had been broken in two.
    Fred is waiting to mail this and is pacing the floor.
                                    Loads of love & kisses from
                                    Your Sweethearts

Ft. Riley, Kans
[July 12, 1925]
Sunday, A.M.

Dear Sweethearts:—

Yesterday afternoon I was so homesick to see you I didn't know
what to do. I drove to Manhattan and it was all I could do to keep from
just taking the road and going home. I hadn't signed out though and the
round trip would have made me so tired I couldn't have acted with any
satisfaction on the firing. We begin firing tomorrow at 7 A.M. and keep it
up 5 hours a day for five days. I have to make up the records of the officers doing the firing. Col. Klemm is giving a cup for it.

Manhattan is a very nice town. Jay Lee's sister lives there. He went
over to see her today.

I went down and watched them unload a regiment of National
Guard artillery this morning. The Missouri regiment— 128th F. A. is to
train here this week & next. I saw some of my old men in the outfit and
it was like seeing long lost friends or kinsfolk. They are a fine looking
bunch of men. One of my sergeants is horse sergeant for the battery from
Clinton and one of my corporals is a Lt. in the battery from Marysville.
One of the 129th Lts. is now a Major. I'm glad I took my promotion. They
can't hightone me anyway. I hope the baby's eyes are all right. I didn't get
any letter today. It makes it seem very long. Be sure and write me every
day.

Your
Harry.

[Independence, Mo.]
[July 12, 1925]

Honey—

This has been a long old Sunday— and a hot one, too— (why do
Sundays always <u>appear</u> to be so much more uncomfortable than any
other day?) until along about five o'clock we had a gorgeous shower and
it cooled off wonderfully.

The baby is sound asleep— she fairly <u>flopped</u> into bed tonight—
I've spent the last hour reading the papers— Katz and the Owl "ads" for
instance. I found the enclosed article— thought maybe you might have
missed it and I knew you would be interested in it.

I think the Nolands have a car— a mighty good looking coach or
sedan— can't figure out the variety. Guess they decided for the car instead
of going East to school this summer.

I'm using the pen Mrs. Kerr brought me from Cuba. It's been many a day since I have used a stub pen. I used to think them the only decent kind made.

I hope I can get down to Jo [*illegible*] for your collars tomorrow if I go to town. I haven't been near K.C. since you left.

There is an expert women's barber in the Baltimore Hotel Barber Shop. Do you think I might go there to have <u>it</u> done? Mrs. Berry went to him yesterday and Natalie says her hair looks better than it ever has.

Natalie and Frank are getting real peevish on the subject of bobbed hair. She is as crazy as I am to have it done but Frank is so grouchy about it.

Well, I'm glad this week is <u>started</u> anyway. Surely hope you'll be <u>here</u> this time <u>next</u> Sunday night.

Has Col. [Maj.] Bachelor been regaling you all with Europe?

> Lots of love
> From Bess

M. looked up at your picture tonight and said "da-da." Later, I said, Where's da-da— and she pointed up at it.

> Ft. Riley, Kans.
> July 13, 1925

My Dear Hon & Baby:—

This day is fine, weather, dinner and everything— I got a good letter. A real sweetheart letter. I like 'em that way. It is fine the baby's eyes are getting well. Do you know where she got them? The shirts came and I'm very glad to get them. They'll be fine this evening after supper.

We went to the firing point this morning at 7:30 started on time and fired fourteen problems. I have seven Lts. in my section to watch but they are all good men and give me very little trouble.

Don't you worry your pretty hair any more, go and cut it off and please yourself. As I said before you'll be just as beautiful to me if you have those curls I'll never forget or if you have none at all. It's you I'm in love with not what you're made of.

I hope it's cooler there than it is here although it isn't too hot to stand.

The gang is falling in. I'll have to fall in.

> Yours,
> Harry

Kiss the baby.

[Independence, Mo.]
[July 14, 1925]
Tuesday— 9 a.m.

Honey—

This will probably be brief— you know how limited time is in the morning. It was so blazing hot last night I didn't have the nerve to keep on enough clothes so I could have a light long enough to write a letter.

We [had] a big storm about 3:30 and it cooled things off considerably but sad to say it's warming up again right now. I sure wished extra hard for you about that time— you know what a nut I am about lightning— we surely had a bird of an electrical storm. I got my book and read until it was over.

I went to K.C. in spite of the heat yesterday. I needed the thing at Katz's so badly— I didn't get your collars because I couldn't have carried them to save me. I went in and came out on the street car— saved thirty cents and really enjoyed the trip. But Great Scott it was hot in town.

The baby's eyes are much better. But she has a lot of mosquito bites that are quite disfiguring.

It was great to get two letters yesterday. I was almost glad you were homesick.

Goodness but I'm glad you didn't really make that trip Sat. night as much as we would have loved to see [you]— you would have been a wreck Monday. Can't you compete for the cup too? Or does your job keep you from it?

I'm ashamed to send this messy letter but it will be afternoon before I have another minute & then it might not get off—

Lots of love—
Bess

[Independence, Mo.]
[July 14, 1925]
Tuesday— 10 p.m.

Dear—

Not a sign of a letter today so it's been a very punk day— and I was hoping you would call up tonight but it's ten o'clock so the chances are slim. Wasn't sure I knew how to reach you or I would have called myself. I remembered the number alright but I didn't know whether I had to call through Junction City or not— I couldn't understand all you said about calling the other night.

The baby is sound asleep on the sleeping porch. I'm rather afraid she will be most <u>too</u> cool out there tonight— as it's decidedly chilly.

Quite some change from yesterday!

I have an idea there'll be a wedding in the family this fall— Jack Yantis' mother died last night— The Nolands' car is a new Overland Six.

How are you coming on the firing? Is it some job?

That was great— your seeing those old men of yours— and under those circumstances too. Made it a lot more interesting than just meeting them on the street somewhere.

The hair is still intact! But I wish it were not.

The baby's pictures won't be finished until the 24th. I had most of them made like the one you liked best.

Poor old [*illegible*] is just this minute pulling in. He's had a lengthy day of it. Left this morning exactly at seven.

If I don't get two letters in the morning I'm going to burn up the wires.

Loads of love—
Bess

Ft. Riley, Kans.
July 15, 1925

Dear Sweethearts:—

Your letter was here when I came in at noon. I think I told you I don't care what they look like so long as I get 'em. I think it looked pretty good. I am certainly glad the baby's eye is improving, but I am so sorry to hear of the heat you are enduring. If I was any good I'd have the where with [wherewithal?] to send you where it's cooler. You see what worries me is the fact that you and the kid are entitled to the world and an acre on the outside and I can't give it too [*sic*] you.

The General and the officers of the cavalry school came over to our dance hall last night and gave us a reception. It was hotter than blazes with my best bib and tucker on. The Gen. and all the reserves stood in line while all the post officers and their wives and the N. G. officers walked around the circle and [told] who they were and [shook] hands. It was a long drawn out affair. Then they showed us a picture of activities at Riley. It was very interesting.

We went out firing this morning and I fired the first problem. It was not very well done. Bachelor fired an excellent one. I can still fire however although I'm out of practice and can't see as well as I once could. I'm afraid I won't get the cup.

I do hope you have better weather and that you both feel better.

It's only three more days. But keep writing. Kiss my kiddie for me.

Your
Harry

Ft. Riley, Kans.
Thursday, July 16, 1925

Dear Hon:—

Your letter was waiting for me when I went in to dinner today. You should not have missed any because I've mailed one every day. I sent one into Junc. City day before yesterday by a 2<u>nd</u> Lt and he may have failed to mail it. I'm glad Miss Mary Margaret is getting on so well. It is a long time since I've seen you both and you don't know how badly I want to see you.

I finished my problem this morning and muffed my chance for the cup. For some reason my brain doesn't function as quickly nor half so clearly as it formerly did. I can figure everything out in advance to the dot and I can stand and watch the officer firing and make every change as it ought to be long before he is ready and then when I get up to do it my mind goes dizzy on me and blooie I miss my chance. If it was on the front I'd do it right but a critical audience spoils the game. You've four things to do every time the guns go off. You must get the direction correctly, they must be properly distributed in relation to one another, the height of the burst must be properly adjusted and you must be able to see if they are short or over. Your mind must be clear and you've got to think of nothing but what you're doing. I've an idea Batchelor [*sic*] will win the cup. He fired another good one today. I'm sorry I didn't call you. I had the urge at the same time you were thinking of it. Kiss my kiddie.

Yours always,
Harry

[Independence, Mo.]
[July 16, 1925]
Thursday—

My Dear—

This is morning again and a delicious one— the thermometer took a tumble during the night some time— I surely hope you are having some of the same.

I was so <u>very glad</u> to get your letter yesterday morning (Monday's letter) and it was a dear one, too. <u>I</u> like that kind, too—

Just when are you coming home? You said something about being here Saturday in one of your letters— but I thought the encampment lasted through Sunday so I was wondering whether you really meant it or not.

Frank & Natalie went to Platte at six-o'clock this morning— Guess Frank wanted to be sure of catching Mr. Kyle <u>in</u> this time. Mr. Southern really got off to G.A. so May and George are out there for three or four weeks.

We miss you like the very mischief, but your daughter has <u>not</u> forgotten you.

Ethel & Nellie still look <u>grand</u> with their short hair.

It's bath time so I must hurry— also to get this out for the post-man.

Lots and lots of love and please keep on loving me as hard as ever. You know I just feel as if a large part of me has been gone for the last ten days.

Devotedly,

Bess

There isn't anybody else on earth I'd stop to write this time of day.

[Independence, Mo.]

[July 16, 1925]

Thursday night.

My Dear—

This was a very <u>full</u> day— <u>two letters</u>— it beat yesterday all hollow. Your Tuesday letter didn't arrive until this morning.

I think Margaret's eyes are much better— altho' they looked pretty red when she went to bed to-night, but she has been driving with Frank and Natalie and the wind may have irritated them.

I took the plaster off my ankle today— with much <u>tribulation</u>. Used most of the benzine in the county doing it. I hope I never have to have any more dealings with adhesive tape.

They surely are <u>putting you all through</u> up there. I'll bet the rest of the men were extremely grateful to you for getting Col. Elliott to allow you to use the cars. I'll bet tho' that walk was about what all of you need. But it's mighty hot to have to do it. Look out for that icy pool that you don't get one of your attacks of cramps.

Why do you so studiously avoid the subject of hair-cutting? Did I tell you that Ethel had <u>Lisle</u> do hers? She said every man she knew in town came into the barber shop while she was having it done.

I'm going to try to get a couple of our soft shirts off to you tomorrow. I should think they would feel good these hot nights. It hasn't been quite so warm today but tonight is close and sultry.

Well I hope you get home tomorrow night but I expect you would rather stay.

Anyway your daughter and I want you, badly—

Love—

Bess

⊛1926

Grandpa may not have held elective office during this time, but he was by no means out of politics. He remained close to the Pendergasts and maintained a wide variety of contacts through the Army Reserve, through his work with the Kansas City Automobile Club and the savings and loan, and through his presidency of the National Old Trails Association and membership in the Masons. In fact, by the time these letters were written, he was already slated to be the Democratic candidate for presiding judge of Jackson County. He had hoped to run for county collector, which paid better, but Tom Pendergast had promised to back someone else.

My grandmother, as always, aided and abetted. She passed on a request from Grandpa to Tom Pendergast to have Senator Jim Reed visit the encampment (he didn't make it) and she herself had wanted to attend a dinner for the senator in Kansas City but had to beg off because she had no one to watch Mom. More directly, she intervened when attorney J. Allen Prewitt asked her if Grandpa would serve on a couple of committees for an event in support of Democratic U.S. Senate candidate Harry B. Hawes of St. Louis. Sensing conflict, she contacted Pendergast through an intermediary and was told that Grandpa should steer clear of "all fights." She promptly called Prewitt back and lied to him, saying that Grandpa wouldn't be home from camp in time for the event. She didn't think Hawes had much of a chance with Prewitt in his corner anyway.

Otherwise, while Grandpa was gone, my grandmother and mother went riding in the family Dodge with Frank and Natalie and attended tea, bridge, and birthday parties, which, to my grandmother's chagrin, were a regular feature of the scorching Missouri summers. As usual, she and Grandpa chided each other for not writing more often and shared a running commentary on reserve officer and fellow politician Jay Lee, who disapproved of Grandpa's favorite diversion, poker. My grandmother held no such prejudice, joking with Grandpa that he might—or might not—use the dime games to add to his campaign funds.

She cared for her ailing mother, felled by an attack of intestinal distress that may or may not have been caused by the water in the cistern. While Madge was sick, my grandmother was her sole caregiver and gofer. Madge's visiting friend, Bess Anderson, called "Auntie Bess," was not much help, nor was someone named Nannie, a maid or possibly a family member who was away.

Frank and Natalie may have been thinking of cutting the apron strings and making a break for it. My grandmother reports that they were looking at a house on Lee's Summit Road. This was probably Natalie's suggestion. Frank was actually very solicitous of his mother, spending half an hour with her every day on his way home from work. Madge may have hoped to quash the rebellion by adding doors to the "barn," now used as a garage, to make it easier for Frank to get his car in and out, thereby enticing him to stay.

When not caring for her mother, my grandmother reported on the search for a misplaced insurance policy and worried if Grandpa was resting and getting enough to eat and if he had shed the ever-present headaches that plagued him even when he was out of office. She also pleaded with him not to go up with any of the reserve pilots after he reported that one of them had been killed in a crash. She was deathly afraid of flying, something she passed on to Mom. In the 1960s, my brother, Will, took advantage of this on a trip to Missouri. "Mom," he said, looking out at the wings as they taxied for takeoff, "do those rivets look loose to you?" She'd have hit him if she hadn't been gripping the armrests so fiercely.

Eddie McKim was a close friend of Grandpa's, a former member of Battery D, and a goof-off. He was so averse to work that a lieutenant subbing while Grandpa attended artillery school demoted him from sergeant to buck private. McKim appealed to Grandpa to reinstate him and was told something to the effect of, "Hell, no. I'd been figuring on busting you to private myself." Nevertheless, McKim was well liked and went on to become a captain in the reserves and a senior White House aide. Unfortunately, Grandpa had to fire him in 1945 after McKim ordered White House secretaries to quit answering Eleanor Roosevelt's condolence letters, noting for the press that Mrs. Roosevelt was "no longer riding the gravy train."

C. C. Bundschu was a fellow reserve officer and son of A. J. Bundschu, who ran Bundschu's Department Store in Independence in the 1920s. Bundschu's was considered the nicest store in Independence and was known for it's friendly and personal atmosphere. The family sold the business in 1959. C. C. and his wife socialized with my grandparents, although they were probably about fifteen years younger.

Spencer Salisbury, another fellow reserve officer, was a former artillery battery commander during the war and childhood friend of my grandmother's, which explains how she knew of his riding ability. In fall 1925,
Salisbury and Arthur Metzger went into business with Grandpa, running
the Community Savings and Loan in Englewood (near Independence).
In April 1926, Grandpa became president of the Savings and Loan and
opened an office in Independence, from which he also sold insurance with
Robert Barr, soon to be eastern judge of Jackson County. Salisbury and my
grandfather eventually had a falling out, apparently because Salisbury was
stealing from the company. Sadly, Salisbury became a lifelong enemy, one
of the few Grandpa had.

Ft. Riley, Kans.
July 5, 1926

Dear Sweetheart:

We arrived at 11:55. I took a bath and ate as much as a horse.
Salisbury and Bundschu arrived about two hours later. They went out
to Olathe instead of taking the Victory Highway. We waited for them in
Topeka and lost about forty minutes. Had a good breakfast in Topeka of
grapefruit, oatmeal, toast and a glass of milk.

It has been pretty hot up here today, but there is a very good prospect of rain. It is much cooler this evening.

I am going to have a real job. The regiment was organized this evening and my labors have started. There is one thing certain I won't have
time to worry about things at home politics or finances either.

I wish I could see my honey and my baby this evening and I'd then
be perfectly happy. This is a sloppy and terrible letter but I'm here I'm
thinking of you, I['m] as busy as the law can make me. Write at once. Kiss
my girl.

Harry

[Independence, Mo.]
[July 5, 1926]
Monday Night.

My dear—

I have just gotten your daughter settled (without any <u>undue</u> strug-
gle) and if she will cease her conversation for a minute or two I will get a
brief note off to you.

I do hope it wasn't perfectly unbearable driving through Kansas to-day— in that <u>wool shirt</u>. It has been a <u>stinger</u>, as you would say— Auntie Bess, Mother, Margaret, & I took a little drive after dinner and cooled off for the time being.

You evidently decided you wouldn't need your straw hat after all— Was Dr. Crandall's car loaded to the guards? Did you have to wait on Eddie McKim?

M. just rolled over in bed scratching her head where the heat is broken out on her and said in the most forlorn way, "O my Dosh." She has asked forty times when daddy was coming— She told George this morning you had gone way, way, way! and wouldn't be home to-night. I asked her just now what I should tell her dad and she said, "Tell dad I <u>hied</u>" (cried). I just gave her a <u>small</u> paddling for taking her nighty off. I think everybody in the county must know you are out of town— the phone hasn't rung once.

You are going to have a guest Thursday or Friday— but I won't tell you who it will be.

I am sitting up here with my eyes almost shut.

Will write again tomorrow— Hope you are <u>comfortably billeted</u> and have mighty good food.

All my love—
Bess

Ft. Riley, Kans.
July 6, 1926

Dear Bess:—

Why don't you write? I have not had a line from you since I arrived. I'm going to call up this P.M.

I have my outfit going likety [*sic*] split. I've passed the buck in B. G. [brigadier general] style and have even got Salisbury working. I have invited Jim Reed to come out and see us. I wonder if you would call up Buck and ask him to see Tom and get Tom to request Reed to pay me a visit. I'd be sitting on top of the moon if that could be done and Col. A. J. E. [Arthur J. Elliot] would have a spasm.

We are having a 3 hour suspension of duty while we go to an aviator's funeral. He fell yesterday and was killed. I'm not going up with these half baked reserve fliers.

I am getting as hard as a rock feel fine and it's doing me good. If you and my girl were here I'd be happy.

For goodness sake send me a letter. Kiss my baby. Wish I could carry her awhile.

> Your
> Harry

I wrote Reed today.

> Ft. Riley, Kans.
> July 6, 1926

Dear Bess:—

We've had a very busy day. I have organized this 443rd into batteries and Battalions and have also made a firing battery out of it. The schools are going good and it looks very much as if we are to have a good tour of duty with plenty of work to keep us all out of devilment.

A train just went by headed for K.C. and I wished I was on it. I'd sure like to see my honey and my baby. How's my girl? I almost called you up yesterday evening but the good for nothing exchange here would not accept the call and I was too tired to go to Junction City.

Jay Lee is looking out for my morals and telling me what to do to be saved as a Regimental Commander. I will write more at length tomorrow. Dr. Crandall is going to mail this for me.

Be sure and kiss my baby. Why don't you write.

> Your
> Harry

> [Independence, Mo.]
> [July 6, 1926]
> Tuesday night.

Honey—

Your daughter and I were mighty glad to get your good letter this afternoon, and to know you arrived safely etc. It did a lot of good for you to wait for C. C. and Spencer at this end of the line that morning— didn't it? What happened to them— did they think they picked the better route?

We've had a glorious change in the temperature— only hope it isn't temporary— rained a little dab, not enough to really wet anything— but it brought a nice cool breeze.

I found the enclosed clipping in last night's *Star**— thought maybe you wouldn't see it.

Margaret went riding with Natalie and Frank to-night. She

---

* The clipping announces that Grandpa, now a lieutenant colonel, is in charge of the encampment.

demanded loudly to be taken out to "Nat's pop's," so they went out and visited the Otts.

I went up and had Lisle curl my hair to-day and that's the extent of my day's excitement.

Arthur's stenog called up this morning and wanted your address so I guess you'll find out soon what it was he had on his mind (?). * I told her to tell him you tried to call him about 8:30 Sunday evening.

I will call Mrs. Hawthorn tomorrow & Mr. Long and see about that policy.

Margaret insisted upon knowing just where you were. She kept asking where is my daddy? Finally I explained very elaborately to her— and at lunch she came forth with "My daddy gone two weeks." The first thing she said this morning was— "Where is daddy?" She is chattering just as hard as she can right now. She didn't wake up until 5:15 so I guess I'm in for a long session.

Today didn't seem to have any beginning or any end— but the letter helped a lot. Hope you can write every day—

> Loads of love—
>
> Bess

> [Independence, Mo.]
> [July 7, 1926]
> Wednesday night—

My dear—

I was so glad to get your good letter this afternoon— it was the next best thing to seeing you. I am greatly relieved about your morals— I am very sure if they are in Mr. Lee's keeping, they are safe. He couldn't lead you into temptation if it were staring him straight in the face. Has marrying made him any different? any more human and like other people?

Am glad you are all organized that was probably a job— You haven't mentioned food— are they treating you well that way?

Natalie and Frank & Margaret and I went out to Mrs. Steele's to get some black-berries to-night. Frank thinks the new car is great. He's had a touch of the heat and is almost sick. It has been pretty warm again this afternoon. The clouds looked terrible while we were out at Steele's and the wind blew a gale— but the real rain passed us by— but they must have had a big rain south and south west.

I called Mrs. Hawthorn this a.m. She was at home with a bum

---

* She added the question mark, which, according to my mother, was a swipe at Arthur's intelligence.

tooth— Miss Bessemer was at the office— but she will go back tomorrow and will look for that policy the first thing and then I will call Mr. Long if she doesn't find it. She said she remembered you showing it to her— but she thought you put it back in your pocket. She had a telegram from her mother this morning saying she will stay another week in the <u>sanitarium</u>. What's the idea of Christian Scientists having a <u>sanitarium</u>?

The baby is sound asleep and I am on the road—

Lots of love—

Bess

Ft. Riley, Kans.
July 8, 1926

Dear Bess:—

The letter came yesterday before I got to the phone and I was sure glad to hear from my babies. I never wanted to come home so badly in my life as I did last night after the young lady said she'd ci-ed. I can some-what sympathise [*sic*] with these birds that lose all respect by going over the hill to see their honies [*sic*].

Two letters just came but one of them was the Ins. Co's letter. I'm very glad you sent it. I'm most always easier to get along with after getting your letters; the gang here found it out and usually make their requests after I get one. [...]

[...] Be sure to kiss my baby and tell her to kiss her mamma for ddy [*sic*]. I'll write more fully tomorrow.

Your
Harry.

[Independence, Mo.]
[July 8, 1926]
Thursday night—

Dear Husband—

I came mighty near not writing this— as I didn't <u>get</u> a letter today— thought I'd give you a little dose of your own medicine— but I decided maybe you had <u>tried</u> to get a letter here today and it wasn't your fault— Besides, I didn't want you to be as disappointed on <u>Saturday</u> as <u>I</u> was <u>today</u>. (I hope you <u>would</u> have been <u>disappointed</u> if one had not arrived.)

Mrs. H. called early this morning and said she had found your policy in the safe. Also said she was feeling much better.

I am forwarding a letter from Mt. Wash. Lodge. Was afraid it might be something that should be attended to at once.

Mrs. Twyman called this morning and asked me to go to the Jim Reed dinner with her— and Mrs. McConnell— I was really sorry not to go— so didn't have to fib for once— but I couldn't leave the child.

Frank and Natalie went out to see that place on the old Lee's Summit Road to-night. Frank says he is sure going to try to get it.

It's trying to rain tonight— here's hoping it succeeds marvelously. Today has been lovely tho.— could stand a whole summer of this kind of weather. I hope it has cooled off out there, too.

Are you still working hard? Have you had a chance to go swimming yet?

According to your theory, the change in the weather is working on your daughter and she is loudly demanding that I "wock her"— so here goes—

I surely am looking for <u>two</u> letters tomorrow and it's going to be a punk day if I don't get them.

Loads of love—
Bess

Your daughter sends a large kiss— She just asked— "When's he toming [sic] home?"

Ft. Riley, Kans.
July 9, 1926

Dear Bess:—

I got another letter just now. They are sure fine. The day is always much better for their comming [sic]. We are getting good food and lots of it. I am glad you sent the *Mo. Democrat* and the editorial from the *Examiner*. I suppose the campaign will get pretty hot on the Court House Bonds shortly. We can get along very well in our present Court Houses.

Miss Holland [Hawthorne?] wrote me that she had found my Insurance Policy for which I am thankful. Mr. Lee is still carefully watching my morals. I dodged him last night though and won 2^{\underline{00}}$ in a 10¢ poker game. He asked me where I'd been this A.M. and was much scandalized that I'd been gambling the night before.

How's my girl? I want to see her so badly I don't [know] what to do. Only one person I want to see worse and that's her mamma. Kiss her and keep writing to

Your honey,
Harry

[Independence, Mo.]
[July 9, 1926]
Friday night

My dear—

I called Buck (as instructed) and he said he would see Mr. T. J. tomorrow sure— if he, T. J., was in town.

This was a grand and glorious day— <u>two letters</u> in the morning mail. Yesterday's letter caught up with Wednesday's. I was surely glad and was right on the job looking for them.

I am so glad you are feeling so fine— keep it up!

May and I went to K.C. this afternoon in the Dodge— it's working very fine— but I must confess needs another bath— I wiped all the dust off this morning but it needs some <u>soap</u> & <u>water</u>. If I had left it out in the yard last night it would surely have had an honest to goodness bath— My word— but the rain we had! Never heard or saw anything to beat it.

I sent a dear little dress out to Luella to-day. Your mother said she hadn't gotten half enough dresses—

Your daughter is probably going to her first party Tuesday— Louise McCoy is having one for little Deb McDonald & Ross Harris. Do you suppose she will break up the meeting?

The Woodsons are having a bridge tea to-morrow and Marnie one on Monday— and Helena a tea on Wednesday. No doubt the parties are just starting. There are always a world of them in a red-hot summer.

I do hope Mr. Reed will have time to go to Ft. Riley—

Did you see the article about Dickey suing the *Star* for 3 million? If <u>his</u> standing and reputation are worth <u>3</u> what are <u>yours</u> worth? Would send this special but don't suppose it would do any good—

All our love—
Margie & Bess

(M. is sound asleep.)

Ft. Riley, Kans.
July 10, 1926

Dear Bess:—

Your letter came today. The day is perfect <u>now</u>. The weather is cool, regular summers resort kind. I saw that you'd had a four inch rain. I don't understand why you didn't get a letter because I haven't missed a day. With all the business I've had I don't let it interfere with your daily letter.

This is a very fine bunch of men. They have co-operated wonderfully with me. They are asking me to take permanent command of the regiment. It makes me feel pretty good. We are going to have an exhibition drill and riding contest Saturday morning. I wish you'd come up. I am sorry you couldn't go to Reed's dinner. I imagine it was a great affair. The Mt. Washington letter was a report for the Grand Lodge. Had a letter from Metzger enclosing a proof of my buttons. Don't like 'em. Be sure and kiss my baby and tell her to kiss her mamma. I'm healthy, sleeping well and if I had my honey I'd be happy.

Harry

Ft. Riley, Kans.
July 11, 1926

Dear Bess:—

This is Sunday. I got up at 7 A.M., ate some apricots, puffed wheat bacon and scrambled eggs. Took the chaplin [*sic*] and Eddie McKim to church, went over to the hospital to see my sick Lieut. and took him a morning paper, and then took about a dozen officers for a horseback ride. We had an elimination jumping contest to see who would ride for us in Saturday's competition. Salisbury and a Lieut. by the name of Calhoun were the best. One of my lieutenants by the name of Fisher who was formerly in the 129th F. A., got too much sun and did[n't] take enough salt so we had to send him to the hospital. He'll be home today. Edgar Hinde came to see me Thursday. He sure wanted to stay. We are having a fine time. I hope I get a letter today. Wish I could see her.

Loads of love
From your
Harry

[Independence, Mo.]
[July 11, 1926]
Sunday morning—

My dear—

I was so glad to get your special— <u>was looking for it</u>— and would have been mightily disappointed if it hadn't arrived. I didn't send mine that way for I was sure you told me last year that it didn't help a bit.

I didn't write last night, was too tired to think straight— but you will get this as usual any way.

Am so glad you are feeling fine— Have the head aches quit? Surely hope so.

Margaret has gone riding with Frank & Natalie. They took her out to the golf club earlier this a.m. and she went around taking all the balls off the tees that the men had set up— They had to give her a ball and club of her own to keep her from breaking up the other games— They drove the

Dodge on the first trip. F. thinks it's pretty fine. The weather is great! I am absorbing all of it that's possible.

Auntie Bess, Mother & Margaret and I drove out to Raytown last night— It was a gorgeous evening for a drive.

The Woodson party was lovely and May got first prize—

Am enclosing some clippings from *Examiner* I thought you might be interested in.*

I wish I could have seen the drill yesterday morning. Know it was fine.

Please promise me you <u>won't</u> go up with any of those aviators— <u>half-baked or otherwise</u>.

I am going up to mail this myself— Fred has gone to Ex. with Miss Watts and Bob— so I have to be my own post-man today— I want it to get out on time. I asked M. this a.m. if she wanted to see you— and she said yes she wanted to give you a kiss— She's learning!

Lots of love—
Bess

[Independence, Mo.]
[July 11, 1926]
Sunday night

Dear Harry—

This has been a long dragged-out day. Couldn't do any ironing or sewing or anything much to help speed the time. Nannie didn't come tho' so there were several extra stunts to do— She went to Jefferson City on an excursion. Think she has been saving up her money for three weeks for this performance.

Emma and Foy breezed in late this afternoon for a few minutes— They were on their way home from K.C. They gave us a <u>very special invitation</u> to come the very first Sunday possible after you come back. I told her we would do our best to make it.

Mother has a touch of ptomaine or intestinal flu— is pretty done up to-night, but won't have a doctor.

I had to put your letter in the outside box this afternoon and if it doesn't get there tomorrow, I'll surely be peeved. Whoever heard of a P.O. being closed up so tight you couldn't even get inside to mail a letter.

---

*The clippings were on a special meeting of the Jackson County road overseers, contributions for a new county courthouse, a feature on American involvement in World War I, and a "We Wonder Why" brief on the county court waiting until just weeks before the primary to oil roads in a nearby township.

Another example of bum management under this Republican regime.

What did you hear from Mr. Reed? It's almost midnight and as I will probably have to arise to get breakfast, I will quit— this trip.

Your daughter is still demanding to be told when you are coming home.

Lots of love from us both

Devotedly
Bess

Ft. Riley, Kans.
July 12, 1926

Dear Bess:—

Your letter came Sunday and I surely appreciated getting it. It made the day really worth while. We are on our way to Manhattan this morning to look over and study a G.P.F. 155 Rifle. It will shoot ten miles and make a hole in the ground you can throw a house into. It rained last night and we are going over on the streetcar hence this shaky writing, so don't accuse me of being drunk as you once did when I wrote you a letter on a French train.

[…] There are lots of politicians here. We have a great time trying to get our campaign funds out of the poker game. Be sure and kiss my baby. Wish I could see you.

Your Harry

[Independence, Mo.]
[July 12, 1926]
Monday night—

Dear Harry—

I think this will be right brief— I've had a rather hectic day— Mother in bed and Nannie not here— and Auntie Bess worse than no help— Mother is better tonight— Doc says the town is full of that intestinal trouble— and if Nannie will only turn up tomorrow— will be greatly pleased. Guess she had too much excursion.

Didn't get my letter today— Suppose Sunday upset the mail schedules— Hoping for two in the morning.

Am enclosing this from Elec. Com. [Election Committee]. I didn't know whether it should be answered at once or not.

What did you do all day yesterday?

It is chilly enough tonight for sweaters and coats.

Mother is having three doors put on north side of barn so Frank can get in and out without wrecking things. He can go in almost straight now.

Natalie & I are going to have a big party a week from Wednesday
for Carrie and Can— and get a lot of our indebtedness paid up. I had to
miss Marnie's today and won't be able to go to Louise's in the morning,
either— but I'm not heartbroken over either of them.

M. is sound asleep— and I will be soon.

Hope you are still feeling fine and thinking about your <u>family</u> right
now.

Lots of love—
Bess

Ft. Riley, Kans.
July 13, 1926

Dear Bess:

I tried to call you up all day yesterday but failed. I was afraid my
Sunday A.M. letter didn't go out until Monday.

We were supposed to fire this morning and yesterday morning but
the schedule was changed on us and we failed to get started out. We went
to Manhattan yesterday and did duty as gunners on a 155 gun they have
up there. [...]

We have a map problem this afternoon and tomorrow we fire. There
is a shortage of ammunition and we can't fire but about 350 rounds.
We are entitled to 1,000 but our poor gov't would rather keep a bunch
of good for nothing prohibition enforcement officers or build a useless
canal across Cape Cod rather than let us learn to defend the country.

I hope that Saturday comes awful quick. I'll probably be home
either Saturday evening or Sunday morning. I'm afraid my daughter won't
know me.

I am certainly pleased with your letters haven't missed but the first
two days. Be sure and keep it up. Kiss my baby and tell her to kiss her
mamma.

Sincerely,
Harry

[Independence, Mo.]
[July 13, 1926]
Tuesday night—

My dear—

Two nice letters today!— and both of them had been mis-sent to
Excelsior Springs— Can you beat that? "Independence" was as plain on
them as could be.

Am so glad you are having some outside pleasure as a diversion— Bet on you finding the <u>politicians</u> in the out-fit. Has your own campaign fund been augmented to any extent? Or depleted?— Eh?

Fancy Spencer being chosen for his excellent riding when he dislikes it so. I remember tho. that he <u>used</u> to just look like part of the horse— and I guess the knack of it must still stick.

I went to see Mary Sturges this afternoon— she looks pretty badly— but seems to be in pretty good spirits. She is almost through <u>one</u> of her <u>eight</u> weeks in bed.

May & George & M. & I took a short drive in the "new har [sic]" this evening.

Mother is better and Nannie came back to-day so I haven't been quite so busy.

Hope your shirts arrived OK. I mailed them Sat. eve. Of course last week of all weeks, the laundry didn't come back 'til Friday night. Have you had plenty of clothes?

Will you be home Sunday or Monday?

Don't know whether these clippings are worth sending or not—

Aren't you <u>glad</u> Dickey didn't get the *Star*? We surely would have been out of luck—

Lots of love—

Bess

M. said today she wanted to send you a letter all by herself— She wrote you one but I can't find it.

Ft. Riley, Kans.

July 14, 1926

Dear Honey:—

Your letter came and I was sure glad to get it. I was afraid my Sunday letter was a dud for I saw my orderly emptying the mail box the next morning.

We went out this A.M. and fired a bunch of problems. The officers did very well, but of course they are not so good as the gang last year because they haven't had the experience.

There is a young man by the name of Fisher who is a Lieut in the regiment. He was a pvt. & sgt. in the 129th F. A. He's crazy about photography and has taken pictures of us in every position possible. There'll be so many of them that you can see what has been done all the way through.

I thank you for the sample ballot. It is all right as far as I can see.

I am thinking of my family. I don't do much else. I haven't missed a day on letters and I'm sorry you missed. I tried to call up but didn't get you. Keep on writing.

Love to both from
Your Harry

[Independence, Mo.]
[July 14, 1926]
Wednesday—

Dear Harry—

This has been a poor day— no mail— suppose they went AWOL to Excelsior again or elsewhere. Surely hope it comes in the morning. Natalie and I are going to K.C. tomorrow to get prizes etc. for our ball— Friday, I am going to try to get up the courage to take M. in to Woolf's to have her hair cut— it's a perfect sight. Saturday, Mrs. Sawyer has a party, Tuesday, Mrs. Stanley Watson has one and ours on Wednesday and I hope to goodness that <u>ends</u> them. We went to Helen's today to a tea— she has a guest, too.

I hear C. C. has been considerate enough to send a <u>post-card</u> home each day— even sent one <u>special</u> on Sunday.

Another notice (like the one from the K.C. Elec. Com.) came to-day from P. J. Kelly but I guess it can wait 'til you return to be attended to.

There is a letter here from J. Allen Prewitt! asking you to be on a reception committee for Hawes on the 23rd also an executive com— but he wants to know tomorrow at the latest— (his letter just came today)— so I guess the best thing to do is to phone him tomorrow & tell him you are out of town etc. and accept for the reception committee anyway. He wants the exec. com. to meet Friday night in his office. I'll say he needs some of you live ones— I'm afraid Mr. Hawes won't get very far under his patronage. I'll call Arthur or Buck before I call J. Allen— & find out what to tell him.

Hope you are still feeling fine—

Lots of love—
From
Bess

I've enclosed Prewitt's letter. Won't need it to call A. or B.[*]

---

* She also included a two-page note from my mother, the first page reading: "Dear Dad— Please come hom [*sic*] soon and take a […]" Despite its brevity, it is suspiciously well written for a two-year-old, plus it is covered with scribbles. The second page features a drawing of a cat, also very well done for a toddler, and more scribbles.

Ft. Riley, Kans.
July 15, 1926

Dear Bess:

Your good letter came this noon and I was sure glad to get it. Mr.
Southern seems to be taking some active interest in politics. He usually
does that when there is nothing to fight about.

I hope your mother is much better. You'd better have that cistern
water analyzed and not let the young lady have any but boiled.

This has been a very busy day. We fired from 7:30 to 11:30 and came
in had dinner and then I had to assemble my Majors & Colonels and
give them all a paper job in a map problem under the direction of Major
Gruber, the artillery officer of this post. He's a very bright man and a class
mate of Col. Danfords. We then fought an imaginary war in the mess
hall. My job was to keep everyone else busy and not be busy myself.

Last night I called on the general and had a very pleasant evening.
I wanted him to help me get some slides made of firing pictures. He
accommodated me and I had a pleasant visit besides. He always kids me
about my political ambitions and I told him that politics and the army
were equally uncertain.

We are having a party tonight. The annual banquet of the reserves is
some affair. There'll be a badger fight some boxing bouts and speeches by
unit commanders. I was so rushed today that I didn't get to write this at
noon as I should have, and I doubt if you get it as soon as you should.

There's a rumor around here to the effect that we can't leave until
Monday but I hope it's unfounded.

Keep writing. Kiss my baby. How I'd like to see her! and her <u>mamma</u>.
XXXXXXXXXX
50–50
From your
Harry

[Independence, Mo.]
[July 15, 1926]
Thursday a.m.

Dear Harry—

Just two lines to tell you that I called Arthur in reference to Mr.
Prewitt's letter— and he thought it best to call T. J. [Tom Pendergast] & <u>he</u>
<u>did</u> for me. Mr. Pendergast said he considers it better for you to keep out
of <u>all fights</u>— so I called J. Allen & told him you would not be home until
<u>next</u> week sometime— and couldn't be any help to him on his <u>executive</u>
committee for that reason and that I didn't feel like accepting a place on

the reception committee without consulting you— and I couldn't reach
you over a telephone (?) so we would just have to let the matter rest
until you came back & he agreed with me. He said he wanted your moral
support more than anything else— & I felt like telling him he needed it.
Thought I'd better tell you all this in case you felt inclined to write him
when you get that letter I sent earlier this morning.

Lots of love—

Bess

It's raining again this morning and is nice & cool.
Your letter came OK. Hurray!

🏵1927

By now, Grandpa was presiding judge of Jackson County, having won the November 1926 election. His plan was to propose a $6.5 million bond issue to improve the county's deplorable roads and to build a new hospital and courthouse, among other things. Tom Pendergast was lukewarm to the idea. Voters, he said, would assume he, Tom, was going to steal the money and/or fix the contracts. Grandpa, however, was going to promise voters that he would award contracts to low bidders and appoint a nonpartisan oversight board to make sure the work was done properly. This kind of honesty was so rare in Jackson County that Grandpa suffered headaches maintaining it.

His fellow judges, Howard Vrooman and Robert Barr, were a couple of playboys; Barr also turned out to be a thief. Their only saving grace was that they liked to play craps behind the bench during working hours. When Grandpa had work to be done, he simply let them start a game and pushed business along while they were occupied. Grandpa was more upset

The Jackson County Judges in 1927 (TL 58-677).

by Barr, who was his own choice, a fellow wartime and reserve officer, and a member of his own Kansas City Democratic faction—the "Goats"—than he was by Vrooman, who was loyal to Democratic boss Joe Shannon, a "Rabbit." In fact, things were so contentious between the Goats and the Rabbits that Shannon ordered Vrooman to treat Grandpa with total disrespect. Vrooman, who was essentially a nice man, couldn't bring himself to do it, and Grandpa actually came to like him, despite his disdain for Vrooman's womanizing. Ironically though, he never cared much for Mrs. Vrooman.

At this point, Grandpa was not the only one suffering, for my grandmother had become prone to "spasms," "nervous fits," and dreams during which she was gunned down. Whereas Grandpa worked himself into a frazzle, she was a professional worrier, as was my mother. Both inherited the trait from Madge, who fretted endlessly over her four adult children. "She just pestered the kids to death," said my Great-Aunt May, "because she wanted to keep track of every one of them."

One morning, May Wallace caught her sister-in-law, Natalie, uncharacteristically leaving her next-door house by the back door. Natalie announced that she was going to town,

Natalie Wallace in 1935, above (TL 2009-1602). Natalie and May at May's home, below, where May caught Natalie sneaking off to town (TL 82-125).

but without stopping by the big house first and without going by her usual route. "I'm going to Kansas City," Great-Aunt Natalie said. "I'm not going to do anything I shouldn't, but if I go, I'm going up to Pleasant Street and get the car, because if I go through the [front] door, she [Madge] will want to know where I'm going and why."

My grandmother's focus was primarily on Grandpa's health, then on my mother's. In these letters, however, you'd never know Mom was prone to all sorts of childhood ills. She was fighting my grandmother tooth and nail at bedtime and was active enough to pick up "a million" chigger bites. She was so rambunctious that my grandmother complained to Grandpa that she couldn't rest or get anything done unless Mom was out cold.

Grandpa, in turn, thought Mom, at age three and a half, needed a saber...and he bought her one. Maybe he thought it would hold off the tornado he feared had hit Independence in his absence. In fact, all the town got was a lot of rain. Grandpa seems to have been an indulgent parent and, in general, my grandmother thought he was too easy on adults as well. He reported that he'd had a flat tire on the trip to the annual National Guard encampment and found that his leased or borrowed car had no jack. He threatened to "unburden" his sentiments to the owner when he returned, but my grandmother knew he wouldn't.

Attorney Rufus Burrus was a longtime family friend and legal counselor to my grandfather. Like Grandpa, he was a member of the reserve, from 1927 to 1975, and served as an officer during World War II. In addition to his private legal practice, he was assistant counselor for Jackson County from 1927 to 1941.

Vietta Garr was my grandmother's full-time cook. My mother nicknamed her "Pete." Vietta helped raise my mother and acted as her chaperone early in her singing career. She was also one of the few people who could handle Madge Wallace. In fact, Madge wouldn't agree to live in the White House unless Vietta went with her. One of my grandmother's last public appearances was in 1973, at Vietta's funeral. My grandmother's letter mentioning Vietta is one of the few places where she used a racial epithet. In this instance, it's to dismiss the motives of Carrie Pool, who proposed to work for my grandparents temporarily, possibly in an attempt to regain a former job.

Sunday Night
July 10, 1927

Dear Bess & Margie:—

We arrived on schedule, that is in time to take a bath and have our noonday meal here at Ft. Riley. We'd have been about forty minutes earlier but for a nail in the right front tire at Manhattan. It happened right in town and only one block from a garage or we'd have been in a nice fix for there was no jack in the car. I shall probably unburden my sentiments to friend Oliver when I return. If he had my job and I his I'd expect a good going over under the same circumstances and I'd probably get it.

I am very nicely situated, have a room with a would be closet and another with a washstand and toilet. It pays to be a Lt. Col. I have Eddie McKim in my room at my request. He promoted me a table a couple of chairs and a bureau with a mirror, so we shall live in fine style. [...]

Kiss my baby and tell her to write me and you do the same. Not a sign of headache tonight and I hope you haven't.

Your sweetheart
Harry.

[Independence, Mo.]
[July 11, 1927]
Monday 1:30 p.m.

Dear Harry—

I got your raincoat off about ten this morning— hope it arrives before you really need it— Judging from the looks of the clouds in that direction you may be needing it desperately right now.

It's horribly sticky and cloudy here today— and I hope it pours.

It's going to be awfully stupid going to Helen's dinner tonight without you, but I suppose it will have to be done.

Hope you have found pleasant quarters and that the food is extra good this year.

Yesterday was a bum Sunday— I slept most of the afternoon.

Did you get into Ft. Riley in time for dinner?

Marg is so cross today— we've been continuously at war. No doubt you would lay it to a change in the weather. Personally, I think it is the heat and original sin.

Am enclosing a letter that had to be attended to in side of ten days. If you want anybody back here to attend to it— let me know.

Wiley Pendleton and Buck were sitting back in your office this a.m. having a grand time— and Miss Fraher was sitting there with her hands folded. Why didn't you give her a vacation now too? You might as well have.

Have a dozen things to do while M. is asleep—

Hope I get some sort of a letter on this afternoon's mail—

Much love—

Bess

Ft. Riley, Kans.
July 11, 1927

My Dear Sweethearts:—

Bess & Margie

The first half day has gone by with only one casualty. One of the Lts. stuck his finger into the breech mechanism of a 155 Howitzer and a piece of it was amputated. Someone looked at the gun trail and noticed this piece of finger lying there and asked who had lost it. Everyone looked to see if he was the guilty party: in the meantime the man to whom it belonged was hotfooting it across the field toward the hospital. One of the boys picked up the piece and started after him, but in the excitement he lost it and the surgeon over at the hospital found it necessary to graft on a piece of skin, so the invalid won't be permanently injured. He was back on the job in an hour.

We are going out to fire on Friday morning. That is the only part of the performance I care much for. I am feeling fine and I hope you both are. Bess you kiss the baby and tell her to kiss you for me.

Always your
Harry.

[Independence, Mo.]
[July 12, 1927]
Tuesday— 2 p.m.

Do you get KC papers every day or should I send you County Court clippings?

My Dear—

Your daughter and I were very glad to get a letter from you this morning.

Am sorry it's so warm out there— but goodness knows you wouldn't be any more comfortable at home— it's blistering hot.

Too bad about the puncture but you were pretty lucky after all— weren't you— for it to have happened in a <u>town</u> instead [of] out on the prairie somewhere. Yes, I think Mr. Oliver <u>ought</u> to hear about it— but you'll calm down before you get home— and he'll never know anything about it. Maybe it would be a good idea to say nothing and let the same thing happen to him— & hope for the worst. That's a Christian spirit— eh?

Helen's dinner was perfect, but I missed you awfully— kept occasionally looking for you all evening. We all went over with Fred. Had a <u>breezy</u> drive but he was very decent about driving at a moderate gait.

Am enclosing dep. [deposit] slip which came today— Also insurance receipt came, but just put that away—

Am glad you have Eddie McKim with you— know you will enjoy him.

Want to get this down on the front porch before the postman arrives— have to hurry.

Don't work too hard— take good care of yourself—

Love and lots of it from—
Marg and Bess

Ft. Riley, Kans.
Tuesday 12 July

Dear Bess & Margie:—

Another day. Everyone was furnished with a horse and went out with Bty A. 9th F. A. for what is known as reconniasance [*sic*] and occupation of positions. The Bty Commander is usually some Reserve Officer, in this instance Dinwiddie Groves and his detail of officers represent noncommissioned officers in the Bty. They ride around and pretend to go to war and learn a lot of stuff that's never used on the front. It's all very pretty and looks fine in print but it works somewhat differently when the shells are bursting around you sure enough.

I got my raincoat and I am obliged to you, but I'd rather have had a letter. None has come to date. I'll have to call you if it doesn't come tomorrow. It has cooled off and is very pleasant up here now. The mosquitoes are a fright. I have seven bites on one shoulder.

I hope you and Margie are getting on well and that both of you are behaving nicely.

Be sure and write to your lonesome sweetheart
Harry.

[Independence, Mo.]
[July 13, 1927]

Dear Harry—

I just about have time for <u>a line</u>— but I judged I'd better send <u>that</u>

than nothing. I'm breaking my neck to get off to Helen's luncheon at the Bellerive and am of course having a hectic time to make it.

Was so glad to get a <u>note</u> from you this a.m.— (it certainly wasn't any <u>letter</u>) but we'll be even after this one I daresay.

Am enclosing this with billet-doux— no doubt it won't be very welcome but I thought I'd better send it.

Will try to write again tonight.

We're freezing to death today. It just poured from two o'clock on— Hope you are having cooler weather, too.

Lots of love—
Devotedly
Bess

Ft. Riley, Kans.
Thurs. 14, July '27

Dear Sweetheart & Baby:—

I got <u>your</u> note today in return for mine. It's what I deserved all right and I am thankful for small favors. I hope you had a good time at Helen's luncheon. She seems to be doing the high social right. I'm very much pleased and flattered that you miss me so. There are two little girls in the other end of this barrack daughters of a Capt Clayton who is on duty here. Every time I see them I get so anxious to see you and my daughter I can hardly stand it. They keep us pretty well occupied here and in times

Presiding Judge Truman in 1927 (TL 64-1514).

past I'd have thought I was being worked to death but being presiding
Judge of Jackson County has shown me that there is no limit to a man's
ability to stand punishment. When I get in this crowd of soldiers out here
and they don't make a grand rush for me and begin pulling me one way
and another to get my ear for a road or a contract or the right to sell soap
or tacks to the County, I'm rather at a loss. My right arm is almost well
and my left is sore from holding a dancing horse. [...]

Wish you could see a battery fire once and then you'd appreciate
what a powerful weapon of destruction your old man had in the war.

I'm glad it's cooler there. It is here too. You can't say this is a note can
you. I bought Margie a saber today. I guess I'll have to file the end off it to
keep her from poking her eye out. Kiss her and look in the glass for me.

Your
Harry.

[Independence, Mo.]
[July 14, 1927]
Thursday afternoon

Dear Harry—

I have an idea that this letter is going to be <u>late</u> for I am very sure I'll
not get it down in the mail box in time for the postman. However, I'll go
to town before dinner and mail it.

Your daughter and I are being extremely lazy while you are gone—
we didn't even wake up this morning until 8:30. It's just what I need, I
guess— because I'm surely feeling better— haven't had a spasm since
Monday a.m. Had a terrible dream then and it brought on one of those
<u>nervous fits</u>. Wasn't that silly?

No letter from you this a.m. but I'm hoping for better luck this
afternoon. Got <u>two</u> yesterday and that was great!

Helen's luncheon was wonderful. The Bellerive is <u>some place</u> to eat!

You haven't mentioned food— are they treating you as well as usual
that way?

I bought a centennial membership for you yesterday— Mrs. Henry
Ott was selling them— so—

She spent a good half hour telling how wonderful she & all the
DAR's thought the present County Court— I kept thinking about the
<u>marker</u> she wants.

Just found your letter in mail box— am so glad about the head
aches being minus— Hope you don't have a single one in your whole
two weeks— Judge Vrooman's name was not among those listed in this

a.m.'s *Times* who are going to France next month— Maybe Mrs. V. made
some more threats.

Lots of love—
From—
Margie and Bess—

Ft. Riley, Kans.
Friday 15, July '27

Dear Honey & Baby:—

This day has been successful. I have a letter from you, have been
horseback riding, watched the battery fire 9 problems, had an hour swim
a good meal and am tired as I can be without any <u>headache</u>. I am certainly
glad you and Marg are resting in my absence. We'll have to arrange it so
you can keep it up. I never need any breakfast and if that would keep you
from having any more indigestion for goodness sake let's do it. I'm glad
Mrs. Ott is satisfied with the Court. I am too. I see the said Court is func-
tioning. The *Star* said they had ordered Koehler to pave Fairmount Ave.
Had a letter from Vrooman saying the Court was not taking any chances
on anything but holding all doubtful matters for my return.

I called on the old General out here and asked him to our party next
Friday. It's to be a Badger fight so ladies can't come. Eddie McKim is waiting to take this to Junktown [Junction City] so I'll have to make it another
<u>note</u>. Be sure and keep writing. Kiss the baby for your

Sweetheart
Harry.

[Independence, Mo.]
[July 15, 1927]
Friday—

My Dear—

Enclosed you will find a letter from your daughter. She hunted up
a piece of paper and pencil for herself and announced she was going to
write to "my daddy." I was sitting here sewing, hadn't even tho't about
writing so it came entirely out of her own head.

Am hoping the postman is going to be good to me this afternoon—
there wasn't a <u>piece</u> of mail this a.m. I don't know when that has happened before.

I tried to get Mrs. Barr this morning to see if the Major went out to
Riley today. This was the day you were expecting him wasn't it?

I am sending your underwear and an extra suit of pajamas— tho't
you <u>might</u> need it.

Marg has a million chigger bites and I don't know where in the world she got them.

The *Journal* was giving the Pendergast-Ross combine the dickens this a.m. I will send it to you in case you shouldn't get it. Do you get the K.C. papers regularly?

Think I'm going to K.C. tomorrow. Mother is buying furniture for the downstairs bed-room so we'll probably spend the next week <u>looking</u>.

Everybody in the County must know you are gone— haven't had but one call since Sunday or Monday.

Must quit and get a bit of rest while M. is asleep— certainly can't get any at any other time.

Lots of love—
Bess

Ft. Riley, Kans.
Saturday, July 16, 1927

Dear Bess and Margie:—

I can't understand why you don't get a letter everyday. I've never missed and I've mailed nearly every one of them in town. It's like everything else under this Republican gov't I guess just a lack of efficiency. Yes I get the *Times & Journal* every day, but not the *Post* or *Star*.

I don't know whether it's the city edition or not but I've seen most of the articles on the paving combine. I think they are nearly true. Murray had an interview in the *Star* that was substantially correct. They are getting what the specifications call for and that would naturally make it more expensive.

I had a horse back ride this morning and a nap before the noon meal and I'm going to a polo game this P.M. and probably a bridge or poker game this evening. There are some extremely high powered bridge players here. One fellow they call Mr. York or whoever it was wrote the book.

Tomorrow is going to be a dead one. I hate to see it come. I'm almost tempted to come home. Kiss my baby and write as usual.

Your honey
Harry

[Independence, Mo.]
[July 16, 1927]
Saturday afternoon—

Dear Harry—

I surely was glad to get your "special" this morning— but I hope
it doesn't mean I won't get one tomorrow. Sunday will be long enough
any way. But Miss Sallie is coming to dinner and Gates and Lee will be in
some time during the day— they are coming for golf— so they will help
some.

How did your dinner turn out? Hope everything was fine. Were you
dressed within an inch of your life when you went to see the General?

Eddie called up this a.m. to tell me he couldn't leave the store
tomorrow but he expected to go later in the week. He asked me to go
with him— but I told him I simply couldn't drive that far. The one thing
I try to avoid is getting absolutely tired out. A six hour drive would about
finish me.

I talked to Mrs. Barr yesterday evening and she thought the Major
was to go up next week some day— but she didn't seem to know much
about it.

Is Rufus Burrus enjoying his first camp?

That St. Louis Colonel certainly believes in keeping you busy—
doesn't he? Is he more popular than A. J. E.?

Am mighty glad you haven't been bothered with those miserable
head-aches. Guess you are right about the cause of them—

Marg is fine— I was giving her the very dickens last night about
bedtime as usual— and she was sitting down here crying & crying and
finally she burst forth with "When is my daddy coming?" That settled all
the discipline— I just had to howl— it was so ridiculous.*

Lots of love—
From
Both of us

Ft. Riley, Kans.
Sunday, July 17, 1927

Dear Bess and Baby:—

I'm glad Miss Margie made you laugh when you needed it most.
She knows her daddy would take her part if he dared. I was surely glad to
get a special this morning. It came while I was out riding. Lt O'Shea of the

---

* My mother recalled my grandmother laughing at her as hurtful. She had already, at the age
of three, decided my grandmother was the disciplinarian and Grandpa the pushover.

2nd Cavalry took us for a ride up over the reservation. He's a second Lt. West Pointer and a very fine boy. Plays polo and everything.

I saw two polo games yesterday afternoon. One was good but the other was only a punk exhibition. They both went on at the same time. The fields are alongside of each other and the spectators stand between. Tomorrow we fire in earnest all day long. Also Tuesday Wednesday & Thursday. Fleming isn't making any stars for himself. Everyone here is down on him. He's Elliot's executive officer and supposed to be senior instructor here. I received a pass to the Newman & Royal good for two yesterday. I'm almost afraid to mail it to you for fear it will get lost. Barr seems to be doing fine. I'm sure glad. I hope the cyclone didn't do you any damage. I'm [going] to call you up after a while and see. Please keep on writing. You don't know how good they look.

Love to you from
Your Harry

[Independence, Mo.]
[July 18, 1927]
Monday morning.

Dear Harry—

I suspect you are looking for a letter today and it won't arrive— Mary Paxton came right after Miss Sallie left yesterday— and stayed so late there wasn't any chance of getting a letter inside of the P.O. and I knew there was no use putting one in the outside box that late.

Marg was perfectly delighted to get your letter this a.m.— Her eyes just shone and she chuckled all the time I was reading it. I was mighty glad to get your "special" yesterday, too.

I am going to K.C. this afternoon to do a bit of shopping— We didn't get there Sat. as planned. Mother got her furniture at Tucker's & the manager there gave her quite a bit off as I was with her (so he said). Of course he laid great stress on the fact that he knew Mr. Tucker would want to do it for you.

Hope you are having as decent weather— as we are <u>at present</u>.

I am trying to get hold of Hunter to ask him to take your clothes in to Ted. I dreamed last night I was arrested in K.C. again & they were on the point of shooting me— maybe it's a warning! Anyway it's too nerve wracking right now to try it. I know H. won't object.

Did you get a letter from Moreno? He asked me your address up at Brown's one day last week.

It's time for M's lunch so must go.

Lots of love—
Bess

Ft. Riley, Kans.
Monday, July 17 [18], 1927

Dear Bess:—

This is an off day. No letter. I got a couple of *Examiner*s and a notice that I had a package at the P.O. which Eddie McKim is going to get for me. We were out firing all day today fired some 25 problems and they were fairly successful. I won't get to fire because the officers above the grade of Major are turning over their ammunition to the Lts and Capts because they need it more than we do. […] I sure spent an uneasy Sunday. I tried all day to call you up and couldn't get through. The papers this a.m. were sure a relief. I almost made the trip home because of the tornado. I hope you and the baby are feeling all right. I wish I was home. It seems by the *Examiner* that Barr is handling the situation in fine shape. Be sure and keep on writing. This has been the longest time away from home of any camp. I guess I'm getting older. Kiss the baby and both of you keep writing.

Your Sweetheart
Harry

Ft. Riley, Kans.
July 18, 1927

Dear Bess:—

Have a letter today. Things look a lot brighter. You sure left me on the uneasy street with that storm close to home, no paper, no letter and not able to phone. I'm glad Miss Margie enjoyed her letter. Yes I got one from the Drug Store gang. It was written on toilet paper, a whole roll of it, and a different remark on each sheet. It was the hit of the camp.

We were firing at seven this a.m. The battery was right up close to us. It was like old times sure enough. We picked the four best problems and let those officers fire in a contest for the

Grandpa at National Guard camp
in 1927 (TL 66-2905).

Klemm Cup. Colonel Seigmund, Salisbury, Colonel Leetom the Nebraska politician, and myself were the Judges. There were two officers from the 380th & two from the 379th. They all fired rotten problems and it was finally Salisbury and Seigmund against Leetom and me for a St. Louis officer against a K.C. officer. We finally flipped and the St. Louis man won. Naturally that made a lot of goating but they will all finally be satisfied.

My party was quite a success. The cartoonist from the *Star* made my place cards and they were cartoons on the shortcomings of each man. We have had a very successful camp. I am all sunburned and have a right hefty mustioche [*sic*], haven't lost any money or spent any except for the dinner, Salisbury owes me 9\underline{^{00}}$ and McKim 15\underline{^{00}}$ so you see I'm doing very well.

Kiss my baby and write to

Your Harry

[Independence, Mo.]
[July 19, 1927]
Tuesday a.m.

Dear Harry—

This was a grand morning— <u>two</u> letters! Your Sunday one arrived with the Monday <u>one</u>.

Am sorry you worried about the tornado. We didn't get a particle of wind— just a very heavy rain— Wish you were here so we could go out and take a look at it— some <u>morbid curiosity</u>— eh?

I can't imagine why you couldn't get me Sunday— absolutely wasn't off the place and never out of range of the telephone.

I knew those boys were going to pull off something on you— the way they were <u>giggling</u> about it— and that good-for-nothing D. Perry said, "Maybe Mrs. T. would like to write a note too." Thank Heaven I told them I was too pushed for time.

How do you like my sporty new paper— I just got desperate and bought some.

How does <u>your Buick</u> drive? Do you want to trade the Dodge for one?

Well, say, don't you feel like a millionaire with those two passes? For goodness sake don't risk losing them in the mail. You'd better have them recorded, as you did your army discharge—

Do you think you'll be home Sunday evening?

Lots of love—

Bess

Ft. Riley, Kans.
Wednesday, July 20, 1927

Dear Bess:—

I got a letter from you, one from Barr and one from Gen. King this morning. Your letter was delivered to me over in the classroom by one of the Lt's. They all know how I like to get one and when they see one in my box they bring it to me.

We had one terrific rain storm this morning about 4 o'clock. It came down in sheets. I'd just given a nigger $1 to wash my car yesterday evening. It didn't hurt the wash much but I've got to go out in the mud with it this afternoon. We are going to fire this afternoon what we missed this morning. It still looks as if it might come down in sheets again. Barr said in his letter that he was rather dizzy with the road situation and all but he still had his feet on the ground. I guess they have handled everything in fine shape. I see nothing to kick about and it certainly has been a relief to me.

I hope you and the Missy are feeling all right. It was nice of Tucker to accommodate you. I am hoping to get home Sunday A.M. if the roads are passable. They will be if it doesn't rain any more.

Be sure and kiss the baby. Wish I was home now.

Your Harry

[Independence, Mo.]
[July 20, 1927]
Wednesday—

My Dear—

This may be very brief— had to go to town this morning and it knocked my day galley-west— as usual. So I was too tired to write before my rest and now must hurry up to the P.O.

Hunter took your clothes to Ted this morning. I called Ted and told him what to do with them— and he said he would send them out by Al Saenger Saturday— I thought that was a good idea— to get some thing out of him. Hunter said he sure would be glad to have you back. I don't [know] what was bothering him, but something was.

We had a fine rain this a.m. and Frank has been at home since two o'clock washing his car so I am afraid we'll have another one soon.

Am enclosing the card from Dr. MC. There is quite a bunch of mail here for you but none of it seemed important enough to send. Suspect there is ten times this amount at the office.

Marg is standing on her head to go up town so goodbye.

Lots of love—
Bess

Ft. Riley, Kans.
July 21, 1927

Dear Bess:—

Got a letter today with Dr. McConnell's card. I guess they are having
a fine time. But it's not doing them any more good than my trip is doing
me. We fired shell all morning and all yesterday afternoon. It rained so
yesterday we couldn't fire in the A.M. A shell burst is a wicked thing to
see. You can't blame people for getting shell shock. It is a very real disease.
Some even get [it] by looking at the bursts without even getting in reach
of them. I can't say I blame them. I went to a reception by Col. Oliver
yesterday afternoon. He's the Col. of the 2nd Cavalry. I should have
had cards but they'll never know the difference. At 7:30 we had a riding
contest between the Cavalry Engineers and Art. [Artillery]. We only got
two prizes; 3rd in walk, trot and canter class by Col Seigmund [*sic*] and
second in potato race. The cavalry won 1st & 2nd in the walk, trot, canter,
1st in potato race and third in jump. Engineers won first and second in
the jumps. It was a very good exhibition only I'd been better pleased if
the Artillery had won more prizes. Jozack Miller, Dinwiddie Groves, Crabs
and myself are invited to a picnic by a Major Brown over in the post. I'd
rather stay home and sleep but I guess I'll have to go. You know how
enthusiastic I am about picnics. They are about to leave now and I want
to get this mailed so you'll get it. Hope to see you Saturday P.M. if everything hold[s] together. If not it will be Sunday noon. Kiss the baby and
love to you. I want to see you both badly
                              Love from
                              Your Harry.

[Independence, Mo.]
[July 21, 1927]
Thursday—

Dear Harry—

The clouds look as if they are going to turn loose pretty soon so I
must hurry this to the P.O. It's so sticky hot, it's surely going to do something unpleasant.

Mother just brought your letter up— was mighty glad to get it. I
knew you must have had a little rain yesterday a.m. when the paper said
Manhattan had an inch & a half.

Am glad you are still ahead on the poker game. You'd better quit
before you lose it all back. That's being a good sport!

I saw in the *Ex.* [*Examiner*] that Mrs. Salisbury and her daughter
had gone to F. R. [Fort Riley] to spend the weekend with Spencer! Was he

particularly happy over it? Couldn't keep [from] chuckling over it.

May & Geo. are coming for dinner & I hope they take us for a long cool drive.

Vietta is going to St. L. Sunday and Carrie Pool, the ex-matron at the Colored Home is coming in her place. Violet said she was just coming to get close to you & see if she couldn't get back out there. I told her she had just better stay at home then. Don't niggers have the wildest ideas!

Am mighty glad you're coming Sunday. I certainly wouldn't want another week of this.

Lots of love from both of us,
Bess

M. said to send you a kiss <u>if you have time</u>. Don't know what she meant, but I guess she does.

⊛1928

In May, voters passed Grandpa's road bonds by a three-fourths majority and he set about soliciting bids and appointing a nonpartisan board of engineers to oversee the work. In short order, he was called to Tom Pendergast's office where he faced three of the biggest local contractors, all Tom's cronies and all demanding to know why they weren't getting the lion's share of the business. Grandpa told them they could have all the business they wanted, if they submitted the lowest bids and did the work to specifications. Enraged, they turned to Pendergast, who shrugged and said, "I told you he was the contrariest man in the state of Missouri." Afterward, Pendergast told Grandpa to keep his promise to the voters, and he never again encouraged him to make a back room deal.

My grandmother, meanwhile, busied herself by painting the bedroom floor and trying to keep clothes on my mother, who was apparently fond of sprinting off half-naked. My grandparents were more than happy to save money by making repairs and refurbishments themselves. When the kitchen linoleum wore away at the edges and peeled up, Grandpa simply tacked it back down. When told that it would cost extra to wallpaper behind some fancy decorations on the door frame in Madge's bedroom, my grandmother had them sawed off. Rather than install a light

Mom in 1928 (TL 82-321-01).

The family at home in 1928 (TL 82-318).

switch at the base of the stairs to turn on the light on the second-floor landing, Grandpa ran a twenty-foot piece of twine from the light cord down the stairwell. It still works today. In January 2010, the U.S. Park Service, which administers the Truman Home, was in the middle of a million-dollar overhaul to address, among many things, places where my grandparents had filled gaps in broken floor joists with rolled up newspaper.

When she wasn't painting, my grandmother divided her time between friends and family. Midday Sunday meals at the Truman farm in Grandview were a regular feature and in stark contrast to meals at the Gates-Wallace house. Madge expected dignified dinners during which everyone, her four-year-old granddaughter included, was to exhibit perfect manners. Conversation was subdued, polite. At the Truman home, it was raucous. My grandmother loved her mother-in-law, Mamma Truman, who was every bit as hard on people as she was and even more outspoken. She got along less well with her spinster sister-in-law, Mary Jane. Though an accomplished farm manager and respected member of the Masons' sister organization, the Order of the Eastern Star, Great-Aunt Mary Jane could be prickly about her old maid status and quick to take offense if she thought she was being snubbed.

One letter refers to Grandpa's cousins Fred and Murray Colgan, sons of his father's younger sister, Emily. They and their sisters, Myra and Mary, were roughly the same age as Grandpa and very close to him—he had even lived with the Colgan family for a time in 1905 when he was working in a Kansas City bank—but this was apparently the first time my grandmother had spent any time with Fred. Years earlier, during a picnic in 1905, Fred and another young man put their names and addresses in a bottle and tossed it in the Missouri River. Grandpa, Murray, and the others fished it out and corresponded with Fred, pretending to be two Mississippi girls who had found the bottle. They went so far as to find someone in Mississippi who would send responses, including photos. Only when Fred and his friend announced they were planning to visit the fictitious girls did the pranksters confess. Fred had fallen a little in love and was upset enough that it cooled his relationship with my grandfather.

Another letter refers to "Daw." This was Uncle George, my grandmother's younger brother. Mom couldn't pronounce "George" and called him Daw. Aunt May received an even stranger nickname, "Boofy," for her habit of kidding my mother, or "spoofing" her. Oddly, on paper, my mother spelled it "Beufie," as though Aunt May were something on a French menu. Aunt May was ten years younger than my grandmother and lived to be ninety-eight. She was the family jokester, the person I always wanted to sit next to at dinner or any other social occasion. I have only a dim memory of Uncle George, who died when I was six. He was easygoing and kind, something that I learned years later masked an on-and-off battle with alcoholism. When the Park Service inherited George and May's house upon May's death in the early 1990s, they found the basement crawl space stacked three-deep in places with empty liquor bottles. While Frank visited his mother daily and practically lived under her wing, George rarely went near her. To do so was to start a fight.

Ft. Riley, Kans.
July 9, 1928

Dear Mudder & Margie:—

Eddie & I had a very pleasant trip down. The air was cool and refreshing and we didn't have to drive hurriedly. This end of the road, from St. Mary's to Manhattan was somewhat rough on account of rain a day or two ago and because of detours. They are paving the last gap now and next year will have pavement all the way. The road is open from Manhattan to Riley.

We have nice quarters with plenty of furniture and all that it takes to make our existence pleasant while here. They had assigned me to a place over the dance hall upstairs but I had it changed to the same barrack that the balance of the regiment is in. That is the reason it pays to come a day earlier. I'd have probably been uncomfortable all the two weeks if I hadn't got here and made arrangements to suit me yesterday.

I am going over to the hospital for a physical examination and I'll bet you I am a hundred percent when I come back except, of course my eyes which never were any good. I hope you and Margie are having a lot of fun riding around in your new car and that it is giving you entire satisfaction.

I am looking for a letter today. Kiss my baby and look in the mirror for me and do the same thing.

Your Harry.

[Independence, Mo.]
[July 10, 1928]

Dear Harry—

I'm so hot I'm just about to run away— so you probably won't get more than a few brief lines. If it's as warm out there as it is here, you be glad they are <u>few</u> and <u>brief</u> so you won't have a heavy job of reading them.

I was <u>mighty</u> glad you called last night— it looked so cloudy in the west all day I was afraid you had run into rain early in the day.

Your Aunt Emma is having a family picnic to-night and Marg and I are going. I talked to Mary R. this a.m. and she was <u>extremely sorry</u> (so she said) that you had to leave just at this time.

I want to have all of them into luncheon some day this week— don't know how long they are staying but will find out to-night.

Got Hunter this morning & he had attended to the check just as you said.

Hope I get a letter this afternoon— and most certainly in the morning—

Lots of love from both of your sweethearts—

Yours—

Bess

Which F. A. are you attached to now? I told Mr. Boxley— the 443rd. Hope I was right!! I never can keep numbers in my head.

Ft. Riley, Kans.
July 10, 1928

My Dear Honey and Little Honey:

[…] At nine o'clock we got on horseback and rode until eleven-thirty. There are copious calls for new skin to be grafted on places where these fat men sit down. The ride was under the direction of a cavalry officer who has, as all cavalrymen have, leather where he sits instead of skin and naturally can't appreciate the tenderness of some of the office-bred boys. They'll get all right in a day or two. I am not the least bit uncomfortable. A lieutenant colonel has opportunities to take care of his hide that the lower ranks don't have. Some advantage in that, even if it is a useless office except on payday.

[…] There was not a letter today. I am looking for one this evening. Be sure and kiss my baby, and tell her to kiss her mamma for daddy.

Yours with love to burn,
Harry

Ft. Riley, Kansas
July 11, 1928

Dear Bess and Margie:

I had a very pleasant noon meal. There was a letter from my two sweethearts. I am hoping it wasn't so hot for the picnic. […] I went swimming yesterday afternoon in the coldest pool this side of the Arctic. It was plumb full of kids from two years on up. A little girl about the size of Margie made a high dive from the top of the thing where the expert divers show off. You'd undoubtedly have heart failure if you'd seen her.

Yes, I am a member of the 443rd Field Artillery. J. M. Lee has a notion in his head that sounds all right. He wants Mrs. Lee to drive out here a week from Friday and bring you with her. Then you can go home with me Saturday or Sunday. What do you think of it?

Tell Margie I will answer her letter this evening. It is nice of her to write me such a fine letter. Be sure you both keep it up. Tell her to kiss her mamma for her daddy. Tell her mamma to return it.

Love to you both by the largest measure you know of.

Yours
Harry

[Independence, Mo.]
[July 11, 1928]
Wednesday—

Did Col. Jackman get there?

Dear Harry—

I didn't get a letter off to you yesterday— The day just zipped by before I knew it— I'm surely sorry for I almost strongly suspect that I'll be missing one about tomorrow or Friday and I won't like that at all. Please don't be so stern this time.

Your Aunt Emma's picnic was quite a success— You and Roy were the only missing ones. Roy was quite too busy to quit and go to a party.

Your cousin Fred is very attractive— good looking and intelligent— and a very interesting talker and so full of poise. He certainly puts brother

Murray in the shade. But even so, I bet you like Murray better— now
don't you? Fred seems to be different from the whole family— I am still
waiting on Mary to tell me which day she can give me— her short week is
full to the guards.

Be sure to write Myra a card or something if you can about Saturday.
She is expecting it. I knew perfectly well you could hardly come for such
a brief time but it wasn't up to me to tell her so definitely when you had
sort of left it up in the air.

Am glad you got the quarters you wanted— Hope they are treating
you well in the culinary department.

We had a <u>big</u> storm last night and it is far more pleasant today—

M. is waking up so I must dress her in a hurry & get off to the P.O.
or you'll miss another letter—

Lots of love—
Bess

Ft. Riley, Kans.
July 12, 1928

My Dear Miss Bessie & Margie:

This day was a dud when I came in at noon and found no communication from home. For some unknown reason there was no letter for
me. Do you know that just exactly ten years ago yesterday morning I was
placed in command of Battery D, 129th F. A.? I'll never forget that morning as long as I live. Klemm told me the evening before after he'd asked
me how I'd like to command a battery. I answered him that some time
in the future I hoped to be able to command one. He said, "You'll take
D Bty in the morning at Vencille." I almost died of fright. I was Gates's
adjutant so I went back and told him what the Colonel had said and
reminded him that "D" had had about five in command and would probably have six before another month. He didn't give me much sympathy
and I've always thought he probably was at the bottom of it. We finished
the war together D and I and I suppose I made more crazy friends, that is
the kind who would fight and kill someone for me than I ever will or can
again. We are still working in damp weather, but it looks as if the sun may
shine later. Kiss my baby and take a car load on credit for yourself. Please
write. I do like to get them.

Yours
Harry

[Independence, Mo.]
[July 12, 1928]
Thursday—

Dear Dad—

Margs and I were surely glad to get your letter this morning and we are going to the post-office to mail this one just as soon as M. gets dressed.

We hope you are enjoying this lovely cool day as much as we are. It's a great change. Do be careful about staying in that cold water too long and for goodness sakes don't spend too much time in the rain. How is your <u>bogus cold</u> any way?

How did your physical examination turn out? Don't hold anything back! We are enjoying the new car immensely and it is behaving itself beautifully. May, Daw, Marg and I drove to Blue Springs last night— long and lengthy trip, eh? I can't get much kick out of that trip with Mrs. L. They have to leave <u>by</u> 5:30, if not earlier, and that part doesn't appeal to me either. And then you'd have to bust Eddie out to bring me home.

If you were staying on for a week or two after the trip then I'd consider it very seriously, but as long as you'd be coming home the next day I'm pretty sure I'll decide not to come. I'll call Mrs. L. and make some excuse.

Marg and I have moved out to the southeast room and I am painting one floor since it was seriously needed.

M. is wandering around in this chilly breeze minus any clothing so must quit and dress her.

Lots of love,
Bess

Grandpa at National Guard camp in
1928, wearing another moustache
(TL 2002-308).

Ft. Riley, Kans.
Friday, July 13, 1928

Dear Bess:

My health is excellent. The medical examination showed perfect except eyes. One of them was nearly blank. The other reasonably good.

I am writing Marger a little letter today. This day being the 13th was all it should have been. We put in the morning riding some ten miles at a trot and then having a regimental problem. The colonel is a wonder. He has brains by the bushel and he knows how to use them. There is one thing though I am sure he is a widower or a bachelor. If he had a wife he would be a more careful dresser. He's no dude. Hyde & I have been by diplomatic means trying to dress him up. We all appreciate the goating [*sic*] our wives give us when we see someone who hasn't had the proper going over.

One reason this day was perfect was because it brought me two letters. Well really three because Margaret's was in yours. I am glad you like Fred and I wish I could see him, but I can't. Murray is worth a pair of him to stand behind you. Glad the Lizzie is behaving. Don't fail to write me. I can see a brighter side of life when they come.

Kiss Margie and love by the largest measure to you.

Harry.

[Independence, Mo.]
[July 13, 1928]
Friday—

Dear Dad—

Marg has almost written her letter and is standing right here waiting to put it in mine. She thinks I am pretty pokey—

We were greatly pleased to get your letter this morning and hope to continue to get them.

I am sorry you are still having damp weather. How is your cough?

I didn't get to your mother's picnic last night— I was afraid to drive home alone and Mother didn't feel like going. Was sorry to miss it. Am afraid I won't get to see Mary again.

Keturah is coming out tomorrow to spend Sunday with us. Know you are glad to miss that.

Do you mind very much if I don't go out with Mrs. Lee? Mr. Lee said she would drive 50 or 60 miles an hour and I would be a wreck by the time I got there if I did get there.

Do you have to get up early? Marg & I have been getting up at seven. The sun gets into this S.E. room with a bang.

The county judges have put <u>one</u> over on you— they ordered that no more cars are to be washed between the court-houses!

I must get dressed and go to town or you [will] be minus another letter tomorrow— anyway maybe you'd telephone.

                              Loads of love—
                              Bess

                                        Ft. Riley, Kans.
                                        July 14, 1928

Dear Bess and Margie:

This is another day that is not so bright. I had no letter from you today. Something must be wrong. It is going to rain very soon. Eddie McKim Hyde and I were swimming. It was cold as Sam Hill because the sun was under a cloud.

We went out on a rode [*sic*] march this morning down to three mile creek, made the Lts and Captains ride the horses and unhitch & unharness and put up a picket line. It was right interesting to watch some of these city men try to take off the harness and then attempt to put it on hind part before maybe.

The Col., Jay Lee and a Major Jones from Omaha took a cross country ride from nine to ten thirty. It is a very sorrowful bunch of horseback riders today. Most of them are complaining of sore seats etc. ad lib. You'd be surprised at yours truly. <u>I am not sore</u> anywhere and I haven't missed a ride or a trot.

Vivian and Gilbert Strode were up to see me yesterday about Washington Twp. I tried to tell them what to do. Wish I'd come home over the weekend but I was afraid it might rain and I couldn't get back. Kiss my baby, and take a load of love for Miss Bessie.

                              Yours
                              Harry

                                        [Independence, Mo.]
                                        [July 14, 1928]
                                        Saturday—

Dear Dad—

We were a couple of disappointed women this morning when your usual letter didn't arrive. Marg had been watching for the postman ever since breakfast and was standing at the front door waiting for him when he came— and then when I told her none of the letters were from dad— I wish you could have seen the expression on her face. I suspect the letter is right up here in this miserable post-office but as there is but one delivery on

Sat. will have to wait until Monday— Here's hoping for a special tomorrow.

We moved back into our room this morning and Marg was as delighted to get back as if she had been away on a trip.

We are driving in this afternoon to get Keturah. Fred went to Columbia this a.m. so we'll be glad to have company tonight. Fred and Major Barr had a meeting of some sort this a.m.

Don't fail to mention the "enclosed letters"— they are a matter of great moment.

Hope you are perfectly well. We are fine.

Will miss you an extra lot tomorrow— being Sunday—
Loads of love—
Bess

Ft. Riley, Kans.
July 15, 1928

Dear Bess & Margaret:—

I got your special delivery this morning and I am more than pleased to get it. You should have had a letter from me every day because I've never failed to write a note of some kind every day at noon. I even answered Margie's letters; they were so nice and well written I couldn't overlook them. Everybody I showed them to thought I must have a mighty smart four year old girl at home. […]

I have been intending to tell you about Jay Lee's attempt to clutter up the stag party for Friday night. You know it has been customary for some years for the reserves to have a "Badger Fight" either on Thursday or Friday night of the last week. Well a Badger Fight is not a very lady like affair nor is it intended to be one. But it makes a very fitting climax to two weeks of very hard physical labor and it is customary. Jay has tried to get it changed to a dance so he can bring his wife and make a lady affair out of it. […]

Kiss my baby and take a lot of love for yourself and keep writing. I haven't missed a day in spite of the fact that you've missed <u>two</u>.
Yours
Harry.

[Independence, Mo.]
[July 15, 1928]
Sunday Morning—

Dear Harry—

I thought I had better get this off <u>early</u> today as long as Keturah is here— for if she gets started talking, I won't get away again probably. She used to laugh at the way Dicie used to converse so incessantly but as far as I can see K. can keep up with her <u>any</u> day and without the intelligence behind it either.

No "Special" as yet— worse luck. But I'm still hoping.

We had a hard shower in the night and it's down right chilly this a.m. We have a fire in the grate. I surely hope it's dry out there. I worry considerably about you being out in the dampness so much.

Fred Colgan is coming back here around the 24th so you will get to see him after all. He is driving home with Mary to-morrow and will stay a week with her. Mary came down in a very lovely Hudson this time. I heard her tell someone it was <u>not</u> a stock car.

Thank goodness the sun is coming out— let's hope it warms up some.

Lots of love—
Bess

It seems to me it's been a week since I had a letter from you. If I don't get one tomorrow!!

Ft. Riley, Kans.
July 16, 1928

Dear Bess:—

After I got your special yesterday I got another one in the regular way about noon with a nice letter from Margie enclosed. That is the only reason you are getting this one because here is another morning without any letter. You'll probably get gipped [*sic*] tomorrow because we go to Manhattan to stay all day and practice on the G.P.F long gun up there.

We had a pistol shoot this morning and qualified some twelve officers with that weapon. I wrote Major Barr yesterday and asked him and Veronica to come out next Friday. If you want to come with them I am sure they would bring you in the County car. I'd sure like to see you. It is a good thing I did not try to drive home Saturday because those who did go haven't got in yet. I am hoping it will quit raining before next Friday.

Has Margaret been a good girl? I hope she has because if she has she'll be glad if she hasn't she'll be sorry when I get home. Don't miss any more days. Please write.

Kiss my baby and a load of love to you.

Yours
Harry.

[Independence, Mo.]
[July 16, 1928]
Monday—

Dear Harry—

Marg and I were mighty glad to get <u>three</u> letters from you this morning— Your <u>Friday</u> letter arrived along with yesterday's. I had a perfectly
good hunch it was right up here in the P.O.

I quite agree with you about Mrs. Lee's trip— there's no point to
it. If they want to make a visit somewhere on the road to Manhattan, let
them do it some other time. I guess J. is too lady like to enjoy the Badger fight anyway— Mrs. L. called me yesterday & I told her that Mother
was planning to be gone over the weekend (which of course is always
a possibility. Fred wanted her to go down last Saturday with him but
Keturah's visit wrecked that) and I wouldn't have anybody to leave Marg
with. I intend to stick to it— so you may still enjoy Friday night. I would
like to be there for Sat. a.m. and for the drive home— but as for the
dance— la-la!

Am relieved about your physical condition. I only wish they had
discovered what caused the head-aches. Have you had <u>any</u> since you left?

Your "Special" yesterday just saved the day— It didn't come 'til dinner time & I was really beginning to get a little worried—

Loads of love—
Bess

Ft. Riley, Kansas
July 17, 1928

My Dear Sweetie:

I got a nice letter from you and one from Margie all sealed up and
with a stamp on it. They were both mighty fine. I am sorry you are not
coming out but I don't think you are making any mistake under the
circumstances. This has been quite the hottest day we've had. We went to
Manhattan and spent the day studying the long gun and practicing the
laying of it by all the methods in the book. It is located on the Campus of
the Kansas State Agricultural College and is a very nice place to work.

We ate in the College Cafeteria and had a wonderful meal for 40
cents. Tomorrow we fire and as usual I guess I'll have [to] give my ammunition to some second Loui who needs it worse than I do.

The National Guard arrived yesterday. There is a battery over there
commanded by one of my privates and he is a good B. C.

I hope you and Katura [sic] had a wonderful time. I'm glad you got
away from her long enough to write me a letter. Keep it up according to

count you've only missed one. Eddie is waiting to mail this and I'll have
to quit.

Love to you in gobs. Kiss skinny.

From your
Harry.

[Independence, Mo.]
[July 17, 1928]
Tuesday—

Dear Dad—

It's <u>good</u> and warm again to-day and I am most melting away— but
here's for a short note anyway. I don't know <u>why</u> you didn't get a letter
yesterday— I mailed one early Sunday morning. It's this miserable service
we have here— if some of your business men would do a little earnest
kicking maybe we would get a change. You'd better do it while Mr. Reed is
still in Washington— You won't get any intelligent effort from either one
of those other birds from the looks of them.

I talked to Myra this a.m. She said Mary & Fred got off yesterday
morning at 6:30.

Frank had two teeth pulled yesterday. One of them was pretty nearly
as bad as yours.

I'll forgive you for not writing if you went to Manhattan today. I
don't want it to be any <u>task</u> to you— I'd rather do without the letters by a
good deal.

You have had a rainy old time out there— I don't remember you
having ever had so much rain on any of your camps before.

Mrs. L. called again this morning & I told her definitely I could not
go. I told her to call Ellen— maybe she would go with her. She had called
a Mrs. Adams I think she said— but she couldn't go either.

I must hurry or will not get to the P.O. in time for this to get on the
inside.

Lots of love—
Bess

Ft. Riley, Kansas
July 18, 1928

Dear Bess:

Your letter failed to arrive again today and I'll make a bet it is in the
Junction City P.O.

We have been firing all day and I've never seen a hotter one. My
hands and neck are as red as a barn door. But I can stand it. There was

no chance to write today at noon because we had our lunch brought out
to us in a cart. I had to dress up in my thick shirt and act as President of
an Army Court. We had a lot of fun trying an officer but it was right hot
while we did it.

Well there are only three days more and then I can see my wife and
baby and I hope I never go again unless you can go with me. It is hotter
than the inside of a stove here but I don't mind it. I'm as brown as a [*illegible*] and as strong as an ox. I can go for another year and a half.

Kiss my baby and tell her to kiss her mamma.

Loads of love.
Harry.

[Independence, Mo.]
[July 18, 1928]
Wednesday—

Dear Harry—

No mail today but as I was <u>warned</u> there might not be any, I am not
worried anyway.

It's so hot I don't even feel like exerting myself to the extent of writing
but thought maybe you would rather have a <u>brief</u> one than none at all.

I sent flowers to the Hays today— Mr. Whitmore or Whitmeyer of
McDonald Lodge called up last night and said he had promised to let
you know Mr. Hoyt died so you could come in for the funeral. I told him
I had already sent you the paper about his death but I felt sure there was
no chance of your being [able] to leave camp long enough to come in—
& that the roads were in terrible condition too. He said all of the Masonic
end of it had been attended to—

Hope to have a good long letter tomorrow—

Are you coming in Saturday or Sunday?

Lots of love from both of us—
Bess

Ft. Riley, Kansas
July 19, 1928

My Dear Sweetheart:

I felt very properly rebuked at what you said about my letter writing being a task and not a pleasure. If I inadvertently implied that it was
a task, the implication was not intended. It is a pleasant duty as you by
this time ought to know. I am the only person here who has written his
wife or sweetie as many as two a week and because I write every day it
is a cause for comment. It is also a cause for comment that I don't go to

picnics or dances or any of the other feminine entertainment, but as you
ought to know I didn't come out here for but one thing and that is mental relaxation and physical employment. I have gotten both. We have a
physical instructor who has loosened every muscle I have and artillery has
kept my mind so busy that I haven't had time to think of court or have a
headache. There is only one thing that would make a vacation complete
and that would be to have you along. It is the most satisfactory vacation
to me except for your absence both from a financial and a physical stand-
point that I could have. I had two letters today as I had hoped I would
have. There was also a nice one from my girl. By the way, you didn't mention her in either one. I have written her two letters of her own which you
didn't say had arrived. The mail service is rotten. There never has been a
day that one wasn't mailed to you and then two to daughter besides.

I have been grading officers on firing all day today and yesterday
and I got to fire a real shrapnel problem myself. Never expected it but this
Colonel is a peach. Quite the smartest man I've been under. The Doctor is
going to take these to Junction City. So kiss Margie and tell her to kiss her
mamma for
Daddy

[Independence, Mo.]
[July 19, 1928]
Thursday—

Dear Friend-Husband—

Was most pleased to get a letter this afternoon— Am sorry it's so
hot out there— It's hot enough here and sticky!— It's been trying to rain
ever since yesterday but has not succeeded to any extent as yet.

Am rather glad I am not making that trip with Mrs. Lee this hot
afternoon— Ellen is going with her. She had three children to leave & I
had only one but she is off & gone anyway.

Your daughter balled you out properly last night— We went driving
with May & Geo. & Marg & May were singing and improvising as they
went along in their usual fashion— & one of Marg's was— "I saw my
daddy— once he was here." Well, it brought down the house— or rather
the car— 'once he was here.'

Must get to town & Mrs. Pleasants before it rains— the prospects
seem better—
Lots of love—
Bess

Probably won't write tomorrow as long as you will be home Sat.
Hooray!

🏵1929

Grandpa was now more stressed than ever. While his $6.5 million Jackson County bond issue had passed with a three-fourths majority (he only needed two-thirds), the $28 million Kansas City bond that Boss Tom floated had been whittled down by the voters to just $700,000. The city manager had become Grandpa's bitter enemy and contractors were apoplectic over the dearth of city money and Grandpa's refusal to fix bids. During this time, he began to lament privately that he sometimes felt a fool for maintaining his integrity when all around him were cheating and stealing and profiting by it. He even signed his July 17 letter, "Your good-for-nothing but loving husband." He was so frazzled he was taking tonic for his nerves and my grandmother was trying to talk him into taking an extra week of vacation.

One minor fracas he did not have to worry about involved the county farm, a combination poorhouse and old folks home. Apparently, someone sent an elderly man out there over Grandpa's protest, and his fellow judges, Robert Barr and Thomas Bash, promised an investigation, which drew the attention of the *Kansas City Star*. The issue was resolved quickly, but with Grandpa fretting, my grandmother spoke to Colonel Southern, publisher of the *Independence Examiner* and Aunt May's father, who said he that thought the *Star* had overblown the story and planned to pass on it himself.

Otherwise, my grandmother was pinching pennies by painting the stairs and a table herself and making a dress for my mother. She also gently chided Grandpa for the extravagance of asking them to visit. "Are you homesick already?" she wrote on July 10. "I don't see how I can make it— the train fare for both of us would be around $15— not to mention hotel bills etc." In a July 13 letter, she added: "You needn't get so up-stage about our coming out. I'd surely like to, but I'll take that money and have our daughter's tonsils out."

My grandmother's father had never been able to make ends meet and her mother didn't care to know how. Even now, Madge was more inclined to spend the inheritance from her own father on drapes and furniture than on clothes or a tonsillectomy for my mother. Not that Grandpa would have accepted her charity, but she also never offered to help him and my grandmother pay off the debts from the haberdashery.

As for my mother, the tonsillectomy would be a bust—halfway, anyway. Although the offending organs, blamed for a rash of colds, coughs, chills, and fevers, were duly removed, one of them, obstinately, grew back. Thankfully, the same could not be said for Grandpa's hemorrhoids, which he so thoughtfully mentions in his first letter home.

Ft. Riley, Kans.
July 7, 1929

Dear Bess & Margie:—

We had a very pleasant trip up with no casualties of any nature. Not even a hot motor. We stoped [*sic*] at Manhattan for lunch while it poured down rain and then drove to Ft. Riley in the rain arriving about 3 P.M.

Eddie McKim pulled in about 7 P.M. and several of the boys arrived along during the evening. I slept like a log last night got up at 5:15 and am in good physical condition. Had a complete physical examination at 8 A.M. and they didn't see my cut [hemorrhoid operation], so I got by. They gave my eyes a real test though and my heart too. The heart was all right. They ordered me to be vaccinated for smallpox but I didn't do it. He also told me that I'd never need another typhoid inoculation. [...]

I came away without my slippers at last but I can use my low-cuts instead so you needn't mail them. If anything worthwhile shows up in the *Examiner,* please mail it. Kiss my baby and tell her to kiss her mother for me.

Always your,
Harry.

[Independence, Mo.]
[July 7, 1929]
Sunday afternoon—

Dear Harry—

Just a few lines, so you won't feel <u>neglected</u> right off at the start.

I hope your slippers got there <u>today</u>— considering I put a 15¢ Special Del. stamp on them.

This has been a nice cool Sunday— but is warming up this evening and that suits me. I called to ask about your mother just now and Mary said she is feeling a lot better today.

Frank had three teeth pulled last night and is feeling pretty fine today and of course can't eat anything.

George Arrowsmith's girl called yesterday and wanted you to come in [and] get the bridge finished <u>before you left</u>!

Must get this in the P.O. if it's going out tonight.

Lots of love from us both,

Bess

Marg was awfully disgusted that you didn't <u>wait</u> to tell her good-bye.

Ft. Riley, Kansas
July 8, 1929

Dear Bess and Margaret:—

I have the finest wife in the world. The slippers almost beat me here. I am going good today. The Colonel has excused me from duty to prepare a lecture on an artillery subject. He and all the rest have gone horse back riding. I am feeling fine, sleeping well and doing something I like to do. I weighed 154 on the official scales which is a pound more than I weighed at home. There is nothing to tell you except that I'm all right.

I hope you and the young lady are all right. Are you coming to see me? Let me know if you are so I can make arrangements. Be sure and write me every day.

Love to both of you

Harry.

[Independence, Mo.]
[July 9, 1929]
Tuesday—

My Dear—

Please don't string me up for not writing yesterday— I simply couldn't get it in. I surely was glad to hear from you yesterday and today and am so <u>very</u> glad that you are feeling so well. Are you getting your orange juice and butter milk? Is the food <u>good</u> this year? Last year I remember you said it was <u>not</u> so good.

Maud Louise was here for a brief visit this morning. She is on her way back to Phil. after a week with her mother in El Paso. They couldn't amputate Mrs. Chrisman's arm after all— and two of her fingers have turned black but the doctors insist she may live some time.

Auntie Myra and Helen are spending the day here and Helen and Mary are now taking a nap. (?)

I am going to scoot right on up to the P.O. with this so it will get there tomorrow sure.

It's been raining off & on for twenty four hours. Hope you haven't had much of it. I'll look the *Examiners* over carefully & send them. Mr. Southern asked for your address yesterday & said he wanted to send you a paper.

Everybody is fine— but nothing interesting to write about.

Do hope you feel like a million dollars by the 22nd. Be sure to plan to go to the Ozarks. You really need that extra week.

> Lots of love
> Bess—

> Ft. Riley, Kansas
> July 10, 1929

Dear Bess and Marger:—

Got a letter last night! It sure made the day brighter. The card was from a Jewish attorney who is a friend of Vrooman's & Metzger's. I am sorry that the young lady didn't get to tell me good bye but I thought she needed the sleep more than she needed to tell me good bye. Arrowsmith was supposed to be at this camp and he ought to have known I was gone. He is getting anxious to finish up so he can get paid I guess. We are going out on a terrain problem this A.M. I am going mounted in the car the rest go horse back. My health and nerves are getting as good as new. The weather has been ideal and everyone sleeps like a log. The worst thing is to get up at 5:30 in the morning. Everyone is good to me and I am having the usual pleasant and instructive time. I'll write you a better one tomorrow. Maybe I'll have another letter.

> Love to you both from your
> Harry.

> [Independence, Mo.]
> [July 10, 1929]
> Wednesday

Dear Harry—

I was mighty glad to get your letter this morning. Marg and I were pretty cozy and it came while we were at breakfast. I don't believe <u>we</u> would last long getting up at 5:15.

Why do you keep asking if we are coming out? Are you homesick already? I don't see how I can make it— the train fare for both of us would be around $15— not to mention hotel bills etc.

I opened a C of S letter this a.m. and decided I'd better send it on.

Thought at first I'd send it to the Courthouse but was afraid they wouldn't know what it was all about. Saw the Major get out of his car and go over and hang over Louise Duke's [car] yesterday— she apparently was parked there waiting for him. They're a hot combination— aren't they?

[*Illegible*] told Fred last week he had applied again for insurance & been turned down very recently & the doctors gave him from 1½ to 4 years.

This is a rainy old day and down right chilly.

Hope you don't take cold with all that dampness out there.

Lots of love—

Bess

Ft. Riley, Kans.

July 11, 1929

Dear Bess and Margaret:—

Another good day— got a letter last night. Sure glad to get it too. It rained all night last night and most of yesterday. Nearly all the outfit went out without raincoats and nearly drowned. I went in the car and so didn't get wet. The rest of them have gone on a demonstration this A.M. but it is so muddy out where they are going that I'll have to stay in. They are to have a cavalry and artillery demonstration, using regulars. National Guards and Reserves, all together. It ought to be a fine war the way it is raining. I had a year of that sort of war under real conditions so I guess I'm not missing very much. We are having a very pleasant and instructive camp. This Colonel we have is as well informed on all subjects as some I've had are ignorant. There's only one thing wrong with him. He won't dress the part. If we could get him dressed up there'd be no equal to him. All of us have some screw loose, I guess. I hope my baby is well and happy and I'm awfully pleased you called Mamma. Please do it once in [a] while. Kiss my girl and tell her to be good.

Your Harry.

[Independence, Mo.]

[July 11, 1929]

Thursday—

Dear Harry—

I was most awfully glad to get your letter this morning— and was particularly glad to hear your <u>nerves</u> are getting back to normal. Are you still taking your tonic or have you passed the point of needing it? I expect the life you are living is a better tonic than that green bottle.

Have you thrown the roll of cotton away, too?

Did Spencer & C. C. get there? What became of Geo. Arrowsmith? Did Jay Lee really not go?

It has rained most of the time since night before last— mostly drizzle— but it certainly has made it miserable and chilly.

May had the club yesterday and we had a very fine time but May sure was disgusted that it was such an icy day as she had prepared a lot of food for a sizzling day. However, it was mighty good.

How are all of the McKims?

It's almost five o 'clock and if I am to get to the P.O. on time— I'd better be moving.

Wish you could walk in and have dinner with us tonight— well, one week is almost gone already.

Don't fail to write. I look for a letter each morning. Marg is weeping because I won't give her time to write you a letter this morning.

> Lots of love—
> Bess

> Ft. Riley, Kans.
> July 12, 1929

Dear Bess:—

I got another letter last night and it made the day perfect. I thought that you and Margaret might want to come and see me while I am out here was the only reason I asked you if you could come, and as to finance that would have been my problem and I'd have solved it. But maybe we'll have better luck next time. My physical condition is almost perfect. I think another ten days and it will be.

The county farm seems to have made a name for itself while I'm gone and Mr. Bash seems to head the column. I wonder what Barr was doing? He never knows when to grab off the lead. I guess I'll have to phone him and tell him something about this case. These people sent this old man out there over my protest alleging that he was not in his right mind and that they could not care for him at home. It seems to be different now. Please keep on writing and let me know how the reaction is.

I get the *Star* and *Times* and have received two *Examiner*s by mail so I guess they are sending it.

I hope Margie has been a good girl and that she'll tell me when I get home that she has minded her mother and never cried a bit while I'm gone. Lots of love to you and kiss my baby.

> Your Harry.

[Independence, Mo.]
[July 12, 1929]
Friday—

Dear Harry—

It's almost six o'clock so this must be brief to get into today's mail. I spent the morning painting the back porch table— consequently I've had to spend the afternoon doing the regular things and am somewhat behind time. I was mighty glad to get your good letter this a.m. Am happy to know there is <u>some</u> reason for keeping you out of the pouring rain. I should think all of those men would have pneumonia by tomorrow. Now, you <u>please continue</u> to take care of yourself at least as far as you are able.

Marg has had a cold but it seems to be alright again. I kept her out in the sun today (the first we've had since Monday) and baked the last of it out of her.

I meant to call your mother today but simply didn't [get] around to it. Will do it tomorrow.

Do you get the K.C. papers? Let me know & I will send them.

Lots of love, even if it is sent in a hurry—

Yours
Bess

Ft. Riley, Kans.
July 13, 1929

Dear Bess and Margaret:—

Yes I am still a slave to cotton. Not because I need it so much but because I can't bring myself to quit using it. I am still drawing a little but no blood. Walked about a while today without any serious results at all. You asked about McKim. All the family are all right but he said his boy is getting hard to handle. They all had scarlet fever last winter. Jay Lee didn't arrive, why, I don't know.

[…] Wish you and my baby were here. Every time I see a <u>little</u> girl I want to kiss her but I don't like the look of the army women. They had a dance last night but I played cards in my own billet. Keep on writing. I'll be perfect as to health when I get home. Kiss my girl twice and tell her to kiss her mama for her daddy.

Your Harry

[Independence, Mo.]
[July 13, 1929]
Saturday—

Dear Dad—

Was glad to get the good news that you are feeling so fit. Am also mighty glad you are going to have a little more time to get on your feet. You needn't get so up-stage about our coming out— I'd surely like to but I'll take that money and have our daughter's tonsils out.

I saw Mr. Southern last night & he rather laughed at the County Farm scandal and said no doubt it was principally a newspaper story. Also said he had told Bash what a silly thing he did in promising to <u>investigate</u> when he really had nothing as yet <u>to investigate</u>. I'm glad you are not here to be bothered with it all and don't let it <u>worry</u> you. There hasn't been another word in the paper & the *Star* has realized probably the foolishness of publishing the story. You might call Barr and tell him <u>what to do</u> and <u>what to say</u>. Mr. S. says those "two fools up there don't know what to do."

He told me he was sending the *Examiner* so I won't double up on them.

It has surely warmed up <u>some</u> today.

Just talked to Mary and she said your mother was fine.

Must quit & hurry to [the] P.O.

Hope to hear tomorrow— from you.

Lots of love—
Bess

Ft. Riley, Kans.
July 14, 1929

Dear Bess:—

Sunday morning and I am feeling fine. Got up at a quarter of six and had breakfast at seven. Some of the boys went over to ride after hounds at 6 A.M. I didn't go. There was church in the Godfrey Court dance hall at 6:30 A.M. where they had a dance last night. They opened with "Onward Christian Soldiers" and I wanted to see my girl so badly that I wanted to come home at once. If I could get a plane I would.

Yesterday was a day of accidents for our organization. Rufus Burrus sprained his ankle and a Lt. by the name of Carruthers ran into a car at Manhattan on his way home to Topeka and wrecked himself and his car both. He is in the hospital here and it will take a week to fix the car. I think I told you yesterday that I walked a mile and climbed the highest hill on the reservation without serious results. I am eating like a horse, sleeping well and getting sunburned in good shape. If I had you and Margaret here today I'd be completely happy. Be sure and keep writing. The letters have come every day and so have the papers. Got the *Digest* and appreciate it a lot. Kiss Margaret and tell her to be a good young lady.

Lots of love to you both

Harry.

[Independence, Mo.]
[July 15, 1929]
Monday— 9 a.m.

Dear Harry—

No doubt you'll feel like wrecking me when you don't get a letter today but a letter was beyond me yesterday. Most of the Platte City aggregation spent the day here. The boys arrived at 8 a.m. for golf and May and I met the girls and infants at 11:45 at the Interurban and I didn't draw a perfectly good breath all day. And it was one red hot day! It has rained this morning and is a degree or two cooler.

Your good Sunday letter just came and I feel guiltier than ever. I was powerfully glad to get the special early yesterday morning— It made the day more complete.

Am sorry about your casualties— it sort of puts a damper on your spirits— hope the young Lt. was not <u>badly</u> hurt.

Well, if the camp hasn't done anything else for you— it got you to church once more anyway— and that's a large item.

We will probably put in this week getting ready for Auntie Bess & Madge. They come on the ten o'clock bus next Sat. night. Will you be in on Sat. or Sunday? Can't you plan to go right on to the Ozarks without any court sessions in between or even going up-town? I'll have your clothes ready. I think Mr. S. is very anxious to go. He is going to Canada early in Aug.

Lots of love from us both.

Bess

M. is struggling over a letter. Don't know whether my patience & hers will last through it or not.

Ft. Riley, Kans.
July 15, 1929

Dear Bess and Margaret:—

Your special came yesterday and I was more than glad to get it and I hope you got mine. I am still in good shape physically— walked up another hill without stopping and I am as brown as an Indian. The

Battery went for a road march this A.M. and I went in an automobile. I went up to the National Guard firing point and saw my private who is now a Battery Commander and a good one. They were doing some good firing. Condon then brought me in and I inspected his kitchen. It was sure clean. His wife said she'd never invite an army officer to dinner.

I am going down there to dinner tonight at 6 o'clock. This has been a good vacation for me and I think I'll be as good as new when I get home. Mr. Southern has diagnosed my associates correctly. There have never been three like the three I've had to deal with. They are in a class by themselves. If I can win in spite of them, there ought to be more credit for it. Keep on writing and be sure and kiss my baby and tell her to kiss her mamma for me.

I am more than glad you heard from mamma.

Love and lots of it.

> Yours
> Harry.

> [Independence, Mo.]
> [July 16, 1929]
> Tuesday—

Dear Harry—

Glad to get your letter this morning to know you are still improving. I know you have missed the horseback riding but I do think you were wise not to try it. Maybe you can make it up later in the summer with Mr. Holland.

Marg had a great time this morning— Mrs. Cox took eight of them out to the zoo— and for a trip in the launch— and then stopped at old Richard's field on their way home and one of the mechanics out there let each one of the youngsters climb into a plane he was working on.

She got a great kick out of it.

Fred never has gotten his passes to Los Angeles— and now Lillian has gone up to the ranch so he isn't so keen about going.

Ethel, Nellie, your Aunt Ella, Jodie, J. A., & Jack are leaving tomorrow for a drive through the Ozarks— They are planning to stay a week. How would you like to take the same trip late in Sept. after it gets a bit cooler? They would like to have had us go with them— at least they asked if it would be possible.

Have to take your daughter to Stanley's to get her hair cut, so farewell for today.

Lots of love from us both

> Bess

Ft. Riley, Kans.

July 16, 1929

Dear Bess:—

I thought today was going to be a dud. We went out to the firing point at 7 A.M. and stayed there until four o'clock, having our lunches sent out. It has been my custom every morning after breakfast to write you a letter while the rest are out riding. I couldn't do it today. Every day at noon I get your letter. When I went to dinner tonight I saw only the *Examiner* and Miss Margie's letter but none from you. I didn't enjoy the meal a bit but felt as if the day had been a complete failure. I made up my mind that the mail orderly had put it in the wrong box so I took another look in the adjoining box and there it was. If I'd missed two days in succession there'd have been war, really.

We went out on the hill and I sat in the sun and fired the officers of the regiment. My hands are as red as beets and my neck and face are full of violet rays. I am physically fit but still having some drainage.

Will see you Saturday or Sunday and I am sure I'll be very fit when I arrive. Had a letter from Mary and she says mamma is better. That makes me feel better. I worry about her a lot. Don't miss any more days please.

Love to you & Margaret

Harry.

Ft. Riley

July 17, 1929

Dear Bess:—

Well another perfect day. The letter was in the box when I came in from the firing point. I am glad that the baby had a good time at the park and the flying field. I want her to do everything and have everything and still learn that most people have to work to live, and I don't want her to be a high hat.

I took my field glasses to the ordinance officer of the 128th F. A. and had them cleaned. They are just as good as the day I bought them now and I wouldn't trade them for a new pair because of the sentimental attachment. Maybe you don't know it but I guess I am two thirds damn fool and the other third sentimentalist. Whenever I see a yellow headed little girl I want to pick her up and squeeze her, when I meet a member of my battery I don't care how ornery and good for nothing he is he can have whatever I've got— and when I think of school days I always think of a pretty little girl with curls down her back who grew into the best and sweetest sweetheart a man ever had and I wish I could see her now. Kiss my baby and look for me sometime Saturday I hope; will phone you if I am later.

Your good for nothing but loving husband
Harry.

[Independence, Mo.]
[July 17, 1929]
Wednesday—

Dear Harry—

Margaret will be <u>thrilled</u> when she wakes up and finds her letter waiting for her. <u>Our</u> letters didn't get here 'til afternoon today and I was on the ragged edge of calling you at noon to see what the trouble was but I knew Mr. Boxley was calling so I thought I'd better wait a bit— I hated to give him your number, but I wasn't sure that I'd be doing the right thing in telling him I didn't know how to get you— and after all it might be important!

Mrs. Barr called up a while ago & said the Major wanted to know how you were. Guess he's been up to something else.

Am glad you are getting such a good healthy coating of sunburn— I've been putting extremely few clothes on Marg and getting her out into the sunshine (whenever there <u>was</u> any) but she just <u>won't</u> tan. It's so provoking.

I've been busy today painting the front stairs and making a dress for Marg.

It looks as if it is just going to pour down for a change. George & Frank are out at Blue Hills playing golf with Lee so they will probably get well soaked.

Hope Dr. N. can get rid of that drainage as soon as you get home.

Lots of love
Bess

⊕1930

Grandpa's political mentor, Mike Pendergast, Tom's younger brother, had died in September 1929, just weeks before the stock market crash. Whereas Tom viewed Grandpa's honesty and integrity simply as political capital, Mike had truly appreciated his character and ability and had actively encouraged him. Grandpa, in turn, had loved Mike "like a daddy." With Mike gone, control of the eastern half of Jackson County now fell to my grandfather. He was in the middle of a campaign for reelection and was also planning to propose another $7.95 million in county bonds to continue improving roads and public buildings. Tom Pendergast was pushing an additional $31 million in bonds for Kansas City.

The established road project was going well. The old "pie-crust" roads were so bad that my mother recalled Sunday drives during which Grandpa would pull over periodically and easily stomp the shoulder to pieces with his foot, hence the name. Now, my grandmother reported that the new road to Winner, a community north of Independence, "looked mighty fine."

In order to help sell the new bonds to voters stunned by the Depression, Grandpa had halved the salary of every county worker, himself included. The worst squawking came from my mother, whose allowance was cut from fifty cents to a quarter. He could placate her with an occasional extra quarter or two, much to my grandmother's consternation, but there was little he could do to help the scores of people who begged him daily for help. With thousands of residents unable to pay their taxes, the county's finances were shot. Grandpa worried about his own finances and lamented his lack of success with them, perhaps wishing that he could help his mother, who had been forced to take out a second mortgage on the farm.

On top of all this, he had become director of the National Conference on City Planning and been elected president of the Greater Kansas City Plan Association. He was so wiped out that on the second night in camp he slept for twenty hours.

Harry, John Snyder, and Harry Vaughan cutting dashing
figures at training camp in 1930 (TL 64-1339).

Both he and the family dealt with scorching heat. My grandmother
reported that the temperature in her bedroom had reached ninety-eight
degrees one day and one hundred degrees on another. Everyone at home
was in a foul mood and laid low, my mother and Vietta included, although
Mom was fit enough to skin her knees in the driveway and try her hand at
golf. At camp, another soldier's toddler kept cool by hogging the poolside
shower and screaming every time someone tried to move her out of it.

In the final ignominy, Grandpa's backside, which had been immune
to saddle sores during the summer encampments of 1928 and 1929, was
now hurting him so badly that he had to ask my grandmother to send him
his salve.

[Independence, Mo.]
[July 18, 1930]
<u>Friday</u>

Dear Harry—

I hope you made the trip safely and didn't <u>scorch</u> on the way out. It got so awfully hot here along about four o'clock yesterday— (and is still <u>hotter</u> today).

Captain Fletcher (I <u>thot</u> he said his name was) called yesterday evening and wanted to get some information about camp. Said he had been attached to your regiment and he had just gotten in from a trip. Said he would go on up Sunday anyway.

Will you get the K.C. papers every day or do you want me to save editorials, etc. There is one today on the 23rd St. entrance. I'll send it in case you haven't seen it.

Margaret wiped up the whole drive way on her knees last night and is a sight.

We took a little drive and cooled off temporarily. I managed to get M's bed out on the porch so we slept comfortably.

Hope you got there in time for the dinner & had a good time. I called [*illegible*] and ordered flowers for Judge Hall's funeral.

With much love—
Bess

[Ft. Riley, Kans.]
July 18, 1930

My Dear Sweethearts:—

Rufus & I arrived quite hot and dusty as well as somewhat grimey [*sic*], yesterday afternoon about 7:15. We stuck a wire fence staple into one of our tires just east of Manhattan and had to get out and get under. The first time I've changed a tire in a long time. It was just about such a place as the one where we stuck the stake into the same tire.

The party was in full swing when we arrived and was a grand success. There were a great many candidates to pull the badger; And the Engineers tried to give me a lesson in probabilities at five cents ante and a quarter limit. I made them pay me at the rate of about a dollar and a half an hour for the time of the session.

At the horse show this morning Eddie McKim's horse failed to take one of the barriers and both horse and Eddie did a wonderful Prince of Wales. He sprained his elbow and was wondering if he could make his wife believe he had fallen out of bed or something. [...]

I hope you are both enjoying the heat as well as I am. Write me as often as you'd have me do it and kiss my baby if she's good.

Your boy friend and sweetheart,

Harry.

[Independence, Mo.]
[July 19, 1930]
<u>Saturday</u>—

Dear Harry—

I surely was glad you called last night but you sounded so tired and hot I'm afraid you are not enjoying it as you ought to. Take it as easy as you possibly can.

It's red hot again this morning and I'm due for a permanent at one o'clock— am rather dreading it, but I can't keep on having marcels* at 50¢ each this hot weather.

Vietta leaves tomorrow for her <u>Grand Lodge</u>— of course she'd pick the hottest weather to go. She is in such a terrible humor today, tho, it will be a relief to get rid of her, if that's going to keep up. Guess the heat is "getting" her too.

Margaret's knees look better this morning. One of them was cut pretty deep.

I saw C. C. pass this a.m. How did he get away so soon? Guess he felt he <u>had</u> to be here for Saturday.

We may possibly go to Lexington for dinner tomorrow. I'm not sure though but what it would be cooler to stay at home and <u>cook</u>.

Hope a nice bunch of men turn up tomorrow so you will enjoy the camp this year, too.

Lots of love from us both—

Bess

Fort Riley, Kans.
July 19, 1930

Dear Bess:—

You'd never guess that I have been sound asleep for nearly twenty hours but I have. Apparently I was nearer all in than I thought. Slept all night last night got up for breakfast and then slept until noon and then until three o'clock. Then went swimming. There was a little girl over there about one and a half years old who insisted on staying under the ice cold shower and she'd yell her head off if she wasn't allowed to do it.

---

* Marcel waves were made with a special type of heated curling iron.

I suppose you are roasting. The wind out here is hot but I'm not suffering with the heat. Hyde and I are very nicely situated with a barrack all to ourselves. It will be full I guess by tomorrow noon. I wish you were here with me. It would be a most satisfactory situation if you were. I am looking forward to your coming down so don't disappoint me.

There's a train leaves at 10:40 and gets here at 2 PM and one leaves at 6:15 PM arriving here at nine o'clock which I think is the best one to come on. How is my girl behaving? I hope she's good and well and that you are enjoying the heat. Your letter hasn't come yet but I may get it at supper. Tell Margaret to kiss her mother for daddy. Love to you both.

Harry

Ft. Riley, Kans.
Sunday July 20, 1930

Dear Miss Bessie and Margaret:—

This has been the first day of duty. Went over and had a physical and found nothing wrong. They insisted on vaccinating me for smallpox and I dropped and broke my reading glasses, a wonderful start off. Colonel Williams who commands the 128th Field Artillery had me down there to dinner. You know one of the batteries is commanded by one of my former privates. It was a very pleasant meal and I enjoyed it. We went swimming this afternoon again and they had changed the water. It was about as cold as the Antarctic Ocean.

I am having an officers meeting to let them know who's boss and to get started right. Your letter has never come, but I still have hopes.

Please come and see me. Kiss my baby and I'll write you a good letter tomorrow.

Your sweetheart,
Harry.

[Independence, Mo.]
[July 20, 1930]
Sunday

Dear Harry—

I feel as if I am going to melt and run away but maybe I can get this letter written first. It's 98 right here in this room and that's plenty warm enough, even for me. I do hope you can stay out of the sun for it might really make you sick. I am glad you had that twenty hour nap— for I am very sure you needed it— You looked so tired when you left Thursday— only Thursday? it seems at least a week ago. Was powerfully glad to get your special this a.m. just as I got back from Sunday School. I didn't send mine Special for I thought I remembered that you said the Specials didn't reach you any sooner than the others.

Mr. Connor says it's going to be cooler the middle of the week and if [it] does cool off, which day will suit you best for us to come? I think the 6:15 train would be the best one, too— for I could get some one to take us to the station at that time of day— and then you could probably meet us. I will let you know very definitely of course before we leave. The heat is even getting on Marg's nerves— she is so cross today.

Jodie has a boy— Robert Allen. They are both alright now but both had a pretty tough time for a day or two.

I want to go to town and mail this before six or I'm afraid it won't go out before morning— Guess we will have to drive tonight to cool off at all— it's just breathlessly hot—

Love from both of us

As ever

                                    Bess

Hello dad— Margaret

                                    Ft. Riley, Kans.
                                    July 21, 1930

Dear Sweetheart:—

Got two letters today dated July 18th & 19th. The pinheaded postmaster on this Post would be holding them until the camp is over I guess if I hadn't just made him give them up. We managed to get organized after a fashion today. I have three majors, three captains, two 1st and twenty second Lts. A very nice outfit and I believe I'm to have a real camp.

Don't you have any rain? It sprinkled here last night and once or twice today. It has been very pleasant all day. If you decide to come you'd better phone me instead of wiring because a wire might not get me until two days after you arrived. I am now living in 4A Godfrey Court and you can get me by calling Ft. Riley and asking for that address.

I am sorry my baby hurt her knees and I hope they both are well by now. I am wondering if she's had to go to bed anymore.

Be sure and keep writing. I've got to go and make up a lot of problems for tomorrow in order to keep this gang busy. Kiss my baby and tell her to kiss her mamma for daddy.

Love to you both.

                                    Harry.

This phone is Ft Riley 339

Ft. Riley, Kans.
July 22, 1930

Dear Sweetheart & Margie:—

The day has been fine and ended perfectly— your letter came just
before dinner. You say it has been a week from Sunday to Thursday* I
say it's been a month and getting a week longer every day. I overslept this
morning, which kept it from being quite so long. I usually get up at 5:30
and beat everyone to the shower and shaving trough; today I didn't arise
until the whistle blew. I have three majors whom I have to keep busy and
it makes my head go around to do it. They are smart and well informed
men. I have them studying now on an order for tomorrow but tomorrow
I'll have to give them another for the next day.

If we have another war I am going to arrange to take my honey and
my baby along. It is a wonderful thing how absolutely dependant a man
can become. I don't see how I got along until I was thirty four [five] without you. Just think of all the wasted years that could have been pleasantly
and profitably spent. I might even have been a financial success if I'd
started with you sooner.

Went out and watched my former buck private fire his battery. He's
a good battery commander in the 128th F. A., Mo. Nat. Guard. He writes
his wife every day too. You see I even trained them right in every respect.
Kiss my baby and a regular one to my sweetheart from hers
                          Harry
The lense [sic] and the collars came. Needed both awfully.

[Independence, Mo.]
[July 22, 1930]
Tues. a.m.

Dear "Huzz"—

Please don't hold it against me that I didn't get a letter off to you
yesterday. By the time I got home after going for your lens and delivering
it to Mr. Long it was too late to write & get it in the P.O. I do hope you can
get the lens put in a hurry. Also hope it has turned cooler out there— as
it has here but not a drop of rain, so far. If this weather lasts, we'll try to
come the last of the week & spend the week-end if that suits— if some
other day is more convenient let me know, because any day will do for us.

I opened a letter from Ernest Kellerstrass [a Kansas City brewer]
thinking it might be something of immediate importance & it was a
check for $50 for your campaign fund. Shall I send it on to you or put it

* Actually, my grandmother said Thursday to Sunday.

away?

Don't you think I had better write a note to Mrs. Boyles and thank her for <u>everything</u>?

Don't short change me on letters now just because I missed <u>one</u>!

I talked to Mary this morning and she said your mother is feeling fine & enjoying the cooler weather.

It looks like it's going rain! So I am going to town before it does—

Let me know what about us coming out Friday or Saturday—

Best love to you

from Marger and Bess

Ft. Riley, Kans.

July 23, 1930

Dear Bess and Marger:—

Your letter came today along with Mr. Kellerstraus' [*sic*]. I'll have to turn the money over to the Democratic committee I guess. It is a compliment to me because he is normally a Republican.

I am going to Manhattan and make arrangements for you and Miss Marger to stay over there. The hotels are better and it is a nicer town than Junction. I would suggest that you come down Friday evening and stay until you get tired or until I go home if you like the place.

We are having a good camp. I made everyone turn out in uniform complete tonight and they looked very well. The men seem to be satisfied with their C. O. and I am pleased with them so everything is right.

I am going to Manhattan to mail this. Kiss my girl and love to you both.

Harry.

I'll get even with you for the skip.

[Independence, Mo.]

[July 23, 1930]

Wednesday—

Dear Dad—

At last it's raining— a <u>real sprinkle</u> anyway— and is delightfully cool— a most wonderful and welcome change.

I am busy getting a dress ready to wear to Riley and must take it to Geo. Leach's now to get rid of a few spots.

If everything holds— we will take the 6:15 Friday evening.

George says he will take us to the train. I will call you between 12 & one o'clock on Friday tho. so you may be sure of the time etc.

Marg and I were delighted to get our letters just now and are answering at once.

I wanted to go to K.C. <u>over Van Horn</u> today but as long as it's raining, think I shall wait. There'll be plenty of slippery mud, I fear.

I went out to Ackerson's yesterday afternoon to send some flowers to Jodie & then went on west to Winner & it looked mighty fine— shoulders etc. in splendid condition— You'll get quite a thrill when you come back won't you?— the first time over it.

No Court today or yesterday— guess B & B are exhausted.

Marg wants to add her letter— so will quit.

Lots of love—

Bess

Dear Dad I hope you are having a nice time shooting off the cannons love Margaret

Ft. Riley, Kans.
July 24, 1930

My Dear Sweethearts:—

Got your letter today and you can tell Miss Marger that I have not fired the big cannons yet. I will fire them next Tuesday and if she stays I'll show her how to do it.

I am sure glad you are coming down, and I am also sure you'll have a good time. The sun shone down on us today but there is a fine cool breeze now and there has been a necessity for cover every night even on the hottest days. Please bring my "Anthony" salve. I have a tender place on my saddle connection. Kiss my girl and don't fail to come down.

Love to you both

Harry.

Ft. Riley, Kans.
July 27, 1930

Dear Wife and Daughter:—

Well here I am doing what I said I wouldn't. I've been waiting and waiting for the phone to ring, but I've waited in vain I guess. If I remember correctly, I phoned when I arrived (after a four mile trip) and I phoned you Saturday night, (under like circumstances.) and just because I don't raise sand and have spasms doesn't mean that I never worry about you or that I wouldn't highly appreciate a phone call— especially tonight. I haven't been so homesick since I went to France. It was almost a tragedy when you left. I guess I am a damn fool but I wanted you to stay, though I thought you'd be cooler and happier at home.

I'd better get a letter tomorrow, at least.

Don Fitch had dinner with me. I guess the fat Col. [Elliott] and all his crowd are in by now.

Kiss my baby.

Love to you both

Harry

[Independence, Mo.]

[July 28, 1930]

Monday afternoon

Dear Harry—

We had a nice hot trip home but arrived ten minutes ahead of time & that helped some. I was surely thankful for the Pullman seats tho. for I honestly don't believe we could have stood the car chair for three hours— and not have been able to move from seat to seat as the heat increased at times & my word! that hot wind. It isn't <u>quite</u> so bad today but I have an idea it won't be less than 100. It was exactly 100 in our room when I came up here at five o'clock yesterday.

Gates and Lee had lunch with us yesterday evening. They had been playing golf with George.

Natalie & I went in to Foster's shoe sale this a.m. & both got a pair of shoes for fall wear.

The afternoon mail has come & no letter from you— however I'll forgive you this time for it was certainly too hot to write yesterday.

I do hope you had a good lunch before you went back and that you didn't just <u>scorch</u> on the trip back.

We enjoyed our brief visit very much— & I wish things had been so we could have stayed longer.

Did your *Examiner*s ever arrive? If I don't hear tomorrow I'll be calling up.

Hope you are feeling fine & that it is a <u>little</u> cooler out there anyway.

Best love from us both

Devotedly—

Bess

Ft. Riley, Kans.

July 28, 1930

Dear Bess and Marger:—

This has been a dreary day— no letter, no phone call, no word of any sort from home, but the weather has been much cooler. The wind came from the northeast this morning about ten o'clock and it is very cool and pleasant. The sun came down in all its power this morning however I wish you'd stayed but I guess it is more pleasant for you at home and I shouldn't be so selfish.

We fire tomorrow morning and the next day too. My army is improving wonderfully and I expect them to go away better equipped as national defenders than when they came. I hope you and my daughter had a pleasant trip home. You no doubt got very warm because it was hot in the barrack and it has to be extra hot for that to happen.

I hope I get some sort of word tomorrow. I got one *Examiner*. If you see anything else worth publishing send it to me.

Your loving
Harry.

[Independence, Mo.]
[July 29, 1930]
Tuesday—

Dear Dad—

I am sorry about the phone call— It didn't occur [to] me you would worry in the least. Fred asked me if I wasn't going to call you & I said— "Oh no! he won't worry— he'll know we got here or Mother would be firing up the wires—" I'll know better next time. Was <u>delighted</u> to get a letter this a.m. and another this afternoon. Please keep up the good work.

We are having much cooler weather, too, but it didn't cool off here until about four o'clock yesterday.

You surely must have enjoyed Mr. Fitch!— where did you run across him? It's too bad you didn't see him first! No doubt he is Col. E's first assistant this week— (to hear him tell it).

Saw C. C. today— he said Maj. Barr & Roger were planning to go out Thursday if it doesn't get too warm again. They are driving I think.

Am sorry <u>you</u> were <u>lonesome</u>. I thought you'd <u>enjoy</u> not having any <u>extra</u> responsibilities.

Marg wants to add to this so to preserve peace will quit.

With much love—
Bess

Will be glad when Saturday comes.

Someone from the "K.C. Call" just asked for your phone number & I told him it was almost impossible to reach you— but he said he was going to try anyway. Some hardheaded nigger I guess.

Dear dad—

are you shooting off the cannon? It is Tuesday

love from Margaret

Ft. Riley, Kans.
July 30, 1930

My Dear Sweetheart:—

I missed writing yesterday. It was hot and we'd fired from 7:30 until 1:30 and then examined a lot of officers on instruments and then came in and went to sleep. Today we finished up the firing with shrapnel and tomorrow we'll examine the balance and tomorrow night the regimental dinner, go riding Friday and the war will be over. I'll be very glad to get home and take on the troubles of Jackson County until fall. I suppose the gang will have spent all the available funds by the time I arrive and it will be my job to find the funds to opperate [*sic*] until fall elections are over.

Got a good letter today and was mighty glad to have it. I hope that Barr and Sermon do come down. But I'll bet you they don't come. I am looking for a letter up to Saturday noon. Kiss my baby

Love to you both
Harry.

Dear Marger:— Yes I shot the big guns about four hundred times. They made a lot of noise and you ought to have heard them. I hope you [have] been a good girl today. Write your daddy again.

Lots of love to you.

[Independence, Mo.]
[July 30, 1930]
Wednesday—

Dear Harry—

I guess from what Mrs. Watson said last night, I don't rank any letter today— am mighty sorry but suppose you are just getting <u>even</u>! I was sort of worried after she called, so tried to get you but as you know was disappointed. But I decided there wasn't anything wrong with you if you were visiting.

It looks as if we might have a chance at some rain today— it's so sultry and somewhat cloudy. Here's hoping once more!

Fred left for Chicago at 5:30 this a.m. We won't have much of a family tonight.

I'm thinking seriously of investing in some golf clubs and going to Stayton's Meadows to play with Natalie <u>quite often</u>— early in the mornings before the sun gets too warm and the crowd gets too thick. What do you think about it? I may even get <u>you</u> interested?

Am on my way to town to get my hair laundered & set. It sure needs it after all that Kansas dust that settled in it coming home Sunday.

<u>Don't</u> skip another day, <u>please</u>.

Mrs. Watson said her son would be home Friday night— will you?
With much love
Bess

[Independence, Mo.]
[July 31, 1930]
Thursday—

Old Dear—

Evidently you are not planning to leave Friday night with the Watson child— as you demanded a letter on Saturday— I hope you don't get let down.

It's getting purty durn hot again today— and I've been good & busy all morning getting things cleaned up for Auntie Bess. She will arrive (supposedly) at Indep. Junction at 4:45 tomorrow—

"Herb" is going to work on the oil rigs <u>again</u> tomorrow— Let's hope they turn out alright this time. He said he would send me one of his new cars to use while he had this one in the shop— It was his own suggestion so I hope it's alright for me to take it. Said he would have the battery attended to, too.

Saw Roger this A.M. & he said he was waiting on Maj. Barr to go to Riley— & I told him he would <u>never get</u> there then.

Marg was delighted with <u>her</u> note and I was surely glad to hear this morning after none at all yesterday.

Frank & Natalie are ready to go back to the Ozarks about Aug. 10th. How about Big Spring Inn— just for over Sunday? Or have you had enough <u>tripping</u>?

Much love from us both.
Bess—

❀1931

Although only one of my grandmother's letters survives from 1931, there was a lot swirling around it, including a rarity in the Truman household: an outright fight between my grandparents.

Grandpa had handily won reelection in November 1930 and seen his bond proposal passed by the voters. He reported from camp that "my arm is still stiff from the last bond-signing and I can hardly write." In fact, his reputation on both the state and national levels was such that there was a serious push, starting the spring of 1931, to make him the party's candidate for governor in 1932.

He was also still dealing daily with scores of people pleading for help, in addition to the usual graft and corruption. His two fellow judges, Barr

Grandpa being sworn in for his second term as presiding judge in 1931. His face seems to say, "Oh, my God. Why did I do this again?" (TL 96-387).

and Bash, had been voted out of office and had spent the last two months of their terms trying to line their pockets. The politics had become so dirty in the fall of 1930 that someone tried to kidnap my mother for leverage. A man arrived at her school one day, saying he had been dispatched to pick up "Mary Truman." No one, including my mother's first-grade teacher, ever called her Mary. I didn't even know that was her first name until I was about twenty-six. Under the pretense of fetching Mom, the teacher ran to the back of the schoolhouse and called my grandparents. By the time they arrived with the sheriff, the man had fled.

The strain of all this was such that in February of 1931, Grandpa skipped my grandmother's and mother's birthdays to check into a hotel in Little Rock, Arkansas. He needed to be somewhere that he knew "the phone's not going to ring, and that no one's going to stop me with a tale of woe when I walk down the street." It worked. He slept soundly and his ever-present headaches abated.

However, at the time of the 1931 summer encampment, my grandmother continued to worry that he was still not fully mended. Earlier that year, after he'd had to lay off hundreds of county workers, he'd been sick to his stomach. "I never did hate so to see you leave for camp as I did this year," she wrote on July 26. "I just felt you weren't up to scratch physically and needed somebody to go along with you. But I do hope the decided change of environment and work will make you over."

Grandpa agreed the following day, alluding to the work ahead, including the possible campaign for governor. "I've been so nearly non compos mentis in the last four months that I'd about come to the conclusion I was not fit to live with anyway," he wrote. "When I get that courthouse located and the contract let, we'll take another weddin' tour and maybe I can get back on earth (if I'm not in the midst of a state campaign)."

Talk of a second honeymoon evaporated days later when he came home for a special session of the court and spent the entire break on business, all but ignoring the family. His backside, sore again this year from riding, was the least of his worries. I think my grandmother misjudged just how much pressure the judgeship and all his other duties were putting on Grandpa when she lit into him for spending the entirety of the short break at the courthouse. He often told her that he could not stand the stress on the job if it weren't for her support at home. When she added to his discomfort, it pushed him over the edge. He called upon my seven-year-old mother to keep my grandmother from ever again "spoiling two days in succession" and promised that if he didn't receive a letter from my grandmother immediately, he was not going to write or call for the remainder of the encampment. My grandmother apologized the next day. She was likely madder about my grandfather pushing himself too hard than she was about being ignored.

Mom, meanwhile, had been losing baby teeth, which Grandpa had apparently promised to replace, but only if she wrote to him. This was the beginning of a decades-long nag from father to daughter about letter writing.

[Independence, Mo.]
[July 26, 1931]
Sunday afternoon—

Dear Harry—

I was most awfully glad you called last night. I had been wondering if you had arrived safely etc. It was such a hot day here, I was afraid you'd have an uncomfortable trip. There is a good breeze to-day and it helps a lot. Your daughter and I went to church this morning! I can see the incredulous look on your face— but it's true. The new rector is very fine— (I think even you would enjoy him) and I am about to acquire the church-going habit again. It wasn't very nice to come into this room this a.m. about 7 o'clock and not find you somewhere around. I never did hate so to see you leave for camp as I did this year. I just felt you weren't up to scratch physically and needed somebody to go along with you. But I do hope the decided change of environment and work will make you over. Am really sorry you have to make a break in your vacation.

Would like to know if Mr. Beeman got off with the Navy. He might just as well have stayed here over the third.

Well, here's hoping for mail tomorrow—

Marg's asleep— or she would probably be adding to this.

With much love
Bess

Is it the 381st again this year?

Ft. Riley, Kans.
Monday, July 27, 1931

My Dear Sweethearts:—

[…] How are you two getting along without your dad? I miss you both when I'm not hard at work and wish you were here. Every time I see a little, yellow headed lady I see in what manner she favors my own pretty daughter, and if she has curls I can always see a resemblance to another pretty little curly haired lady who went to a Presbyterian Sunday school in Independence about forty years ago.

My arm is still stiff from the last bond-signing and I can hardly write. We are living in the Second Cavalry barrack and they are living in tents out on the parade ground. You know they must love that. I have the choice apartment with Major Snyder and Ed McKim. There are about 160 officers in the building with twelve wash basins all in the basement. There is a scramble in the morning. Write to me as often as you can.

Your loving dad,

Harry S. Truman

Ft. Riley, Kas.
July 28, 1931

Dear Bess:—

[...] I'm glad you missed me. It makes me feel better. I've been so nearly non compas [sic] mentis in the last four months that I'd about come to the conclusion I wasn't fit to live with any way. When I get that Court House located and the contract let we'll take another weddin [sic] tour and maybe I can get back on earth (If I'm not in the midst of a state campaign) Tell my daughter to be a good young lady, mind her mother and speak respectfully to her grandmother and all her uncles and aunts.

I shall be home Saturday morning and close court and I hope I can arrange it to stay until Monday. [...] Keep sending me letters.

Love to you both from

Your Dad.

Ft. Riley, Kans.
July 29, '31

Dear Bess:

I had another good letter with the clippings this noon. Sure was glad to get it. Have been in the saddle three hours a day every day and can still sit in comfort (on a cushion). Eat enough to kill a horse at every meal and don't gain a pound. That I think is on account of the heat.

I'll be home Saturday morning and you need not bother with me. I'll call you when I get to town and you can come and get me. [...]

Your Harry

Ft. Riley, Kans.
July, Aug. 5, 1931
[postmarked Aug. 4, 1931]

Dear Bess:—

I was very much surprised at your peeve last evening although I expected it. Yesterday was about the worlds worst. I had an accommodation spasm all the way down here besides a headache and Halvorson. The Court room was impassable and every pest in the County was there including Lester and Stayton. I am just about to blow up and another bellows is turned into the balloon, (and it's really the only puff that can count). So I went out to camp hunted up a friend took two snorts and went to bed. This morning I felt better, took the outfit out [on] horseback and road [*sic*] them fifteen miles more or less over a terrain problem. I was in command of all the artillery. It was a success so I guess my head, eye and pests had cleared up.

You tell my daughter that the next time you choose to spoil two days in succession, for her please to remedy the situation. I hope you've both had a good day and lots of fun. If you don't send me a letter tomorrow I'll neither write or call you until Sunday morning.

Love to you both
Your Dad.

Ft. Riley
Aug 5 1931

Dear Bess:—

Your good letter came today and apparently you are over your disgruntled spell. Well so am I. We fired today and will do the same tomorrow. It is a hot strenuous job for me. I fire every problem with every officer and then critique it with the instructor. It looks as if some of them never will fire but we have to have patience. If we can get 90% of them so they will be of some use in an emergency in the future our time and the governments money won't be spent in vain.

It has been a very good camp but the break in it made it seem like two to me. I hope my daughter hasn't forgotten how to write. She wrote me when she was four years old and I still have the letter. Now here she is over seven and can't find the time to write her daddy. I hope to be home Saturday some time. Most of the men will get out Friday but I have to stay and sign reports etc.

Kiss my bad girl and tell her I'll not bring her any teeth if she doesn't write me.

From your loving
Harry.

☸1932

By the summer of 1932, the drive to make Grandpa the Democratic guber-
natorial candidate had fizzled thanks to Tom Pendergast, who was backing
his old friend Francis M. Wilson. "Old" was the operative word, because
Mr. Wilson was sixty-four and in poor health. In fact, he died in October,
at the height of the campaign.

Work on the courthouses was proceeding apace. To build the best
courthouse possible, Grandpa traveled more than twenty-four thousand
miles during the first six months of 1932, visiting courthouses across the
country and talking to architects and planners. He found a courthouse he
liked in Shreveport, Louisiana, and hired its architect to build the one in
Kansas City.

While Grandpa was on a business trip to St. Joseph, Missouri, and
continuing when he went on to camp, the county attorney, Fred Boxley,
was in a snit over contracts for the new building projects. Frederick Gunn,
an architect appointed to the project by Tom Pendergast, had apparently
put Boxley up to calling Grandpa to complain. At the same time, Grandpa
had trouble with another architect, his brother-in-law Fred Wallace, whom
he had hired to work on the new hospital at my grandmother's request.
Fred was a drinker, like his father and his brother George, and was unreliable as a project manager, so Grandpa was doing most of the work himself.

His general irritation may be why he left home without his raincoat
and razor blades. My grandmother mailed them to him, along with an
admonishment not to let the Boxley-Gunn thing bother him. She felt terrible about Fred but saw no way around it. She was obligated to help her
younger brother, even though it put an extra burden on Grandpa.

Mom had begun piano lessons, Grandpa nagged her by mail to practice, and both she and my grandmother were once again wrestling with the
oppressive Missouri summer. Mom, now eight years old and past the nap
stage, was so susceptible to the heat that she was usually completely listless
by the middle of the day and had to lie down. Frank Wallace, meanwhile,
had come down with "weeping eczema," which he initially thought he had

contracted from handling the change in his pocket.

The heat was so bad that more than once my grandmother used it as an excuse to skip writing. Grandpa remedied this by making her responsible for the health and welfare of the camp's second lieutenants, who always had an easier time of it when their colonel had received a letter and was therefore in a better mood. At home, my grandmother's mood was often darkened by her loud and rowdy new neighbors.

My grandparents wrote back and forth about Rufus Burrus, who had brought his wife, his sister, and another, unidentified woman to camp with him. He was ill upon arrival, which my grandmother attributed to the women's company generally, and his wife's backseat driving specifically. It was her belief that the other Guardsmen should treat the summer encampment as she and Grandpa did, as a vacation—from everybody.

Ted Marks was an old friend, a wartime comrade, and the tailor who made Grandpa's suit for his wedding. In one letter, Grandpa complains to my mother about the dearth of newspaper comics in Minnesota. Although he had a lifelong love affair with history, he was also a diehard fan of the Sunday funnies. The "Dearmont meetings" refer to Russell Dearmont, Francis Wilson's competition for the Democratic nomination for governor in 1932. He lost.

[Hotel Robidoux, St. Joseph, Mo.
July 7, 1932]

My Dear Sweetheart and Daughter:—

I arrived about seven-thirty went up to my room, a good one, and now I'm writing you. You've no idea how I wish you were both here. It will certainly be an ideal condition when you can go with me everywhere.

I told you I'd forget something. My raincoat is at the office. Please mail it to me at Camp Ripley so I won't have to buy one, and look in my right-hand top drawer and get one of those full packages of razor blades and mail it to me. Margaret must practice her exercises every day. I hope she will turn over to the front of her music book and learn how to read bass notes while I'm gone.

Whatever do you suppose caused Boxley to call me up and have the fit he did about the arrangement for the courthouse? Old man Gunn is in his dotage and doesn't know what it's all about, but I kidded him into believing he is necessary because Pendergast likes him, but Boxley ought to have more sense than to listen to him. I've made Keene, Wight and Neild agree with each other and with me now the Counselor is having a fit. I sincerely wish that all professionals could be made to wear a straight [strait?] jacket when alterations come on them. I'm not going to think of it anymore for two weeks. Tell Buck to calm the county attorney down.

Kiss Margaret and tell her to kiss her mother for me. My address is

<u>Col.</u> Harry S. Truman

F. A. Reserve, Camp Ripley, Minn.

<u>This is one on you.</u>

[Independence, Mo.]

[July 9, 1932]

Sat. 12:15

Dear Harry—

Was glad to get your letter from St. Jo. It made you seem not quite so far away this a.m.

Buck sent your rain-coat down and I am mailing it & the blades when I go to town in a few minutes.

It is most awfully hot today— & seems worse, of course, after the delightful yesterday.

Don't let Mr. Boxley's spasm worry you. He probably went off just half-cocked & will completely change his mind in two weeks. Anyway, are you going to be able to suit <u>every single</u> lawyer & private citizen in K.C.?

Don't consume too much <u>Omaha liquor.</u>

Hope you find everything fine at the new camp. Am enclosing two papers— didn't know if they were of any value or not.

Lots of love

Bess—

Camp Ripley, Minn.

July 10, 1932

My Dear Daughter and her Mamma:—

We arrived here at one o'clock yesterday and went through the physical examination and got assigned to quarters. We are living in a tent just like Camp Doniphan— sand and all. The wind is from the northwest and right off the north pole, but the sun is shining and it will be warm by noon. There are about 182 reserve officers ordered here, forty of them will be in my outfit. There are no horses everything is tractor drawn, and there'll be plenty of walking. Ted's car broke down below Minneapolis and he didn't arrive until six o'clock. He and George are over at the doctor's now. It's to be a good camp but no luxuries. We have to walk over two hundred yards to the bath house, and it's a hard thing to do at 5 a.m.

with the north wind blowing your bath robe over your head. Pajamas are rather thin about that time of day.

Margaret, I bought a St. Paul paper this morning and all I could see in it I knew was *Jiggs*. Sure wish I had a *Star*. Have you practiced your music? I'm hoping you can play all those exercises without hesitation. If you can I'll teach you to read bass notes when I get back. Kiss your mother and Mother you kiss my pretty girl for me. — and write— write— write.

Your loving dad & sweetheart

Harry.

[Independence, Mo.]
[July 11, 1932]
Monday

Dear Harry—

It was so miserably hot yesterday, I couldn't get up enough enthusiasm to write a letter even. However, today is lovely, so I guess we can pull thru the hot ones if they don't come in succession.

There isn't an earthly thing to tell you— except we are well— and missing you.

I meant to go to K.C. this morning but didn't seem to get around to it— but I will take your suit when I do get off.

Am anxious to hear about the camp etc., and hope to have your Sunday letter tomorrow. I noticed by the paper that Rufus' wife, Porter Montague's wife & somebody else went with him. Poor Rufus, it's too bad he couldn't have had one vacation without being saddled with three women.

Well, (that first letter looks more like an H than a W!) I must get to town so as to get this off.

Lots of love from us both.

Bess

Camp Ripley, Minn.
July 11, 1932

My Dear Sweetheart and Daughter:

Your good letter and my raincoat came at noon today. The razor blades were in the package too. That is all I've missed so far. We have organized the regiment and are preparing to start work in earnest tomorrow morning. Col. Dwight P. Griswold the Rep. nominee for Governor of Nebr. and his men are with my outfit for training. He will command all one day and I the next. He is a fine man and my good friend but he can't be elected Gov. because Bryan can't be beaten and conditions are against him. He doesn't seem to be worried about it.

Speaking of Omaha liquor, I arrived there at 9 a.m. and Eddie and I left at 9:30, arrived in Mason City at 4:30 P.M. and I haven't seen any Omaha booze yet. [...]

The regulars in charge of this camp are all friends of mine and I am sure everything will be fine. Col. Jackman from Minneapolis is here in charge of an outfit. You know he commanded the 443rd a couple of years while I was Lt. Col. and let me run it. He was very glad to see us all.

I am hoping that Margaret is practicing and walking more every day. I'll make it pleasant for both of you when I get home. I nearly froze last night, but the wind is in the south today and somewhat warmer. I wore my khaki yesterday but have on wool today.

We are going to Brainard [Brainerd] this afternoon and I'll mail this from there. Please send me the news and keep writing. Tell Margaret to give you a big kiss and you return it.

Your loving dad & sweety

Harry.

The gang call it Camp "Believe It or Not."

[Independence, Mo.]
[July 12, 1932]

Dear Harry—

Was so glad to get your letter this morning and to know you were settled etc. Can't help worrying about your taking cold bucking that chilly wind every morning in your pajamas. It's a mighty good thing tho that you took your heavy bath robe. How's the food? I hope it's good for that cool weather ought to give you some appetite.

It's red hot again to-day and I'm going down to Natalie's to play contract with Mom & May— I certainly don't care for the idea but I didn't have any excuse excepting the heat & I didn't dare offer that.

What kind of mileage did you get?

Nellie & Ethel got off this morning early. Suspect they are well fried by this time.

Must get Marg out of the tub so I can get in myself or the large bridge party will be sitting and waiting on me.

Write often—

Lots of love—
Bess

Tuesday

Camp Ripley, Minn.
July 13, 1932

Dear Bess—

Got your second letter today. I don't know where Rufus has his wife parked but it's somewhere up the road. He brought his sister and someone else. They haven't seen much of him because he has been sick in camp two days. These young kids can't stand the physical and mental inconveniences that the old heads take as a matter of course. I often wonder how many of them could go through a Meuse-Argonne or Camp Doniphan training and still be whole. They all live in a machine convenience age and when the machine doesn't function for them they are out of luck.

I hope that my beautiful daughter is still doing her finger exercises and practicing as she ought. The day is very pleasant not hot or cold. Yesterday it went to 97 while I was tramping all over six hundred acres trying to put seventeen carloads of tractors and trucks into position as a regiment of 155s. I got it done after a fashion but got a skinning for not doing it some other way. The Nebraska colonel who is Rep. candidate for Governor went out this morning after I'd made all the mistakes in the book before him and made as many as I did. So I don't feel so badly.

I hope you are all well and happy as I am. I'm brown as an Indian eating like a horse and sleeping seven hours a night. Keep writing even if it does get hot.

Kiss Margaret. I had hoped for a letter from her.
                                        Your loving
                                        Harry.

[Independence, Mo.]
[July 14, 1932]

Dear Harry—

I deserted you yesterday— I went to K.C. and it was so red hot when I came back and I was so all in, I just naturally passed up the letter— and felt very guilty all evening.

Was mighty glad to get your Tuesday letter today and to know it had warmed up a bit. It's more than a bit down here. It's 94 right here in our room.

I talked to your mother and she said they were both fine and she would write to you soon.

Uncle B. & Helen & John are coming out to dinner to-night. Mr. Reynolds was here this a.m. doing some work so we had him make a large top to go over the basement table & we are going to eat in the yard, "al fresco"— as it were.

If this wind keeps up tho', I'm afraid nothing will remain on the table.

Yes Marg had your card & was delighted. She had one from Ethel today from St. L. Said it was <u>hot</u>.

Am so glad Ted & Eddie could both be with you this year because I know you will enjoy the two weeks that much more.

My hand is so wet it insists upon sticking to the paper.

Will try not to skip another letter.

Very much love [from] us both.

Bess

Camp Ripley, Minn.
July 14, 1932

Dear Bess:—

I hope you had a good time playing bridge with Norma at Natalie's and that you got Margaret out of the bath. You are very popular with the 2nd Louis because they all know when I get a letter I'm not as cranky. I gave them hell this morning in the firing school and when Rufus brought me a letter the remark was, well it'll be easy this afternoon he got a letter.

It rained nearly all night and was cold as October this morning but has warmed up by now. It never gets muddy the ground is sandy and is easier to walk on and drive over when it is wet than when dry.

Colonel Randolph was here yesterday and we took him to the train last night.

The Camp is all organized and going good. The food is good and everyone is learning to do what he ought. Burrus is around today and feeling all right.

Tell my daughter I'm still looking for that letter.

Keep writing. Tell Margaret to kiss her mamma for Dad.

I am always
Your Harry.

[Independence, Mo.]
[July 15, 1932]
Friday—

Dear Harry—

It goes without saying I hope that I was mighty glad to get your Wed. letter this morning.

Too bad you had such bum luck getting the regiment into position. May be the regular army officer didn't really know as much as he let on.

I should think using tractors and trucks when you've been used to horses would make a world of difference anyway.

I don't agree with you as to what made Rufus sick— I'm sure it was his wife's back-seat driving all those 800 miles. It would flatten out anybody.

Frank is laid up again. Sunday, his head broke out with what he thought was heat but it kept getting worse and spreading & yesterday it very definitely developed into weeping eczema & he is a sight. The Dr. was there for an hour & a half last night treating the places & back again this a.m. He says it takes heroic treatment to stop it. F. is so mad about it & in such a bad humor, it makes it harder to do anything for him. He is convinced he got it off of money. Dr. K. says it has to come from some outside source.

I must get Marg ready for her rest. She is so tired by one o'clock she can't do anything for herself—

> Lots of love—
> Bess

> [Independence, Mo.]
> [July 16, 1932]
> 5 P.M. Saturday—

Dear Harry—

I almost passed up your letter again to-day— It was three o'clock before I arrived at the point where I could stop— and I decided I <u>had</u> to <u>rest</u>. I further decided I couldn't let the "2nd Louies" down since they are depending on these letters to save them a wigging. If <u>your</u> disposition has arrived at that stage then the world <u>is</u> up-side-down. To-day is fairly blistery but not quite so much so as yesterday, or we are getting used to it.

Frank seems to be a little better to-day but it is still spreading.

Did Ted O'Sullivan get there? He was surely anxious to go. Am glad Rufus is alright. Don't work him too hard. You keep his nose to the grindstone all the time anyway. Give him a little vacation!

These people next door are even worse than I thought they were. Such dirt & disorder! They raised the neighborhood last night about 2:30 trying to get their dog to come home.

Hope I hear tomorrow, some way or other.

Your daughter is so lazy she won't write— but maybe she will change her mind.

> Lots of love—
> Bess

[Independence, Mo.]
[July 18, 1932]

Dear Dad—

I guess I'll get another black mark for not writing yesterday but I didn't wake up until six & I knew the P.O. would be closed before I could get there. It was so hot I am not sure I could have made my few brains work anyway. Why is it that Sunday is always so much hotter than any other day.

It cooled off late in the evening tho— and we had to have cover all night on the sleeping-porch but today is another stinger.

Marg was quite thrilled with the E. W. & your regiment pictures. We had to get the magnifying glass to find you, tho.

I just talked to Mary & they are both fine. Fred ran a hay fork into his knee last week & they were a little worried about it but Mary just told me that he was alright again.

Will you be leaving on Friday or Saturday?

I haven't sent any papers for there hasn't seemed to be anything of local interest in them.

Your commission arrived from Washington a few days ago.

Marg is eager to get to her letter so I will have to let her have the pen—

Lots of love,
Bess

Camp Ripley, Minn.
July 18, '32

Dear Bess:—

Got a fine letter yesterday and one this morning. Thanks for sending Norquist's letter. I'll write him. I sure hope Frank gets along all right. That must be a very painful condition. What on earth could have caused it?

We went out to fire this morning and I was disappointed in the showing and told them that I wanted a little less poker playing and a little more skull practice. I don't know what they thought of it but I have never seen such a dull display at a firing point. Only three out of eleven showed any signs of knowing what it was about. […]

Please keep writing to me. I am getting cranky and they help keep me right.

Love to my daughter but I thought maybe she'd surely write me.

Love to both of you— lots of it.

Harry.

[Independence, Mo.]
[July 19, 1932]

Dear Dad—

Here goes the S.L.L.S. (the Second Lieus' Life Saver) in case they need it.

I went to sleep like a nut in that hot room and feel as if I had been parboiled for the last hour.

We are planning to go to see Helen etc. tonight if it cools off a bit after dinner. It's amazing how hot a north wind can be.

I'm sorry the hot weather has hit you again. A tent is about the hottest place in the world.

Breezy Point sounds most attractive. How far is it from your camp? Is that where Mrs. Burrus is?

The Dr. says Frank is better but he is a sight. Mack has it too— so no doubt <u>that's</u> where F. got it.

Have you had a pool to swim in? You haven't mentioned it.

It's almost six & if I don't hurry you'll be minus a letter on Thursday—

Lots of love—
Bess

Camp Ripley, Minn.
July 20, 1932

Dear Bess:—

I got even with you when your letter didn't come yesterday I just refused to write so you'll skip one, too. It was a great pleasure to hear from you and Margaret together. I also got one each from Beeman and Bill Francisco. I don't know what Beeman has in mind but he has been awfully nice to me lately.

We were out on a problem this morning with the Minnesota Natl. Guard. So far as we were concerned we may as well have been in bed. I brought my out fit in and held an artillery firing school. We finish up tomorrow, pay off Friday and I ought to be home Sunday. It has been a rather hot week. We have our Regimental dinner tomorrow. I wish you were here.

Sincerely
Harry.

[Independence, Mo.]
[July 20, 1932]

My Dear Mr. Truman—

You are "in very bad" with your wife and daughter— no letter today & there can be no <u>possible excuse</u> for it. Surely you're not so vindictive as to be merely paying us back!

But, seriously, we were disappointed.

Dr. Brick was here this morning [and] said Marg had been doing
entirely too <u>much</u> & she would have to quiet down <u>considerably</u> for four
or five days & he would be back. Said this hot weather alone has a ten-
dency to wear people out. She is so tired today she can hardly move, but
it's very oppressive so I think that has something to do with it.

Hope it has cooled off at Ripley— Noticed in the morning paper
that Butte had had a hard hail storm. Trust the lower temperature will
come this way.

The Times this a.m. had a splendid editorial on Wilson— but large
groups of Kansas City women have been having Dearmont meetings this
week.

Well, it won't be long now— two weeks from yesterday—

Please let me know <u>about</u> when you will get home.

Lots of love from

Your Family

(in spite of there being no letter)

✿1933

In 1933, my grandparents were at a crossroads. Grandpa was approaching the end of his second and final term as presiding judge of Jackson County and was looking forward to running for the county collector's job. There was even some talk of Tom Pendergast backing him for a newly created congressional seat.

My grandmother would probably have been fine with the collector's job, followed by retirement or even a return to farming, as Grandpa had once suggested. She enjoyed politics, at least vicariously, but was happiest with her family and close friends. She would have been happier still to be married to someone who wasn't so tightly wound half the time.

As these letters begin, in May of 1933, Grandpa was on his way to St. Louis to sell his final plans for the new Jackson County courthouse to the Chamber of Commerce. Bids were going out and work would start soon. The "mill business" he mentions has to do with the Waggoner-Gates Milling Company, co-founded by my grandmother's grandfather, George Porterfield Gates. My grandmother's aunt, Maud Gates Wells, and her sons wanted to sell the mill, while my grandmother's brothers, particularly Frank, who worked there, wanted to keep it going.

My grandparents shed at least one worry. Over the winter, my mother's penchant for illness had reached new heights and she had come down with the flu, followed by pneumonia and rheumatic fever. It was bitterly cold that winter, the house's heating system was abysmal, and the family doctor ordered her to a warmer climate. My grandmother chose Biloxi, Mississippi, and rented a cottage on the Gulf of Mexico. Mom improved instantly. Unfortunately, both she and my grandmother, away from home and family, were bored to tears. My grandmother referred to Biloxi as "this burg" and wouldn't let Grandpa get away with taking even a minute longer than needed to conclude his business and rescue them.

[Hotel Robidoux, St. Joseph, Mo.]
Sunday, May 7, 1933

Dear Bess:

[…] Tomorrow I'll be forty nine and for all the good I've done the forty might as well be left off. Take it all together though the experience has been worth while; I'd like to do it again. I've been in a railroad, bank, farm, war, politics love (only once and it still sticks) been busted and still am and yet I have stayed an idealist. I still believe that my sweetheart is the ideal woman and that my daughter is her duplicate. I think that for all the horrors of war it still makes a man if he's one to start with. Politics should make a thief, a roué, and a pessimist of anyone but I don't believe I'm any of them and if I can get the Kansas City Court House done without scandal no other judge will have done as much and then maybe I can retire as collector and you and the young lady can take some European and South American tours when they'll do you [the] most good; or maybe go live in Washington and see all the greats and near greats in action. We'll see. I'm counting the days till I see you.

Lots of love to you both

Harry.

[Hotel Robidoux, St. Joseph, Mo.]
May 10, 1933
Wednesday.

Dear Bess:—

Well it looks as if I will get off to St. Louis tonight. Everything is set to go at the Chamber of Commerce today and Buck and McCardle have agreed to accept the plans and order the bids advertised for on Monday. It will be better for me to be out of town while the contractors are figuring anyway because they would devil the life out of me. If I'm not here they'll have to figure it out on the square and if we get back on the 4th of June that will be too late to do anything.

[…] The Mill business is going forward. Your mother and Fred are going over to talk to your Auntie Maud and still try for an amicable settlement. I am sure if she were acquainted with the facts she would want to keep the mill running. Those boys are so anxious to get money for that bank they can't see anything else and I don't blame them for that. But I have urged Frank to take whatever steps are necessary to save the Mill and he's doing it. The meeting is Monday and I know things will be all right. Besides it means a good job for Frank and I believe for George too sometime in the future.

You may get a wire from me from St. Louis by the time you get this.
Kiss my baby. Love to you both.

Harry

[Biloxi, Miss.]
[May 11, 1933]
<u>Thursday</u>—

Dear Harry—

Just a <u>brief few</u> lines— we are in an extra hurry to get to B. [Biloxi]
& back for lunch. Then to Gulfport to have Marg's hair cut and let Mrs. L.
attend to some business.

Was mighty glad to get your Mon. letter this morning. Am sorry M's
package had not arrived but hope it got there before the day was over.

Am surely glad you have practically decided on the 15th. But if you
leave St. Louis on Tues. night I can't see why you won't get here <u>Wed.</u>
night instead of Thurs. night. It only took you 36 hours to go all the way
home so we'll be looking for you <u>Wed.</u> You had better bring your seer-
sucker suit— it's in Marg's closet. Bring it like it is— the laundry down
here will do it cheaper than at home.

I noticed by the paper your warm weather has started. I know you
are glad of it.

I am sending candy to Mother & your mother for Sunday— I can't
buy anything decent, otherwise, in this burg.

Must get off— Love to everybody—

Bess

[Hotel Claridge,] St. Louis, Mo.
May 11, 1933

Dear Bess:

[…] Yesterday was quite a day. Said my speech to the Chamber of
Commerce and by working all night they got the model ready and had
it on exhibition. It is a beautiful building and I believe I sold it to them.
Even old Battle said I made a good speech but I am always rather doubtful of my ability in that line […] It was the biggest crowd the Chamber
had had this year. They asked a lot of questions but they were all apparently friendly. Keene, Wight, Gunn and Neild [the architects] were all
there and helped me answer the questions. Everyone seemed to go away
sold on the idea that the building should be put up. When I get that job
done I can probably retire to a quiet job and enjoy life a little bit with my
family. Not that I'm not enjoying it now but it is sometimes pretty hard

on head and nerves. I can hardly wait to see you both, but it won't be long now, I hope. Be good both of you until I arrive.

Lots of love to you both

Harry.

✳1935

By late 1933, Grandpa had all but given up on furthering his political career. Boss Tom, who it seemed could stand only so much honesty, had refused to back Grandpa not only in a bid for governor in 1932, but now in a possible run for the newly created congressional seat as well. He had even given away Grandpa's fallback job, the county collector. Disgusted, Grandpa had threatened to

Grandpa on the campaign trail for the Senate seat, with two cohorts (TL 82-61-7).

go back to the farm or maybe open a filling station. Before he could do either, however, Pendergast offered to run him for the U.S. Senate.

After Grandpa's election and arrival in Washington in 1934, Senator J. Hamilton Lewis of Illinois told him, "Don't start out with an inferiority complex. For the first six months, you'll wonder how you got here, and after that, you'll wonder how the rest of us got here."

For my grandmother, this was the start of a decades-long tug of war, my great-grandmother on one end and my grandfather on the other. Both played dirty. Madge complained that she was "impatient" for my grandmother to return to Independence from Washington.

Bess in 1935, when Grandpa was a new senator (TL 58-607).

142

Portrait of the family from 1937, showing them taking off for D.C. (TL 82-183-01).

Grandpa moaned that when she did, he got headaches from being left alone. Mom, meanwhile, groused at having to spend half the year at public school in Independence and half in private school in D.C.

It was actually an exciting time to be in Washington, with President Roosevelt trying to pull the country out of the Great Depression. Grandpa's job brought him into contact with all sorts of colorful characters, including Huey Long, the long-winded, demagogic senator from Louisiana, and Father Charles Coughlin, the radio priest who started out as a Roosevelt supporter and wound up thinking kindly of Hitler.

Despite the familial tug of war, my grandmother really enjoyed having an insider's view of Washington and Grandpa was happy to provide it, as his first letter shows. He, in turn, was in dire need of advice as to how to remove some obstinate spots from one of his summer suits.

On July 28, Grandpa wrote to my grandmother from New York, where he had gone to see Tom Pendergast, who was on his way home from a tour of Europe. Grandpa wanted to get to Pendergast before Charles Howell, who had run against Bennett Clark for Senate in 1932. Howell hoped to run for governor of Missouri in 1936 and wanted Pendergast's support, which would have enraged Clark and split the state's Democratic Party. Grandpa planned to propose a compromise candidate, millionaire apple-grower Lloyd Stark. It made sense at the time and averted catastrophe but would turn out to be a huge mistake.

Several letters mention Vice President John Nance Garner. "Cactus Jack" Garner, who was from Texas, became a political mentor and close friend of my grandfather's. One letter mentions William Dryden, who was the boyfriend of Grandpa's secretary, Mildred Latimer. An alcoholic, he had had a meltdown on a city bus and was arrested and hospital- ized. Dryden managed to convince Mildred that he'd had heatstroke, but Grandpa wasn't fooled. In an earlier letter, he said that if it was up to him he'd just as soon throw Dryden in the Potomac River. My mother thought that Grandpa's reference to the undependability of alcoholics was also a jab at Grandma's brothers Fred and maybe George, who couldn't seem to take care of their mother, thus depriving Grandpa of his wife and daughter.

My grandmother ends one letter by asking about Huey Long, the grandstanding Louisiana senator, and his bid to replace Roosevelt in 1936. Neither she nor Grandpa had much love for Mr. Long, who used to hold up legislation he didn't like by reading aloud from the Bible or the phone book. Whenever he stood up to speak, most senators fled the room. Even Vice President Garner headed for the door one day, leaving Grandpa in charge. Afterward, Long asked Grandpa what he thought of the speech. "I had to listen to you," my grandfather said, "because I was in the chair and couldn't walk out." Long never spoke to him again.

Washington D.C.
Friday, July 26, 1935

Dear Bess:—

This is turnip day and, I think, Nellie Noland's birthday. You are supposed to sow turnips today. There's no place for me to do it except in the court yard of the Senate Office Bldg and Garner probably would object.

Six new white collar attached shirts came from Eddie's* factory today or yesterday I don't know which I just saw them. They have that new collar on them. I should keep clean now anyway. I'm going to get a couple of white suits while the sale is on and then I can run until fall. I shouldn't have to buy any more clothes until 1941.

[…] The Senate convenes at eleven o'clock today to consider the banking bill. Senator Nye of North Dakota spoke for four hours after he'd introduced Father Coughlin's bill as an amendment. The Priest's cam- paign manager and the President of the American Bankers Assn. sat side by side in the gallery. Neither of course knew who the other was. Most of us thought Coughlin wrote Nye's speech. Nye is one of the good-looking egotistical boys who play to the gallery all the time. He's had the lime

---

* Eddie Jacobson, who was still in the clothing business.

light on the munitions investigation for six months and he never comes
to the Senate except to make a speech or introduce a bill to abolish the
Army and Navy or to get more money for more investigation and more
publicity. Several so called people's friends in the Senate would be in a
hell of a fix if there were not some good old work horses here who really
cause the Senate to function. I can't pay much on Nye, La Follette, Black
of Alabama and that brand. Wheeler and Bankhead of Alabama are
workers. Wheeler isn't as radical as he's painted and I like him. Glass is
a worker, so is Adams of Colorado, Harrison, Robinson, and one or two
others. Robinson's gone high hat but he's a good worker nevertheless.
On the Republican side, McNary, Shipstead, Hale and White both from
Maine, and the ex-prize fighter from N.J. Barbour, are the best workers.
There isn't a so-called progressive who does anything but talk. Your letter
just came. Glad you had a good time at Thelma's. There's a rumor that
August 15 is the day.* I hope it is. Wrote Frank this A.M. about the mill.
    Kiss Margey. Love to you.

Harry

Glad you talked to Mary. Hope the station is worth something now.

Kansas City, Mo.
[July 28, 1935]
Sunday—

Dear Harry—

    Was glad to get your letter a little while ago. It makes Sunday not
quite so long (or quite so hot) altho the thermometer is surely going to
hit the top today. Guess it's a good thing Frank wouldn't go to Bella Vista.
If you get home before Labor Day maybe we can go down there or somewhere. That is good <u>news</u> about Aug. 15th but <u>seeing is believing</u>.

    Am afraid you didn't get off either to Delaware or N.Y. as you didn't
mention it in Friday's letter. Am sorry you didn't have a change of scene.
Seems to me you need one.

    That's a good idea to get some white suits while they are on sale. Did
you try having that suit <u>washed</u> at the laundry to get those red spots out?
They can get most everything out with <u>clorox</u>. I got some yellow spots on
my one white coat the day I had luncheon with Mrs. Strickler & they can't
get them out. I can't figure out what they are— Lord knows they aren't
liquor as long as I was with <u>her</u>— iced tea was the heaviest thing I had to
drink & <u>that</u> ought to come out easily. I tried washing them myself yesterday & they are <u>paler</u> & I'm going to work on them again today.

---

* The day the Senate would adjourn and he would get to go home.

No news— nothing of interest— the days are deadly— <u>could</u> play bridge any & every day but it's just too hot.

Lots of love

Bess

New York City

Sunday July 28, 1935

Dear Bess:—

Well I left Washington at noon yesterday and drove up here by seven thirty which was not so bad considering the traffic. I let the boy at Ft. Meade drive me so I had help in case of car or tire trouble and if the hotel treats me as it did before it won't cost anything but meals and that is a rather cheap cost for a driver.

I am going to see T. J. [Tom Pendergast] this morning and start back to Washington at noon. Hope I find a letter there when I get back and I believe I will. I'll probably get all extravagant and call again. Charlie Howell was in to see me and I wanted to get to the boss first so that's why I'm here. He & Mrs. Howell are going to Europe & I am sure he wants to announce for governor when he gets back. That'll split Clark and T. J. [for] sure. I believe I'm going to prevent the split if I can. Love to both of you. Kiss Margey.

Harry

[Senate Chamber]

August 9, 1935

Dear Bess:—

You don't know how much I appreciated the letter that came in this morning's mail. I was so devilishly homesick— I could see you standing out there in the yard watching me drive away and I don't think you kissed me good-bye or you can put it around the other way if you want me on the defensive. Then I didn't call you from Richmond but it was so late when we got there and I didn't write from there either. We had a very strenuous trip what with high water detours and what not and I found Harry Salsbury being taken to the hospital as soon as we arrived. They operated on him for appendicitis about an hour after I called you. I was over to see him with Johnnie this morning and he was doing fine. Doctor said he could go home Wednesday. I sent his dad a wire this morning telling him about it and that Harry is getting along all right.

When I come home next time we are going to take a week's vacation and then maybe I can see you more than twice. I like the Continental and probably with a change or two will stay. You don't know how handy it is.

Kiss Margey and tell her to write me a letter. I'm getting this off in a hurry.
                    Love to you
                    Harry

                                                    New York City
                                                    August 10, 1935
Dear Bess:—
    I just arrived in this big city. Left Washington at 3 P.M. It is now 8:10
EST 9:10 EDST. If you can't translate those letters it will be too bad. Ben-
nett was supposed to come with me but got cold feet at the last minute.
He and I have been entertaining the Gov. and Caskey [Judge Caskie]
Collett and Sam Hargus all day. They came to my office at 10 o'clock and
as soon as Clark arrived we went to see Garner and Backman [Nathan L.
Bachman, D-TN] and [William J.] Bulow [D-SD], the Senate characters.
    I had dinner with them last night and lunch today and then beat
it up here. They had been to see T. J. and I must try to find out what they
did tomorrow. O'Malley and Paul Dillon are over at the Commodore
and I don't know whether to let them know I'm here or not. They have a
muddle in St. Louis which they want me to help settle. I don't much care
about getting into it. The High hat Mayor was in Washington twice and
failed to call on me and I don't see why I should go to any trouble for him
do you?
    I enjoyed the short note from you today: all I wish was that it was
longer. We may get done next week. Won't that be something.
    Kiss Margey and love to you. Monday is Mary's birthday. Please call
her.
                    Harry

                                                    [Independence, Mo.]
                                                    [August 12, 1935]
                                                    Monday—
Dear Harry—
    Was delighted to get your letter from N.Y. Hope you had a <u>successful</u>
trip. Was Bennett afraid you would sew him up too tight? I guess he knew
the two of you could out-talk him & he was taking no chances.
    Marg and I are going out soon to take Mary's birthday presents to
her. It was too hot yesterday to go out after dinner.
    I hope the big tax bill will be shelved so you can get away soon. The
Dem. Party would probably profit considerably (each one of you, personally) if the thing doesn't come to a vote this session.
    I do hope you can get here awhile before Marg's school begins so

we can take a short trip anyway.

There isn't any news— except that it is slightly cooler & somewhat cloudy— & that is news.

Must get off if we are to get home by lunch time.

Lots of love
Bess

[Independence, Mo.]
[August 13, 1935]
Tuesday—

Dear Harry—

Your Sunday letter didn't arrive until the afternoon delivery which is very unusual— I was mighty glad to get it then— for I was wondering what had happened to you in N.Y. and was glad to know you were back home OK.

I've been playing bridge at Natalie's all afternoon— with Louise [*illegible*] and Grace Minor. Had a nice time but not much bridge.

It's so grand & cool our pep has returned & I imagine there will be a number of "bridges" in the near future.

They plowed up & oiled Van Horn today. We are going right out thru the south yard. It's just as hard as concrete & the cars make no impression on it & there isn't much of a bump at the curb.

We saw your mother & Mary yesterday and they were fine.

It looks as if the tax bill will not be such a stumbling block after all & maybe you will get away soon—

Have you had any more offers on the 1424–16th apt.?

Must hurry; it's almost six— Marge will write soon—

Lots of love
Bess

Washington D.C.
Tuesday, August 13, 1935

Dear Bess:—

Well I'm up to date with my mail today. It is a real task to get up to date and I've had more customers from Mo. than ever too. Jim Dougherty, my old supply sergeant in the army was in to see me yesterday and took me out to his uncle's for dinner last night. The first time I've been out. Today Howard Hall was in to see me with one of his daughters. She's fourteen and looks older. She looks like her mother and is very nice. We had lunch in the Senate dining room and she got as much kick out of it as if she'd been to Hollywood. Clark had up an amendment to the liquor control bill to allow the sale in barrels as well as bottles. It was defeated by 59 to 24. He and I are going to see [Roosevelt aide Harry] Hopkins at 5:15 to talk about Murray. Someone has been knocking him and these bureaucrats have to be sold over. I am finally moved into the Continental to stay. Got all my things out of the office today.

I am sorry I mentioned the fact that you didn't kiss me goodbye at the car. I guess you thought the one at the house was enough. It looks now as if we will be done by a week from Saturday and if we are I'll be home a week after that.

I'm glad you went to the ball game and I hope you go again. If you'd get my pass from Hunter it wouldn't cost you anything.

If Frank buys a farm you can help him build fences and cut weeds.

Kiss the daughter and love to you.

Harry.

[Independence, Mo.]
[August 14, 1935]
Wednesday—

Dear Harry—

Your letter came nice & early this morning. I was down in May's yard conversing while she washed the walks. After they spread the oil on Van Horn yesterday she & Natalie decided they could really clean up once more. They have been living in a thick cloud of dust all summer.

Christine [Wallace, Fred's wife] and I are going up town to look for sandals for the baby [David Wallace]— he is walking all over the place in his Taylor Tot & going straight through his thin shoes just like Marg did. Do you remember when we bought her a pair a week? I don't know how they are going to stand that, but maybe she can get heavier ones now.

Am glad you got Nettie organized— you've surely had a time with Thompkins.

Natalie & Frank are thinking about driving to Santa Fe about the tenth of Sept. & asked if we would be interested in going. I think she thinks the car would be too full tho. with Marg along so I don't see how we could do it for I wouldn't leave her here at home for that length [of] time. Guess we had better do our own traveling— it would probably be more satisfactory anyway— They are both of them so old & crotchety. Hope you get home long before Sept. 1st. The morning paper says you are having plenty of heat. It's great here this morning. We slept under several blankets last night.

This is one letter that will get out on time—

Love—
Bess

[Senate Chamber]
August 15, 1935

Dear Bess:

I was most happy to get the letter. I am glad it's cool and pleasant. We are having a hot wave. Yesterday and today and the day before were scorchers. I guess your hot wave came over here and you received a cool one from Alaska. At least that's the way the weather map looks.

Harry Salsbury was moved to his boarding house yesterday. He seems to be doing fine. I was over to see him last night. We now have another invalid in town and on our hands, one William Dryden. He's made Mildred believe that he's in bad shape and she's all sorry for him and I guess I'll have to help her out with him. I went up to see him this morning and he was tickled to death. He'd made all of them believe he'd had a heatstroke. I said Bill, how much hootch [*sic*] did it take to give you this stroke and he said he only had one drink he could remember. Of course I won't tell Mildred. Let her think well of him. I like him but he's like all the rest of the alcoholics— undependable.

Mr. La Follette is making a speech on the tax bill and most of us are in the cloak rooms waiting for his finish. He has some nutty ideas on taxation that have a lot of merit but I don't think I'll vote with him. If we get him and old man Frazier out of the way we ought not to have much trouble passing the bill and then we can go home.

I wonder if Margey is ever going to write her dad? I'm glad you saw Mamma and Mary and that they were feeling well. I'm looking for letters. Kiss Margey. Love to you.

Harry.

[Independence, Mo.]
[August 15, 1935]
Thursday—

Dear Harry—

That is mighty good news that there is even a chance of adjournments by a week from Sat. Will it take you a whole week to wind things up in the office? Will John come with you? Won't Vic have to come, too, about as soon as you do? Have you broken the news to Bud that he isn't coming? What about his vacation? How about some more questions?

Mother & Marg & I are going to Platte this afternoon. It's fairly cool & I think we had better get off before it gets any warmer.

Betty & Virginia are coming back tonight & Marg can hardly wait. I'll be glad she has them here again, rather [than] such a dose of these two she plays with so constantly. I haven't the nerve to call Hunter & ask for

the pass as I would use it so seldom—
but I haven't seen him out there any
night we have been there. Edgar & the
boys & Charlie & Florence were sitting
near us the last time we went. The
Blums won't be back 'til the 8th anyway
so <u>you</u> can get the pass from Hunter.

    Fred appreciated your letter
yesterday—

    Am glad you are settled again.
Did Huey make any sort of a stir by
announcing he would run for Pres. in
'36?

Lots of love—
Bess

Mom (center back), with friends,
in 1934 (TL 82-182-1).

Washington D.C.
August 17, '35

Dear Bess:—

    It sure looks like an early home
coming. We went through the calender [sic] in short order yesterday and
it looks as if we'd wind up a lot of controversial legislation Monday and
Tuesday and probably begin adjournment on Wednesday. I ought to be
starting home Sunday of next week. I forgot to put a special on yesterday's
letter. My mind doesn't work any more I guess. I have been worried for
fear I'd never find out what its all about. I sat on a committee to hear
all about why airlines should be put under the Inter-State Commerce
Convention. I've posted the bill and got it on the calender [sic] for Sen.
McCarran and then forgot what it was all about. Had to read the proceed-
ings from start to finish. That ought not to happen and wouldn't have
ten years ago. Maybe I need a holiday. I wrote your daughter a letter after
reading about the other baby's shoes in your letter yesterday. It was great
to watch her grow up, and I hope it will be as happy from now on.

    Hope to see you soon. Love to you both

Harry

✸1937

President Roosevelt had split the Democrats over his plan to increase the number of Supreme Court justices from nine to fifteen. Publicly, he said this was to ease the burden on older justices, but some people were pretty sure it was a bid to pack the court with justices friendlier to New Deal legislation. Grandpa studied the plan and found that there was legitimate precedent for enlarging the court, so he backed the president, causing a rift with his conservative colleagues.

As a member of the Interstate Commerce Committee, Grandpa was investigating the wholesale looting of the nation's railroads by their owners. In 1926, U.S. railroad companies employed more than 1.75 million men and had a payroll of nearly $3 billion. By 1938, half of those men had been laid off and ten thousand miles of track, vital to the nation's economy, had been abandoned. In a speech on the Senate floor, Grandpa reminded his colleagues that the Missouri Pacific had been robbed in 1876 by Jesse James, "who used a horse and a gun and got up early in the morning" and "took the paltry sum of $17,000 from the express car." More recently, he went on, the Rock Island Railroad had been robbed by "tin plate millionaires" who used not guns but holding companies and took $70 million. "So you can see," he concluded, "what pikers Mr. James and his crowd were alongside of some real artists."

Grandpa was also working on antitrust legislation that would wrest control of public utilities from Wall Street and was trying to craft a bill that would regulate the nation's airlines. And while he was doing all this, he also had to watch his back. Lloyd Stark, the apple-grower whom he and Tom Pendergast had helped to elect governor of Missouri in 1936, was now turning on both of them. In a letter of November 1, Grandpa reported that Stark had refused to appoint even one Pendergast man to the state election board, this after inviting Jim Pendergast to bring him a list of candidates.

Stark was also cozying up to President Roosevelt. Though Stark denied it, this was a transparent warm-up for a run at Grandpa's Senate seat in

Grandpa
with Vice
President
John Nance
Garner and
FDR aide
Jim Farley in
1936
(TL 58-195).

1940. Grandpa tried to intercede through Jim Farley, postmaster general and architect of Roosevelt's successful 1932 and 1936 campaigns. Although Farley assured him they had no intention of helping Stark, the postmaster was on the outs with Roosevelt over the court-packing scheme. As my grandmother pointed out in November, it had become hard to dissuade FDR in the aftermath of his landslide 1936 victory.

Stark might have also enlisted the help of longtime Pendergast foe Senator Bennett Clark had Grandpa not convinced Clark that Stark would eventually come after him as well. Grandpa wrote to my grandmother in November that he had ended "the Clark-Stark hookup." Pendergast had become increasingly vulnerable. His organization was under investigation by U.S. Attorney Maurice Milligan, brother of Grandpa's Senate primary opponent, Congressman Tuck Milligan. Pendergast himself had developed a serious gambling habit begun, some said, after he wagered ten thousand dollars on a long shot and won two hundred fifty thousand dollars. Now, he was taking more and greater risks to cover huge losses and firing long-serving and loyal aides, presumably those who tried to help him or rein him in. My grandmother, after lunching with the wife of one of the victims, wrote to Grandpa that Pendergast had gone "completely loco."

Generally, my grandmother's letters from this year are upbeat. She enjoyed being a senator's wife almost as much as Grandpa enjoyed being a senator. She had a ringside seat to an exciting time in American history and enjoyed the social life, except for the commute between Independence and Washington. At home, she took up horseback riding again and even persuaded my mother to join her. I cannot imagine my mother on a horse. She always said she disliked animals and allowed us to have only the smallest creatures—hamsters, gerbils, and fish—as pets. This may have been a front, however, because when she decided that my brother was not feeding his pet rabbit well enough, she gave it the carrots and cabbage she had planned for our dinner. As usual, my grandmother worried about Grandpa, who was again working too hard and started the fall by check-ing into the U.S. Army hospital (the "hoss pistol," as he called it) in Hot Springs, Arkansas. Once he was pronounced fit, however, she was happy to have him do all the shopping for apartments in Washington.

In several letters, my grandmother mentions Fred Canfil, who Grandpa met during his time as county judge and became a longtime, trusted Truman aide. My mother described him as being built like a bull with a voice that could shatter glass at a hundred paces. Years later, during the postwar Potsdam Conference in Germany, Grandpa, then president, introduced Fred to Marshal Joseph Stalin as "Marshal Canfil." He didn't bother to explain that Fred was a federal marshal serving in the State of Missouri. Thereafter, the Russians treated Fred with great respect.

A letter from October 18 refers to Harriette and Leighton Shields, a couple my grandmother felt bound to help. Like Fred Wallace, Leighton, an attorney, was an alcoholic who had drunk himself out of a promis-ing career. He wanted Grandpa to make him an assistant U.S. attorney. To help him—and get him as far away from my grandmother as possible—Grandpa persuaded the Roosevelt administration to appoint Leighton as district attorney to a U.S. court...in Shanghai, China.

In late October, my grandmother writes that my mother was singing with the church's adult choir. For Mom, this was the beginning of her inter-est in a singing career. My grandmother, on the other hand, hoped Mom would become interested in the religious aspect of it. That never happened. She and Dad went to church just long enough to get the youngest of us through Sunday school. After that, everybody was on his own spiritually.

[Independence, Mo.]
[September 1937]
Monday—

Dear Harry—

I am enclosing two or three things I thought maybe you would want to attend to before Friday or Sat.

It looks as if the Hot Springs trip is off, too— Frank's bad eye is giv-ing him a lot of trouble again & he is at Dr. Green's this morning. Natalie thinks he will not be able to do any driving. I hope you can be home by Friday— these two weeks have been <u>plenty long enough</u>.

We are calling off the moonlight ride to-morrow— as it has dwin-
dled down to three of us— & I would just as soon Marg isn't up as late as
she would have to be. I would never get her up Wed. morning!

Your mother's cold was better— but not completely gone. She was
glad to get the nuts and pralines.

Mr. Keene has just called & wanted you to have lunch with him as
soon as you get back.

Dr. Musgrave of Excelsior Springs called last night while I was out &
wanted you to help get Roosevelt to stop in E.S. to dedicate the "Hall of
Waters" etc.— but didn't give any date.

Carrie & Webster are going back to Detroit to live. She is having a
luncheon on Wednesday— Guess she is glad to get that far away from
"Jinnie" again.

Have a paint job on hand & must do a little before I dress. Hope
you are feeling really grand.

Lots of love—
Bess

[Park Hotel] Hot Springs, Ark.
Saturday. 9/11/37

Dear Bess:—

I arrived at 9:30 this morning after a seventy mile drive over a very
rough road. You should have been along. It was over a mountain range
and the most beautiful scenery. Goes through Ouachita National Forest.
So you see I got to Ouachita even if it is spelled in a peculiar manner.

Have a beautiful room at the Park Hotel for $3.00 a day tub and
shower a big fan and everything but a radio and I can live without that I
guess. It would cost me at least $4.50 for the same thing at the Arlington
and I believe it's cooler. This is a beautiful day and I wish you were all
here. If you and Margie were along I'd be fixed in good shape.

I didn't know I was so tired. Slept until noon at Tulsa and went to
bed at seven and slept until seven at Russellville. I'm not going to visit the
hospital until Monday— after some more sleep and then I know they'll
find nothing.

Kiss my girl and write me a letter because if I'm not discovered I'm
going to stay a week.

Love to you both and remember me to all the family.

Harry.

[Independence, Mo.]
[September 12, 1937]
Sunday noon—

Dear Harry—

I was glad to talk to you last night— and glad, too, to have your
wire early in the day— You must have left Russellville good and early to
have reached H.S. at ten o'clock. Surely hope you have a good report from
the x-rays tomorrow— What did they x-ray? I wanted to ask that last night
but thought I had better not. Will you please promise to tell me exactly
what the report is?

We are all going horse-back riding this afternoon— all except
George— he wouldn't leave his golf for any thing else. It is one grand
day— just made for a ride. I hope you will go while you are down there. I
feel more limber already & the ride yesterday didn't "faze" me. I will be in
trim for a three mile hike pretty soon.

Christine is going to Chicago with her mother to-night— Here's
hoping the babies stay well 'til Friday morning!

Take care of yourself!!

Lots of love—
Bess

Mrs. Hawes' brother called this a.m. & said that boy would have to
be re-appointed this week— so I told him you could not be reached— &
he had better call Jasper if anything had to be done at once.

Hot Springs, Ark.
Sunday, September 12, 1937

Dear Bess:—

Well it was nice to talk to you last night. You ought to be here. I got
up at six this morning, put on my yellow shirt and walked up the mountain and back. The sign says it is 1.5 miles up. I made a short cut or two
and judge I made it in a mile. Anyway I made the round trip in 35 minutes. No one was up except an old granddad sitting on a bench halfway
up the hill and the negro bell boy delivering papers to the rooms. The
front door of the hotel was lock[ed] when I went out. I didn't know they
ever locked 'em. It was a perfectly grand morning— cool and clear. All
these people shivering like winter time. I came back took a bath, another
nap and had breakfast at 8:30. Wrote my St. Louis speech and sent it to
Vic to type and then took another nap. It was noon by then so I ate a light
lunch and walked to the other end of town looked over the shows but
didn't go in. Got in my car and drove up the mountain. I walked up and
went to the top of the tower— in the elevator and saw the whole country

around here. It is a wonderful view on a clear day. Again wish you and
Miss Marger were here.

Got to the hoss pistol [*sic*] in the morning and I'd as soon it was a
pistol but maybe it won't be so bad. Kiss Margey. Love to you. Remember
me to the family.

Harry

How's that for coming out even?

[Independence, Mo.]
[September 13, 1937]
Monday—

Will send this to hotel so those smart P.O. boys won't know you are
in hospital.

Dear Harry—

I was glad to get your wire a little while ago— and am glad you are
going to be where you will have to <u>behave</u> yourself and have the <u>right
things done for you</u>. I hate like the dickens to know that you <u>need</u> things
done for you— but if you <u>do</u>— you are in a grand place for them to be
done. That sounds rather complicated but I hope you get the drift. Just
what did they say about your eyes— etc. Now tell me the truth— don't
varnish it any. I wish I were down there— I hate to think of you there all
by yourself but maybe you are better satisfied that way.

We had a nice ride yesterday— & went to see "The Lost Horizon"
last night— Am going to town with Natalie this afternoon & that's the
extent of my "goings."

Lou Holland called this a.m. & wanted to know if you would be
here Thurs. for the Winner Road dedication & I told him I didn't think
you could possibly get back & I shall call him tomorrow and tell him
definitely you will not be there. Tell him you are having some <u>eye</u> treatments— but not <u>where</u> you are.

Please let me know how you are getting along— & why can't you
stay two weeks— (or almost)— anyway. You won't have another chance
to rest very soon. What about the diabetic condition?

I hope there is a letter tomorrow morning—

Lots of love—
Bess

Hot Springs, Ark.
September 14, 1937

Dear Bess:—

How do you like my new stationary [*sic*]? The border is a knock out.

Believe I'll have some Senate stationary [*sic*] made on the same plan.

Well I moved into the hospital yesterday morning and they start doing things to me today. Photograph teeth, stomach, lungs and other parts so they say. Make blood tests etc. Say there is nothing to worry about the heart. I told you I didn't trust the navy. I have a northwest corner room on the eighth floor overlooking the town. It is cold as the dickens down here. I had to put on my blue coat & vest last night to witness a picture show on the roof of the hospital. The weather has been beautiful and I wish I'd gone to this place to begin with. I'd have been six dollars ahead anyway. Only have to pay for eats at $1.50 per day and medicine, if any. Pretty soft.

Wish you'd call Lou Holland and tell him I can't be there the 17th. It will take all week to do this job and since I've started I'd better go through. Feel better this morning than I have for a month. They are really feeding me. I was most starved to death. Love to you all. Kiss Margey.

Harry

[Independence, Mo.]
[September 14, 1937]
Tuesday—

Dear Dad—

I tried to get you by phone last night but they insisted you were not registered at the hospital and were not there! I was wondering how you were & knew I would sleep better if I could talk to you— I may try again tonight—

I surely hope you are getting a most thorough rest and that the treatments will do you a world of good.

This is one more gorgeous day and I would like to be taking an all day trip somewhere— preferably in the direction of Hot Springs— If I had had the money, I'd have left yesterday right after your telegram came— but probably it's a good thing I didn't have it— for I suspect you will get more good out of the "rest" without anyone else around.

I talked to Ethel yesterday— They are all well & enjoying the extra weeks of vacation. I hope the board doesn't insist upon them making it up next June.

Margaret Strickler sent Marg a big box of Park & Tilford— she <u>said</u> to take the place of the many pieces of Marg's candy she ate on the way to Wash.

Talked with Roylynn Taylor last night. Harriett's engagement was announced Sunday. To a St. Louis man named Leo— or has Jim already told you all about it?

If I don't get a letter tomorrow, I'm going to send out a "searcher" for you.

Lots of love—
Bess

Hot Spring[s] Ark.
Wednesday Sept. 15 [1937]

Dear Bess:—

I thought sure I'd get a letter today but I was doomed to disappointment. It was a very great pleasure to talk to you last night however and I hope you do it again tomorrow. Today was my busy day. I got up at six thirty, had breakfast at 7:30, a blood test at 8, throat & nose at nine; eyes at 9:30 and a real Hot Springs bath at ten. They really do it scientifically here. Then I had a tooth exam at 11:30. They are going to Xray 'em tomorrow and give me another eye test. There is a very fine eye man here and he seems to be very much interested in getting me properly fixed. My astigmatic axis has changed again and he says that <u>may</u> cause the headaches.

They are really feeding me. I was half starved too I reckon, but I'm eating all they give me now and its plenty. It surely is a place to rest, and they treat me like a King.

Had another picture show tonight— Lily Pons in the "Girl from Paris."* It was good too. Then Cong. Crosser and three army colonels and myself talked until ten o'clock settling all the country's ills. I'm writing this in bed.

Kiss Margie. Love to you— call me
Harry.

Hope I'm not entirely lost down here. You reckon I'll still be in politics when I get back?

[Independence, Mo.]
[September 15, 1937]
Wednesday—

Dear Harry—

Was surely glad to finally get you last night— had to tell who I was— so I guess you are pretty well barricaded. Nobody but Fred Canfil knows where you are— & he and I have been telling everyone you were out of reach of telephones & wire— and I guess you <u>are</u> at that!

I'm afraid you have been holding out on me— judging from your letter which just came the <u>Navy</u> Dr. told you <u>something</u> unpleasant about

---

* *That Girl from Paris*, a comedy released in 1937.

your heart— and you
swore he said it was
O.K. after promising
to tell me exactly what
the report was!

I guess I'll have
to write to the hospital
down there to get the
correct dope on you
this time. Here's hop-
ing it's all fine.

Am glad it's cool
down there. It's grand
here but somewhat
warmer. May, Natalie,
Marg & I are going

Fred Canfil (far right),Grandpa's hulking,
taciturn aide (TL 58-728-02).

riding after school. Marg was delighted about the imminent arrival of your
pralines. She laid me out for not calling her when I got you last night—
but I couldn't have gotten her without waking up both babies.

We had an announcement this morning of Clyde Williams' daughter's marriage. You know what that means.

Mr. Canfil calls every morning to see if there is anything he can
do— I gave him a couple of apple growers' telegrams to answer. He found
out from Mildred they were already working on it in Wash.— Am sending
mail to Vic every day— Stay as long as you possibly can.

Lots of love,
Bess

Hot Springs, Ark.
September 16, 1937

Dear Bess:

Well this is a gala day. I walked down to the Hotel [a] while ago and
there were four letters from you, one from Marger and one from Mary.
Fred Canfil walked in on me about five minutes after two and we had
a fine visit. He'll see you when he gets back. I was glad to get the lodge
letter and J. K. V's* too. Of course J. K. can't make his arrangements until
he knows what mine are and of course he doesn't know. Does the St.
Louis Mayor want us Sunday or Monday? I thought it was Monday. Canfil

---

* James K. "Jake" Vardaman was a St. Louis banker and later Navy aide to Grandpa during
his presidency.

wasn't sure. You make him read you the Mayor's letter and then I'll wire
that St. Louis Lodge.

They photographed my teeth today and finished my eye examination. This eye man is as good as I've had. The glasses needed a change.
The heart photo was analysed [*sic*] and found all right. One valve is
smaller than it should be but it isn't the one that gives trouble so they say.
The blood test isn't finished, but I've had enough to eat four days [*illegible*] running anyway. Fred can tell you how grand I'm fixed up. There are
four doctors giving me special care and I'm nearly rested. Will stay as long
as I can though. Wish you'd come down when the notion hit[s] you. Do
you need any money? Love to you both.

                                               Harry

                                    [Independence, Mo.]
                                    [September 16, 1937]
                                              Thursday—

Dear Harry—

Aside from being half frozen, we are all fine today & surely hope
you are, too (<u>fine</u>, not frozen).

We had a grand horseback ride yesterday afternoon except that the
trails were horribly dusty. We are planning the moonlight ride for next
Tuesday. Won't you be here to go too? We put it off 'til the last possible
night thinking you might get back in time.

I am enclosing Mrs. Hawes' notes she wanted you to have. Did I tell
you Bishop Spencer called up about the boy, too?

Are you allowed to go out and roam around the town or do they
make you "stay put?"

A letter has just come for Marg and I am tempted to open it but
guess I had better not— it wouldn't be a very good example to set.

Must get off up town— or this won't go out today.

Am anxious to hear from eye & teeth x-rays—

                                    Lots of love—
                                    Bess

                                    [Independence, Mo.]
                                    [September 17, 1937]
                                              Friday—

Dear Harry—

I am sitting under a dry-er, having my hair done— so this writing
will probably be even more up & down hill than usual— and it's always
bad enough—

I hope there is a letter at home for me when I get back. I had a telegram from Fred Canfil this morning from Little Rock saying you look so much better— was surely glad to get that kind of news & it was nice of him to send it.

I am hoping to talk to you tonight but thought you might want a letter tomorrow anyway so will send it special as it would not be delivered on Sat. otherwise.

This is another perfect day & I hope we can scrape up a few to go horseback riding after school.

Chris[tine] got in this morning— has quite a cold— but had a good time & her mother bought her some clothes so it was quite a satisfactory trip.

Mildred* sent your speeches this morning but I had so many things to do I haven't read [them] yet— will do it tonight.

Mrs. Hawes called again today & I deliberately told her I hadn't been able to reach you.

Haven't my glasses so can't read this. Hope you can.

I surely hope you are really feeling loads better. I am wondering if they are giving you a less restricted diet. I hope you find you can have more breakfast after those strenuous walks.

> Lots of love—
> Bess—

> Hot Springs, Ark.
> September 18, 1937

Dear Bess:—

Here is a check for $100.00. I should have left you one when I left and intended to but my mind wasn't working.

It was good to talk to you last night. I sat around here hoping you'd call. If Margaret goes to Colorado Sunday why don't you come down here? You can stay at the Park Hotel and we'll go home about Thursday getting there Friday. Wire me if you decide to come and what train you'll be on. The Hot Springs sleeper comes through Independence and down by way of Joplin.

Heard the President's speech last night and it suited me fine. They are still giving me various tests but I feel fine. At least I'll have been thoroughly gone over when I come out.

Kiss Margey. Love to you.

> Harry

---

* Mildred Dryden was Truman's secretary during his Senate years.

[Independence, Mo.]
[September 18, 1937]
Saturday—

Dear Harry—

It was grand to talk to you last night and you <u>sounded</u> as if you felt loads better sure enough— The heart picture doesn't sound very <u>ominous</u> <u>but</u> I shouldn't think those long <u>hard</u> walks you take every morning would be so good for it. Maybe you had better inquire about that!

If you <u>have</u> to have a diet, be sure to get a new diet list— one made strictly for you & not one that has been printed by the hundred. Here's hoping you can eat what you want and plenty of it— even if you do put on a Senatorial front.

M & I were both glad to get your letters <u>this morning</u>— it's the first time one has come in the morning's mail.

The pralines are <u>grand</u>— the best I ever ate and I will get some of them & the nuts out to your mother.

Am afraid the Colorado trip is off. Frank thinks they can't afford it! Marg is quite disappointed— and I am, too— for I felt the high altitude might settle that hay fever. It has been terrible for the last week.

I hope you are having our brand of delightful weather.

Am glad you are staying another week— it will do you a world of good.

Lots of love—
Bess

[Independence, Mo.]
[September 19, 1937]
Sunday—

Dear Harry—

I was glad to get your special this morning & know you are feeling <u>better</u>. Thanks a lot for the generous check. The trip to Colorado is definitely off at present— Frank is <u>supposed</u> to have John R. Green give him a thorough going over tomorrow & he may not get off <u>anywhere</u>. I wish he could have the same sort of <u>thorough going-over</u> you are having but— he just blows up if you mention "clinic"— I guess John R. is the next best thing to one.

Your speech is very good— Have you started one for the Liberty women? It has to be on the "Constitution" too— doesn't it? You had better pile it on thick for them— for it may be some political strategy they are trying to pull in that Milligan territory.

Fred Canfil's girl was trying her best to find him this morning—
"Judge" Long & the boss wanted him at once. Do you get the K.C. papers?
Maybe you don't want them. W. E. Sullivan— (Welfare Dir.) died yester-
day— but guess Jos. B. will name his successor.

I am trying to work on N. and F. [Natalie and Frank] to drive down
to H. Spgs Tuesday or Wed. but I don't know whether I'll have any luck.
It's such gorgeous weather, I think the drive would be great.

They are going out this afternoon to take the nuts and candy to your
mother.

Hope you keep on feeling fine— and can come back in great trim—
Lots of love,—
Bess

If Marg had gone to Colo. I think I would have done <u>exactly</u> as you
suggested.

Hot Springs, Ark.
Monday Sept 20 '37

Dear Bess:—

It sure was a pleasure to get your special yesterday. I have not had
a before breakfast walk since I came here last Monday. They are always
doing something to me by seven o'clock so I don't get a chance. I have
to go to the lab for another and more elaborate blood test this morning.
I saw all the doctors yesterday and told them I'd have to leave Thursday
morning and it was O.K. I am not yet on a diet and it looks as if I won't
be. There are only two more tests and then I'll be reported sound in mind
& limb and salable on any block.

We took a drive yesterday and I didn't get a chance to write you.
They organized a penny anti [sic] game on the 4th floor and asked for
amateurs. I reported and by nine o'clock quitting time I had not only
learned how to play but had $1.²⁵ of their funds. Funny how easy it is
to learn some things and how hard others. For instance, I've been trying
to memorise [sic] the preamble to the Constitution & can't. Kiss Margie.
Sorry she didn't get to Colorado. Guess I won't see you either until Friday.
Love to you. Writing this at 6:30 A.M.
Harry

Hot Springs, Ark.
Sept. 21, 1937

Dear Bess:—

It was a pleasure indeed to get two letters from you this morning,
but it was a disappointment when you didn't come down. Hope the

family decide to drive down. I'll be leaving here Thursday A.M. and will
be home Friday some time. My teeth are 100 %. No extractions necessary; heart all right; and so is everything else. Will hear from the complete
blood test tomorrow. Dieting is overboard. That was principally the difficulty— starvation. The rest has been just what was needed. The staff here
know their business and they have no reason for fooling me. I've about
made up my mind to do it once a year. They say I should have twenty one
baths for a full course. I'll get eight and I'll say they are the real thing.

What has happened to the writing arm of a certain young lady who
calls me dad? She didn't even acknowledge my communication enclosing
check for a stated amount. Is she sick or just sleeping?

Hope you can come down. Love to you.

Sincerely
Harry

[Independence, Mo.]
[October 15, 1937]
Friday—

Dear Harry—

I surely hope you are having better weather for traveling than we
are having here today. It has been raining and sleeting a bit— & is cold &
cloudy now. Mrs. Balfour is having her luncheon way down at Mrs. Rice's
place & I wish I had refused it. I sent the telegram to Mr. Brown early this
morning and got the mail off to the office, too.

We sure missed you last night— I never did hate so to see you leave.
It's a h— of a way to live— the way we do.*

I hope you found Vic feeling fine— & the girls all well.

Wish Mr. Brown could have sent that telegram sooner— but on the
other hand, you will have a little more time to do all that reading.

Must get along & get dressed— or I'll have to take a plane out to the
luncheon—

Lots of love—
Bess

* President Roosevelt had called a special session of Congress on November 15, so Grandpa
had returned to Washington early. My grandmother had been expecting to have him home
for three months.

[Independence, Mo.]
[October 16, 1937]
Saturday—

Dear Dad—

It was nice to talk to you last night— but I hated to think of you being further & further away.

It is raining a pretty good clip right now— so maybe we are <u>at last</u> going to get a decent amount. But I surely hope the sun is shining on you on that trip over the mountains.

I am about to get off to have my hair done & I feel kind of like a cat would about getting out in this rain.

I can see Ethel giving her room a good housecleaning.

I talked to your mother yesterday— to thank her for the pickles— and she said she was fine.

Fred is going to mail this for me & is ready to go.

Lots of love—
Bess

Washington D.C.
October 17, 1937

Dear Bess:—

It was good to hear your voice last night and the night before and the night before. I am wishing you were here already and if I find an apartment you are coming. It is very fine weather here. The sun shines and the breeze is in the south. I stayed at the Hay-Adams last night in a room as big as my office with a bath tub that Taft could have used. They are very anxious to rent it to me by the month. I looked at some rooms at the Raleigh and they were very nice too. The Carroll-Arms has raised the price and are very independent so I'll probably end up by going to the Continental unless the Raleigh or the Hay-Adams make me a very good price.

Ran into Minton as I came out of the Raleigh and he brought me down to the Capitol. His wife is just coming out of the hospital from an operation. They took her gall bladder out. He said they had just returned from Europe. She was sick all the way over and they took her off the boat to the hospital when they got back. He says "to hell with Europe."

Vic is looking fine but is on a vegetable diet. His food has to go through a colander like a baby's. Perry says hello.

The President sent me his latest picture all endorsed and everything. Wasn't that nice? Tell everyone hello! Kiss M.

Love to you
Harry.

[Independence, Mo.]
[October 18, 1937]
Monday—

Dear Harry—

I have just been over to see your Aunt Ella— she is laid up with rheumatism this morning and suffering a good deal. Ardis is staying with her— so she is well taken care of (I strongly suggest there is to be an addition to that particular family.)

I had a letter from Harriette this a.m. dated Sept. 26. Of course they were still in Japan— but a P.S. to the letter said she had just received a cable from Leighton telling her they were to sail October 13th on "Hoover" for Manila— & she was delighted to get out of Japan.

I am going to K.C. to get Harriett Taylor's wedding present this afternoon.

Marg & I went in to the Midland to see "Stage Door" yesterday— Good show—

I hope you are satisfactorily settled by this time.

Paul Knightman is in K.C. & is coming out tomorrow night to have dinner with us. He will be in Wash. Thursday.

Am so glad Vic is better.

With love from both of us—

Bess

Washington D.C.
October 18, 1937

Dear Bess:—

This morning I have two letters— Friday's & Saturday's both came at once. The sun is still shining and things look beautiful, but the weather man says rain tonight. Had dinner with John Snyder and Mr. Schram and his wife. He is a director of the R.F.C. [Reconstruction Finance Corporation]. We ate at the Hay-Adams. They have a very swanky dining room— pipe organ music etc. I'm to have brunch with Scott Faris and Perry today or tomorrow and Mr. Helm on the other day. The Washington papers all noted my arrival in town and the why of it— but our own failed to make a note of it. I guess they are still worrying over Mr. Milligan. Catherine and I almost cleaned off my desk. It was a mile high. I'll get most of my reading done today and my Cape speech written and then I can study railroads tomorrow. I am going to try and see Mrs. Nally tomorrow and also Weaver Ross about Sedgwick. It is a most unsatisfactory way to live but nearly everyone has some sort of difficulty and all life is beating the difficulties and making things as pleasant as possible. Perhaps if we were rich we'd be crazy or some other handicap would [*illegible*]. I spend most of my time trying to figure out something and some day I'll hit if the King of Hades doesn't get me first. Kiss Margie.

Love to you
Harry.

[Independence, Mo.]
[October 19, 1937]
Tuesday—

Dear Harry—

I was glad to get your Sunday letter this morning— and Marg was, too. I hope you are settled by this time— I can't quite see how you can stay at the H-A [Hay-Adams Hotel] as Belle said their rent for one room was simply terrible— and it certainly is not convenient— to the office.

Am sorry about Mrs. Minton's illness— but they can hardly charge <u>that</u> up to Europe.

Mrs. Palmer called this a.m. & asked if I had heard you say whether you & Mr. Haworth had come to any conclusion about her job or if Mrs. Wyatt got it— etc.

I am going to ~~Mrs. Swofford's~~ the luncheon for Mrs. P. [Pendergast] today— Would much rather not, but guess it has to be done.

I am wondering if you have decided what you can do about the Cape Girardeau meeting.

Your Aunt Ella is better & thought she would get up this afternoon—

Love—
Bess

Washington D.C.
October 19, 1937

Dear Bess:—

No letter this morning but I got two yesterday, so I suppose I ought not to kick too much. Vic & Perry and I put Mr. Snyder aboard the train last night and then I tried to write a speech for Cape Girardeau but didn't get very far with it.

Between the painters and the interruptions I couldn't do much. They are painting the office. It'll be so clean I will be afraid to work in it. They've cleaned all the rugs and are getting me a new one for the outside office.

Haven't found any place to live as yet. The Raleigh asked me a terrible price for a room— $125.00 for what I'd pay the Continental $75.00.

The Carroll Arms wants $80.00 straight time. It seems every hotel in town has raised its price.

I'll probably end up at the Continental. I surely miss you & Margey, but I hope it won't be for long. You aren't having all the rain. It's pouring here today, but warm.

Oscar came to see me last night and I had a nice visit with him. Elsie called this morning and said she'd let me know when "anything has happened." Hope I get a letter. Love to you. Address one of my envelopes to me & give to the Indp. P.O. so they can ship my individual stationary [*sic*]. I forgot it.

Harry

[Independence, Mo.]
[October 20, 1937]
Wednesday—

Dear Harry—

I strongly suspect you will be on your way to the Cape by the time this reaches Wash., but here goes anyway.

I was glad to get your Monday letter this morning— also the type-written one— & I will attend to that. We enjoyed seeing Paul last night— He is anxious to get back to W. & will be seeing you Thursday.

Mrs. Swofford's luncheon was <u>very</u> nice & she made a <u>splendid</u> talk.

Mrs. O'Malley asked me to a luncheon today at the K.C. Club. She probably won't <u>feel</u> much like doing it— he [Mr. O'Malley?] was dropped yesterday— Mr. P. [Pendergast] certainly has gone completely loco.

We were <u>all</u> invited over to Annie's for Sunday— Mother, Marg & I are going— & I wish you could make it, too— I hope you are not going to fly.

I am not very eager to go to the Taylor wedding alone— Marg wants to go to Columbia to the game— & I'll save about $20 by letting her do it— as she would have to have a dress and shoes—

Hope you can call me Sat. night anyway—

Lots of love—
Bess

C & O Train
October 24, 1937

Dear Bess:—

I have been very derelict in my correspondence since Thursday and I'm sorry for it. But I couldn't very well help it. I have had a rather hectic time since Wednesday when my R.R. hearings started. Every reporter in

Washington except the *Star* reporter has been after me. I had to write two speeches also. I don't like alibis and never credit them. When anything is to be done nothing should prevent it and you can merely take the above statement as one of fact and no excuse. I should have written just the same. My St. Louis trip was a success. I met and talked to the Young Dems. and they seemed very happy to see me. Canfil took me to Cape Girardeau and I saw all my south Mo. friends. That is Fred took his car and brought me back to St. Louis. I road [sic] down with Clark, John Nangle, and the Mayor in the Mayor's car. Learned a lot about Mo. politics, Mr. Stark and the senatorial situation. We still have things in hand. Though they all have ambitions to control.

Had a good breakfast at Jake Vardaman's and John Snyder put me on the train. I am trying a new train. Will arrive at noon tomorrow and wire you. Kiss Margey. Love to you

Harry.

[Independence, Mo.]
[October 24, 1937]
Sunday

Dear Harry—

We are just about to get off to Platte to spend the day with the cousins. I know they will be sorry you are not with us. It was grand to talk to you last night— I didn't suppose there was a chance of it.

Well, I missed the wedding & was sorry to do it— but I just felt more comfortable being along with Marg at that game. We could have made it home in time if the traffic hadn't been so terrific— I talked to Roylynn & Jim this a.m. & they were very nice & understanding, but I surely did hate not turning up for it.

It's a grand day to drive to Platte County— It was so cloudy last night, I had visions of a rainy day.

There was a picture in the *Star* just like this one.

Lots of love—
Bess

C & O Train at Charlottesville, Virg.
October 25, 1937

Dear Bess:—

If you and Margaret were with me this would be a perfect day. The sun shines out of the bluest sky I've seen this year, and the Va. Mountains are painted every color of the rainbow by frost. Just passed the Farmington Country Club and it certainly looked good. We've been going through some high mountains and a lot of tunnels. The cedars and pines make the oaks and elms stand out. The mountain sides look like patch work quilts with dark green for the main color.

This is rather a slow motion train. Left St. Louis at noon stopped at Indianapolis fifty minutes and stayed forty-five at Cincinnati. It will arrive in Washington at 12:45 if it is on time and it seems to be. It is a very fine train called "The Sportsman." They have one they name Geo. Washington too. Since I'm investigating 'em I wanted to see what they were like. This is the road that the Van Swearengins* used as a back bone of all of their rail empire. It is so rich they couldn't break it. It still pays dividends.

I'm going to open up again tomorrow and really go to the bottom of the Missouri Pacific. Hope some good will come of it.

I'm also going to try to find a place to live and you all are going to come.

Fred said I stole the show at Cape Girardeau. I didn't intend to.

Kiss Margey. Love to you

Harry

[Independence, Mo.]
[October 25, 1937]
Monday—

Dear Harry—

It is now 11:30 and I supposed you are just about arriving in Wash. If I had known you would be in St. L. Sat night, I would have tried to make some arrangements to get there. We could easily have gotten there as early as we got home anyway.

How do you like this dime store paper? I didn't realize it was so small when I bought it.

We had a nice day at Annie's— the first thing they said was— "Oh— Harry didn't get home!"

I hope the trip didn't tire you too much— Was the meeting a success?

Mr. Summerfield Jones sent you a bushel of Stark's Red Delicious— Will you write him or shall I?**

We are doing some housecleaning today & hanging curtains etc. & I'm tired already, & if I don't get some ironing done today your daughter is going to have to wear her riding breeches to school tomorrow. She

* Brothers Oris Paxton and Mantis James van Sweringen became railroad barons to develop Shaker Heights, Ohio. At the height of their success, they controlled 30,000 miles of rail worth $3 billion.

** My grandparents would, of course, want to thank a friend for sending them a bushel of Stark's apples, never mind that the orchard owner might be out to wreck Grandpa's career.

<u>thinks</u> she has made the school play— she will be most awfully disappointed if she doesn't.

Must get to work whether I want to or not—

I've missed your letters the last few days— but it <u>was</u> nice to talk to you—

> Lots of love—
> Bess

> [Independence, Mo.]
> [October 26, 1937]
> Tuesday—

Dear Harry—

I meant to tell you before this that the girl Mr. Tucker is interested in is "Helen Stone" & <u>not</u> Miss Morris— unless she is going under an alias.

I never have gotten down to the Federal Bldg. Both times I've been in K.C. since your letter came— I've been in a tremendous rush & had visions of having to sit & wait to see Mr. Allen— but I will try to make it <u>soon</u>.

I am going in this morning to a Phi Mu Concert in Edison Hall at 11— & then way out to Mag's luncheon at Mrs. Rice's at 1—

Was glad to get a letter from Terre Haute this a.m. Was expecting to have to wait 'til tomorrow for mail— so it was a grand surprise. Was there any sort of a new angle on Stark's senatorial ambitions?

Surely was glad to hear from you last night— It's too bad about the Warrick Apts.— but something else will turn up. If you look at any houses— don't forget the <u>heating plant</u>! I wonder if any of those new apts on 16th have any apts large enough?

I am enclosing a note from Mrs. McDaniel— Please send me her address— & tell me what you told her about us not turning up in Jeff [Jefferson City]— so I can write the same thing.

This is a gorgeous day. Wish I were taking a trip somewhere with you.

Have you worked out any plans for Nov 14th? It looks to me as if you are going to have to fly back unless you can be a day late for the session.

My left hand is giving me hail Columbia* & I'm going to <u>have</u> to see a Dr. and it's going to be somebody besides Jo. G. I am convinced he was tight the other day— I'll wait to hear from you if I can about it—

> Lots of love—
> Bess

---

* My grandmother is referring to the painful arthritis that had started up in her left hand.

Washington D.C.
October 27, 1937

Dear Bess:—

Yesterday was a good day— there was a letter when I got back from the hearing. Mr. Sawyer seems to have made the headlines anyway. He and Salisbury worship money, so if the lady extracts any of it from him it will make a bad wound. I also appreciated the picture. Mr. Alford finally discovered I am in town after the Associated Press had taken care of the hearings. He called me yesterday. Mr. Shoop has been in Topeka helping Mr. Landon on his radio speech. I suppose Roy Roberts wrote it. It turned out to be a flop and a disappointment. Even the *Washington Post* and *Star* could see no good in it.

Wish I could have been with you at Platte. I ought to come home next Saturday and meet with the Senate Committee on Agriculture but I just don't see how I can make it. This committee has witnesses coming nearly every day, and besides it costs too much and no one ever pays <u>my</u> expenses. That Masonic Lodge in St. Louis sent me $20.25 so that's one that did. The Gov. has asked the Committee and Clark & me to lunch that day. Please send me last week's *Mo. Democrat* ours didn't come. I have a nice room at the Carroll Arms but it's a dreary place without you & Margey. Love to you both

Harry.

[Independence, Mo.]
[October 27, 1937]
Wednesday

Dear Harry—

I have your last laundry ready to go, believe it or not. I am sure you have needed the underwear— (or <u>should</u> have).

I was glad to get the letter from Charlottesville this morning. It made me homesick for Farmington, to hear about it. It should be a marvelous spot at this time of year— but I imagine the pool is not quite so popular as it was last July— Am glad you had the trip over a different route.

Marg got the part she wanted in the school play— & they are hard at practice.

Ethel is having the dickens of a time with her eyes. Dr. Allen says her blood count (<u>red</u>) is low & there is a bladder infection. Of course she is feeling pretty sunk. Has been out of school a week already— & no improvement yet.

The concert was lovely yesterday & Mag had a nice party, so it was a nice day.

Your Virginia sky had nothing on ours to-day— This is one of the perfect days you read about—

Hope you are rested by this time.

Lots of love
Bess

Washington D.C.
October 28, 1937

Dear Bess:—

I am uneasy about that hand. I don't know what doctor would be trustworthy if you are off Dr. Joe. He knows more drunk than most of 'em do sober. But have it looked into at once. You've waited too long now. It may be teeth or nose or one of a dozen things. I don't suppose you'd want Elmer Twyman to look at it. He might want to cut it off.

I am sorry I didn't know about being in St. Louis until I had done it last Saturday night. They had so many guests at the Cape that after I'd made my speech in the afternoon I could gracefully withdraw and get a night's sleep in St. Louis. That is how it happened. We had the right girl in the Tucker business. Hope you had a nice time at the brunch and concert.

I am in a quandary about coming home. I should be in Jeff City Monday and also be in K.C. the 14th. I'm in the midst of the most important thing I can do now in this rail investigation and it makes my head ache trying to figure what to do. If I had unlimited funds I could fly back & forth to all the engagements as it is I guess I should stay here and do my job. If I could have gotten through this week I'd have come home and stayed until the 14th but I can't get through. Maybe I just won't do anything but my job here. You work on that hand.

Kiss Margey. Love to you

Harry

[Independence, Mo.]
[October 28, 1937]
Thursday—

Dear Harry—

I got beautifully "left" this morning when I looked for a letter— but here's hoping it comes this afternoon. Had Vic's letter about Miss Stone— let me know how her last trial comes & I will save this letter of Vic's to show Mr. Tucker. He certainly can't ask anything more of you than you have done.

I am enclosing some *Examiner* clippings. The *Star* merely said you & B. [Senator Bennett Clark] were there & spoke.

Thank Catherine for sending Marg's magazine. She will probably
get around to it in time but the poor child is good & busy— practiced
until 5 at school yesterday & at church from 7:30 till 9:30 & she is so tired
today she can hardly move. It's going to be <u>every day</u> after school until the
play— on <u>November 28</u>— I hope they all survive.

Thank Vic for his letter. I will be glad to have that information if Mr.
T. has raises any questions about her.

Have you seen Paul? Did he tell you he bought me a pint of Hiram
Walker and I gave it right back to him? I told him to take it to Wash. & let
you help him drink it.

Lots of love—
Bess

New York, NY
October 29, 1937

Dear Bess:—

You'll wonder what I'm doing in New York. Well I had a date to
see T. J. Sunday and Col. Littlejohn, Post Q. M. [quartermaster] of West
Point who was at Hot Springs with me asked me to come up to the game
tomorrow. Virginia M. I. [Military Institute] is to play Army at the Point
so I'm going. Mr. Stark and Mr. Clark and cotton corn etc will have to
worry along without me. For once I'm doing what I want to and not what
I ought to. I got here at 7:30 called both T. J. and the Colonel and now I
am going to bed and get one good night's sleep.

You know what made me write instead of wire? Well I turned on
the room radio and the Cities Service hour was going over W.E.A.F.* A
couple of kids were singing "They'll Never Believe Me" from the "Girl
from Utah" and I sat here and thought of another couple of kids listening to Julia Sanderson and Donald Brian singing that beautiful melody
and lovely sentiment and I wished so badly for the other kid that I had to
write her to sort of dry my eyes. I hope you remember. I'll never forget it.
And I wish you were here with your second edition and we'd all go to a
show instead of going to bed and I probably would disappoint both T. J.
P. & the Colonel. I needed something to sort of relieve my nerves anyway.
It has been a most trying and patience straining week. I wanted to punch
the witnesses rather than question them because they'd robbed and
abused a great property and a lot of the "widows & orphans" you hear so
much about. I really wanted to verbally pulverize the ring leader yesterday. N.Y. papers had my picture on the financial page and really gave me

* WEAF, a New York City radio station, changed its call letters to WNBC in November 1946.

a nice write up. Even Mr. Hearst gave me the best of it. So I'm calming down somewhat.

Kiss Margey and I wish I could kiss you.

Harry.

[Independence, Mo.]
[October 30, 1937]
Saturday—

Dear Harry—

What with housecleaning etc. I didn't get a letter off yesterday— but we are even at that— I didn't get one on Thursday—

Was glad to find one in the box this morning— so often on Sat. they don't get in the morning's mail & then I have to wait 'til Mon. I wish you were coming home today— but it sure would mean a lot of traveling— this weekend and on the 14th, too— Maybe you could borrow an Army plane for the 14th as long as it is strictly to present Mrs. Roosevelt. Too bad you aren't on the military committee.

My hand is a bit better & it sort of works on the order of the Arkansan's leaky roof.

Today is David's birthday & he is having two or three of the neighborhood youngsters in to eat ice-cream & cake with him.

Jane is spending the day with Marg so she will get in on the party, too. Marg had a whirl at the Lefman child's party last night. I almost <u>bursted</u> when <u>she</u> said <u>she</u> thought they were too <u>boisterous</u>. She is singing with the adult choir at their Harvest service tomorrow evening. I am hoping she will get really interested in the <u>church</u> end of it.

I had a long talk with J. C. while I was waiting for Marg to come out & he said they were all fine. He is such a nice chap.

Ethel went to Dr. Curran & he told her she has a partial paralysis of that right eye— but there is a large chance of it clearing up— that he had had good results in 95% of his cases. She

David and Marian Wallace in 1937
(TL 2009-1493).

isn't very happy about it naturally— but <u>she</u> isn't as sunk about it as Mrs. N. & Nellie are.

I am sending regrets to the Russian Embassy— I judged (from the past) that that was what you wanted me to do.

So, there isn't a chance of me having Elmer T.— in fact I'm afraid <u>anybody</u> I do have will want to extract a tonsil or so— or half a dozen teeth.

I hate to ask it— but will the exchequer stand a little extra pressure this month? My Taylor's bill will be plenty large with the dress for myself & Marg's snow suit— I told her she had to make that suit last the rest of her life.

Well, I am still hoping you <u>may</u> drop in tonight.

Are you still not taking the *Star*? I don't want to keep on sending clippings you have already seen.

Lunch is ready, so—

Lots of love—
Bess

New York, NY
October 31, 1937
Sunday A.M.

Dear Bess:—

Well I had a grand day yesterday. Got up 6:30 and after the usual preliminaries, walked down to the 42nd St. Ferry and caught the 8:30 West Shore train for West Point.

Col. Littlejohn met me in the biggest car on the Post, the Superintendent's and took me on a sight seeing trip over the Post. Had a grand brunch at the Col's house and then went to the game. It was a real contest although the Army beat V.M.I. 20 to 7.

I sat in the General's box and had a grand time with his wife a funny old lady who is proud of her mince pies which she serves at every game at the end of the half with coffee and doughnuts. I found out from Littlejohn that she is the Walgreen Drug Co. so I guess she can afford mince pies.

It was a beautiful day and I enjoyed it. It would have been nicer if you and Margey had been there. The Littlejohns are lovely people and have a daughter just Marg's age.

I had all the boys there I am acquainted with come and see me after the game and they are a fine looking outfit. It seemed to please them very much.

I'm to see T. J. this afternoon and then back to the grind tomorrow again.

Kiss Margey Love to you

Harry.

How's that hand?

[Independence, Mo.]
[October 31, 1937]
Sunday—

Dear Harry—

It was nice to get your special this morning before I even got out of bed— right on the dot of eight o'clock. Have read the 2929 Conn. "prospectus" and it looks very attractive— With a restaurant in the building we can get along alright with a dinette— & I can do without a Nettie, too. Is there any prospect of a vacancy— or were they just talking? Did you ask the Sedgwick manager if the Jaffes on 2nd were leaving anytime soon?

There seems to be plenty of closet space at 2929— & the Venetian blinds will eliminate buying curtains— just drapes— Are the apts too modernistic for other sort of furniture— I can't live with a lot of moderne furniture & I know you dislike it as much as I do.

Orine and Ben Murray spent last evening with us. B. is crazy to go back to Wash. Is there any chance of getting her a filing clerk job with the new Census set-up? Emma evidently got her job— She called me from K.C. Friday & said it was all "set"— & she said somebody else was taking the credit for getting the job for her— but she didn't say who. I'd let whoever it is take care of her in the future, too— because you know darn well that twenty-four hours after she goes to work— the complaints are going to begin coming in.

Uncle Boulware & Helen are coming to dinner— a jolly day ahead of us.

I was downright disappointed when you didn't turn up last night.

Am sorry you have to do all the apt hunting. You & Vic ought to be qualified to take it up as a "side line."

Must get a note off to Mrs. McDaniel.

Lots of love
Bess

Washington D.C.
November 1, 1937

Dear Bess:

Well I'm back in Washington. Left N.Y. at 6:30 last night after a lengthy interview with T. J. P. He looks fine and seems to be in the best of health. He is very much put out with the Gov. He says that Stark asked Jim [Pendergast] to come to Jeff City and mark a number of Democrats on the list he had. Jim made the trip and marked seven— <u>and not one was appointed</u> on the election Board. I don't understand that brand of politics. Evidently he wanted to be sure that we'd have no friends on the Board. You remember how he hounded me for help when he was trying for the job. Conditions evidently have changed. You should have had a letter everyday for I haven't missed. Glad you got the letter about the Stone girl. Hope Margey doesn't work too hard. But I'm very certain that she'll do the job creditably. Here's a letter from Mrs. Bill Taylor. I opened it by "mistake" <u>and read it</u>. I really didn't notice the address until it was opened.

Sorry I can't attend unless it is the Saturday before the 14th. I've decided I'd better come home and introduce the President's wife and fly back if I can.* It seems to be the 13th so we can go if you want to. I've seen Paul but he didn't come across with Mr. Walker. You should have taken it.

Kiss Margey.

Love to you.
Harry.

[Independence, Mo.]
[November 2, 1937]
<u>Tuesday</u>—

Dear Harry—

I am so glad you had that nice trip to N.Y. & especially to West Point & I wish Marg could have been with you— Wouldn't she have had a thrill out of it?

I didn't get a letter off yesterday— Vietta was at home and I simply didn't have a minute until late afternoon & I was so tired, I couldn't hold a pen.

I'll be glad when you get through with that committee— I'm afraid it's going to undo all the good Hot Spgs. did for you. Save the N.Y. clippings for me.

What's the news about Betty Gardelli? We haven't heard anything about Elsie either. I don't think much of that doctor Elsie is having so I

---

* Grandpa flew home to introduce Mrs. Roosevelt, who was going to give a speech in Kansas City. Prior to taking their places on the dais for the speech, my grandmother warned my thirteen-year-old mother not to move a muscle while the first lady was speaking. Mom worked so hard to comply that her arms and legs fell asleep.

am kind of worried about her.

I am going to <u>try</u> to get to the Custom House to see Mr. Allen today.

Am glad you have a nice room— which side is it on? Surely hope you are not over that kitchen entrance again.

How are the girls in the office? That was mighty nice of Catherine's mother to cook the pheasant for you. Did you write to Summerfield Jones & Mr. Saighman of Waverly about those apples they sent us?

Take care of yourself.

Lots of love—
Bess

Washington D.C.
November 2, 1937

Dear Bess:—

I have been gadding again. Went down to look over the Fredericksburg battlefield Monday and then stayed in Richmond last night. Went to Hampton this A.M. and had lunch with Myra. It pleased her very much and also put that Captain in his place. Got back here at 5 P.M. and have been reading the mail ever since. Glad to get your letters of the 30 & 31.

Certainly am sorry to hear about Ethel and I hope she comes out all right. Myra looks fine. She's fully recovered and is getting along with her work now. I was only in Hampton about an hour and a half. The newspaper men were pestering me so I got in my car and hid out. I seem to be the only source of news in town at present. I think I'll probably come home the middle of Armistice week and stay until Sunday and then fly back. I don't seem to be able to get my thoughts together for some reason. There doesn't seem to be anything to write about. I really believe we can get into 2929. The woman at Sedgwick didn't think those people on the 2nd floor would move before March.

Here is a check if it isn't enough we'll dig up some more. Love to you. Kiss Margey. The laundry came but I haven't opened it.

Harry

[Independence, Mo.]
[November 3, 1937]
Wednesday—

Dear Harry—

I was glad to know this morning you were safely back in Washington— Surely hope the brief trip rested you somewhat. I suppose you are hard at work again today with that committee. How much longer will it last— do you think? I <u>called</u> Mrs. Bill Taylor this a.m. & Homecoming

<u>is</u> the 13th— so I accepted & she said she would write the KC Taylors today— I told her not to make any engagements for <u>us</u> for Sat. night tho.— that we would have to come home after the game. I hope that is alright with you— I really thought you would rather do that than to stay up most of the night down there. That means you will be in by <u>Friday night at the latest</u>— doesn't it? She wants us there by 12 o'clock for lunch.

I wish you would organize a committee to investigate the mucilage on the flaps of Gov't envelopes. I have got to get out my tube of glue every time I use one of those brown ones.

Almost everybody in the family has a cold. It's downright funny to hear the chorus of coughs & sneezes. So far, I have escaped— Marg has no temp. but quite a cold & of course I have her in bed— much to her disgust. If it gets any worse I simply don't know what I am going to do about a Doctor. If I call Dr. Jo I shall feel inclined to ask him if he is coldly sober.

Have you been completely free from headaches with those new glasses? I've wondered so often & <u>meant</u> to ask.

Louise and Bill Duke are having a cocktail party this evening— their 20th anniversary. I can't remember whether I told you— but I think I shall skip it. I might not be able to drive home afterwards.

The Graveses have a cousin living at the Lucerne so she and Keturah invited Mrs. G. & Lorene & me in to dinner tomorrow night. Nutty Mrs. Webb is having a luncheon for Mrs. Fenn Friday— (I almost hope I can develop the family cold by that time).

This is a glorious day— & I am going to ditch M. & get out this afternoon.

Have you heard anything more from Leighton?

It's lunch time—

Lots of love

Bess—

Yes, of course, I remember Julia [Sanderson] and Donald Brian— Why should I forget any more than you?—

Washington D.C.

November 3, 1937

Dear Bess:—

Well I waited until the last mail and got fooled. It is 3:15 and I've got to get this off or it will be too late. I am sending Margaret the Armistice Day speech to read for me. You look it over and if you think it goes too far make any correction you think it ought to have.

I went into the R.R. business again today and I think got some more real information. I have a notion it didn't please Mr. Kemper very much. But I can't help it. I'm not working for him. I'm working for Missouri.

I'll try to be in Independence on the night of the 10th at 8:30 P.M. Mo. P. [Missouri Pacific Railroad] That is conditional on my getting done with Kuhn Loeb and Co. and the inimitable Mr. Ayers, the economist and a lot of other important and very rich people who have made their money at the expense of the stock & bond holders of the railroads.

Hope you've done something for that hand. It certainly needed looking after long ago. I can't see why you procrastinate when you know the longer you wait the worse it's likely to be. Kiss Margey.

Love to you
Harry

[Independence, Mo.]
[November 4, 1937]
Thursday—

Dear Harry—

You were an angel to send me the nice fat check— I sure do need it. I wish someone would figure out where money goes— It's as much of a mystery as pins & razor blades— & far more important.

Chris[tine] & I are painting the bathroom fixtures— for a change— black again this time. That awful blue got on both our nerves— (or rather the nerves of both of us).

That was a good idea, going down to see Myra— Did you enjoy the Fredericksburg battlefield as much as Gettysburg?

Marg's cold is better today but she had a pain in her middle & as it's been raining all day— I kept her in. I'm hoping it (the rain) will stop a bit before I have to go in town.

I had the *S.E. Post* continued as one of your mother's birthday presents. Was that alright?

I surely hope you <u>can</u> come by the middle of the week— that will be a mighty short stay at that.

I suspect you have seen this enclosed *Post Dispatch* editorial but am sending it just in case.

Talked to Nellie last night & she thought Ethel's eye was a <u>little</u> better. They are terribly worried about it, of course.*

---

* The letter ends here. I assume a page is missing since my grandmother never failed to sign off with "love" or "lots of love."

Washington D.C.
November 4, 1937

Dear Bess:—

Just got off an air mail special delivery to Margaret and I hope it is on time. Got no letter yesterday but two came in the morning's mail but one was for Vic. Hope Vieta* is back.

We are saving all the clippings about the hearing so you can see 'em when you come. I haven't heard from Oscar since I returned but he is to let me know as soon as anything happens. Haven't been informed as to the Gardellis either but I'll investigate and let you know. The office force are all well. Mildred had the flu but she has fully recovered. Vic is on the mend and I think we'll get through with everything all right. I'm going to bed early and walking in the morning but not as far nor as fast as I did to begin with. I'm feeling all right so don't worry. Hope you have done something about that hand.

I'm off to the War College to hear a lecture by Douglas Freeman on Lee. Have to be there by 8:45 and then back here at 10:00 for my hearing. I've been here since 7:30 and have things in shape.

Kiss Margey. Love to you

Harry.

I guess you forgot about Julia & Donald.

[Independence, Mo.]
[November 5, 1937]
Friday—

Dear Harry—

Marg's speech arrived early this morning & she was delighted. It was a very fine speech & I think is just what Mrs. W<u>ms</u> wants.

I was surely glad to hear this morning that you will be in on the tenth. We will be at the M.P. station at 8:30! But I should think you would be afraid to ride the M.P. Don't let anybody <u>know</u> who you are— they may throw you off in some deserted spot.

Well, we had the news from Oscar this morning. At last there is a Wells <u>boy</u> in the family. I hope Oscar doesn't feel it necessary to celebrate too <u>rambunctiously</u>.

Marg's cold is much better & she will get out some today.

We had a nice time at Keturah's last night— but she just rubs me the wrong way— & it's not very pleasant to be with her for long.

I couldn't develop a cold so as to miss Mrs. Webb's luncheon today

---

* Vietta Garr was the Truman's housekeeper.

I have just talked to Roylynn & they want us to go with them— & they are very glad to come back that night after the game.

Please give Catherine half a day to go down and get my [hair] nets I am writing to her about. They are 30 cts a doz. cheaper there & much better & according to reports are to be very scarce so I am ordering enough to last me awhile.

Lots of love,
Bess

Washington D.C.
November 5, 1937

Dear Bess:

Well I just got in from a walk around the Capitol grounds, waited for the mail but no letter. Maybe it will come in the next mail. I have been looking at ads again and there is an apartment in Tilden for rent one at 2110 19th St. which is right across from the school. I'm going to have Vic look at it today if he can get away. They are both furnished however I thought maybe we could get into one or the other of them and then by taking the furnished one on a month to month basis we could get the unfurnished one fixed up. What do you think of that sort of an arrangement?

I have balled things up again. They are having a celebration in Washington Twp. to open up their water system. The date was set for Nov. 6 and I told them I wouldn't be home on the 6th but would on the 13th. So— they promptly changed the date. My football game has gone a glimmering. Why don't you and Margey go on with the two Taylors and enjoy it anyway?

Here is an invitation from the Gordon's. I don't know whether it has to be answered or not so I'm sending it to you. Elsie went to the hospital yesterday morning and just had a baby boy. The nurse just told me both [are] doing fine. Vic says Mrs. G looks as if it might be triplets. Mrs. V says she'd bet you know how that one came out.

Kiss Margey. Love to you.

Harry.

[Independence, Mo.]
[November 6, 1937]
Saturday

Dear Harry—

I was glad to get your letter this morning & to hear you <u>say</u> you feel alright. I hope it's a <u>fact</u>!

Mrs. Doble called a few minutes ago & I assured her you would be here in plenty of time & she was delighted. They <u>think</u> they will have a "sell-out."

I am going to take Ethel in to see Dr. Curran again this afternoon— Nellie will <u>not</u> drive <u>downtown</u>—

The wind is blowing a terrific gale— & I strongly suspect we'll be getting some "weather" soon.

Marg is out today & seems to feel a <u>lot</u> better— She really had a pretty severe cold.

Marg & I are counting on a picture show or two so please don't fill up <u>every day</u> & <u>night</u> before you get here.

Mrs. Webb's party was quite nice after all and we had good food, too, so I did the poor old gal quite an injustice.

Well, it's lunch time for a change— Sure am glad I'll <u>see</u> you before next Saturday rolls around.

Lots of love

Bess

P.S. Mrs. Sam Pendleton— (the onetime Eastern Judge's widow)— said yesterday her daughter Mary Parker Johns had written you about something or other & asked me if I would write you & tell you who she is etc. She recently moved to Ohio or PA.

Washington D.C.

6-Nov-1937

Dear Bess:—

Well the letter came late mail yesterday. I was glad to get the clipping about the Gov. and the election board. Rather glad you didn't go to Bill Duke's tea if you felt you could get away without driving into a post. Hope you don't get a cold. I haven't had a headache until yesterday and that wasn't caused by any over work here but because I'd mixed things up so for the 13<u>th</u>. I certainly need a guardian. I had a letter from Vivian about the opening of the water plant in Washington Twp. I had promised him I'd come and talk about county planning etc. so as to give the section a boost. He's worked so hard on it and it may mean that we could get a buyer for that 200 acres and save the farm which as you know is my greatest worry because of Mamma. She knows nothing of the extremity to which the mortgage holders have been pressing us for payment. In fact when Vivian & I went to see them last when I was at home they told us point blank if something wasn't done by Dec 1 they'd take over. Well I'm afraid it would Kill her and I want to keep her alive as long as I can. [...]

I've certainly been raising hell in that committee. They had rumors in N.Y. papers that Wheeler was not behind me. I wired him & [he] told me he is for me and to let 'em have it and I have. It's rather a wearing job though.

Kiss Margey Oscar says Elsie's doing fine. Love to you
Harry.

[Independence, Mo.]
[November 7, 1937]
Sunday—

Dear Harry,—

I was disappointed not to get a Special this a.m. but I guess the call last night will have to make up for it.

Ethel called after she had seen Dr. Curran & said that he thought her eye was "definitely better"— but she can not go to school this week— He says now it's some infection & he has to find the source of it.

Miss Jessie is coming out to dinner & I am supposed to go for her— but I had such a pile of ironing to do, I don't know whether I am going to get off or not.

To-day is just like spring (including the wind). I telephoned Rubin yesterday to get my fur coat out of storage & I might have known it would turn warm immediately. I thought I was going to need it next Sat. You wire Bill Taylor— 1312 Bass Ave. I simply haven't the nerve to call them. From henceforth I make no more engagements— The Jim Taylors are going anyway, so it won't make any difference to them except that the Bill T's weren't going to ask them 'til we had accepted. So it's quite thoroughly mixed up.

Marg seems ever so much better this morning— & will be back in school tomorrow.

Henry Chiles' wife is very low. He called this morning & asked for you. Said Vivian said you would be here to-day. I told him that was the first I had heard of it.

I am sorry you are not getting in Wednesday.
Lots of love
Bess

Sunday Nov 7 '37
Washington D.C.

Dear Bess:—

Well I'd hoped to be on the road home today but I'm not only here but it looks like I'll be tied here until Thursday night. This so called committee work is nothing but drudgery and publicity all so depressing sometimes. I'm not so sure that even after I've aired all the Mo. P. dirty linen that any thing but another chance to dirty some more will come of it. You can't change human greed for money in a committee. The money hogs control the country and there's no use trying to keep 'em from it. All we can do is to make the yoke as easy as possible.

It was nice to talk to you last night only I wish I'd been there instead of a thousand miles away. Yours and Margaret's special came promptly this morning just as I was leaving the hotel for a walk. I'll send Catherine down town for the hair nets. I wish you and Margey were here. This is going to be a dreary day even if the sun does shine. [...]

Hope to see you before long. Love to you

Harry.

Washington, D.C.
Monday November 8, 1937

Dear Bess:

Well I worked until nine thirty last night trying to get my investigation in hand. Three lawyers for the committee were here and the situation seems to get worse and worse. Witnesses have been called for every day up to Friday, but I'm going to try and get the Friday session called off. If I don't I can't get home until Saturday night at 8:30 which will ruin all the meetings.

Would you and Margey consider coming back with me? I get so lonesome I don't know what to do with myself and all I can do is come over here and work. Vic and Mrs. Vic took me to the Allies Inn last night for dinner. It is the only place Vic can eat any vegetables properly fixed away from home. He can't get anything but mashed potatoes, mashed peas & beans and cottage cheese. Most of his food has to be run through a collinder [sic]. He's gaining weight on it however and I think will be cured up if he stays with it.

The coal commission had a reception from 5 to 7 last night too. Vic & I went to that and then went to dinner and I came back here and met the lawyers. I'm in for really raising hell this week. I'm afraid all the N.Y. bankers and some in St. Louis & Kansas City will be off me for life. I've got to go through now though or be a quitter. Will call you about time you get this & let you know what happens.

Kiss Margey. Love to you.

Harry

[No envelope or postmark]
[No date]
Tuesday

Dear Harry—

I thought I had better send this on at once—

I am about six hours behind time today. It's bridge club day & I forgot it & did a lot of cleaning & ironing— so now I am in a most awful rush. Hope you will be all ready to start <u>Missouri</u>-<u>ward</u> when this arrives.

Everybody fine—

Love
Bess

Washington D.C.
Nov 9, 1937

Dear Bess:—

Your Saturday letter came at noon yesterday and I was sure glad to get it when I got back from the hearings. I sure want to go to a picture show or two with you and Margey but this devilish hearing is getting really into a bog. We had Mr. George Whitney and S. Parker Gilbert before us yesterday. Mr. Whitney is very much inclined to feel his position. He came to my office at about a quarter to ten and told me what he was going to do. I simply asked him who the chairman of the committee happened to be and he immediately dismounted and went along like a gentleman. […]

If I quit this thing now they'll say that Kemper and the Boss pulled me off and I'm going to go through with it if I don't get home at all. It is a mess and has created a terrible furor in N.Y. Guaranty Trust and J. P. Morgan have used every means available to make me quit. I'm going to finish the job or die in the attempt. I sure hate it but you can see where I am. Kiss Margey.

Love to you.

Harry.

WESTERN UNION
Independence, MO
November 11, 1937
IF CALLING TONIGHT PLEASE CALL BY SEVEN LOVE=
BESS.

Washington D.C.
November 16, 1937

Dear Bess:—

The B & O left St. Louis thirty minutes late. I had boarded it at 9
o'clock after a good hearty breakfast in the Harvey lunch room. Read
Henry Clay for an hour and then the Secretary of the train came around
all smiles and informed me Mr. Shannon was on the train. I ran into him
in the club car talking to Archbishop Glennon, who is a most pleasant
old gentleman. Mary Chiles' boy was on the train too. I left [the] Congressman with the Archbishop and went back to Henry Clay. Read until
lunch time and then went to sleep— after lunch. The Mayfield boy came
around about time we got to Cincinnati and we went to dinner. Mr.
Shannon came along and said he'd looked for me all over the train. My
berth was in the club car right at the end of the club part and in the exact
center of the car. I guess I was asleep and Shannon couldn't see me. Well
he caught me after dinner and talked to me continually until ten o'clock
when I told him I thought he was staying up beyond the hour the doctor
had ordered and he went to bed.

He's against Clark and he wants Aylward fired as county and State
chairman and he's sure we're licked in the city election. I'm writing this
in the Senate and Jimmy Burnes [Byrnes] is trying to talk down the Anti-
Lynching Bill. It looks like a filibuster from now on. We'll probably be
talking about it Christmas day. Farley will call me tomorrow I hope, and
then I'm going to see FDR and find out what he wants to do.

Vic had my desk all cleaned off and in perfect order. It'll probably
take me two days to mess it up again.

Kiss my baby, love to you.

Harry.

Independence, Mo.
[November 16, 1937]
Tuesday—

What do you mean— "raise a political backer?"

Dear Harry—

Yes, I called Roger!

I was glad to get your St. L. letter this morning— it was a nice sur-
prize [sic].

I felt kind of low all day yesterday— didn't even feel like writing. I
called Mr. Canfil to see if you really did go on the train. It's miserable here
today. Cold, damp and very cloudy— we had a few snow flakes yesterday.

I hope you make a point of finding out exactly where Mr. R. and Mr. Farley stand on K.C. politicians— If you can depend on what they say. Because if they think they can get along without us in '40— we'll show them a thing or two. Is the Pres. trying to wreck Sen. Guffey, too? It seems to me you are in the same boat, as far as <u>bossed organizations</u> are concerned.

Polly is coming to spend the day with us— Marg is playing at the Methodist Church tonight with the <u>Harbin</u> girl.

Lots of love—
Bess

[Independence, Mo.]
[November 17, 1937]
Wednesday— a.m.

Dear Harry—

I'll be glad when tomorrow comes and brings a letter. (It had <u>better</u> bring one.)

We had a nice day yesterday— Polly and Mary Bostian and Agnes! (believe it or not) had lunch with us & it seemed quite like old times. Polly is still full of fun but is so fat & looks so much older I've started <u>roll-ing</u> in earnest after seeing her— also dieting. She said she was sorry not to have seen you.

I am about to finish painting my floor this morning. I hope the bed doesn't fall down when I move it.

Ethel's eye is <u>very</u> much better— the double-vision trouble has practically cleared up—

Thank Vic for his letter about Ben Murray— I think she is planning to go to W. some time this week. She thinks she will have a better chance to get a job if she is there in town. She was most appreciative of Vic's letter & she would like to have that sort of a job again.

Did Vic have any luck with the Sedgwick Apt.?

Henry Chiles' wife died Mon. I sent flowers— I wasn't sure whether you would think it necessary— but decided it was better to err on <u>that</u> side.

Love—
Bess

Washington D.C.
November 18, 1937

Dear Bess:—

Well the letter came. I'd threatened to fire the whole office force if
I didn't get it. You weren't a bit bluer than I was. If I'd had someone to
condole with I'd probably have taken several drinks for consolation, but
since I didn't have I had to stay sober.

Our filibuster still goes on & on. My committee is temporarily done
and I'm sure glad. We had the Metropolitan Ins. Co. and the John Han-
cock on the pan all day today.

Senator Guffey has asked me to go deer hunting with him, Garner,
Ryan Duffy and Schwellenback.* Will you mail me my army shoes &
leggings and a woolen shirt. I think I have my sweater. You can put in my
hunting cap that Eddie J. gave me, too. I have a pair of pants. If you see a
pair of wool army pants around there, though, you might enclose 'em.

The *Star* had to publish my picture. Wasn't that too bad? I'm to see
Farley tomorrow and I'm going to know what happens from now on.
Had dinner with Dickens Clark, Cockioue & Tom Hennings last night.
Poor Tom was crocked as usual. We had a very pleasant evening & I got
home at 10:30. How's that? Hope you won't forget to write again. Thanks
for calling Roger. You might ask him about the city Manager Plan. Kiss
Margie. Love to you.

Harry

[Independence, Mo.]
[November 18, 1937]
Thursday—

Dear Harry—

Was glad to hear this morning that you had arrived safely! What
a break to find Jo. B. on the train! And most any of the boys except J. G.
would have been more desirable than F. M.?

It was nice of Vic to have the desk cleared & ready to go!

The ground is well covered with snow this morning and it is still
coming down a bit so maybe will get a little moisture— I am going to
K.C. to have lunch with Polly & to do some Christmas shopping for
Mother. I'd like to get her job done before I start on my own.

There is an article on the financial page of the *Times*— I'll send— it's
A.P. so maybe the same thing is in the other papers, too.

I bought a Kodak-book for $1.25 for Betty Gardelli— Do you think

* Senator Lewis Schwellenbach (D-WA), later Truman's secretary of labor (1945–48).

that is enough or should I get her something nicer as long as Wally did you a good turn on the Venetian blinds. Let me know about this soon— for I'll have to return it in six days if I'm going to at all.

I stayed home all day yesterday & made out my Needlework Guild report.

Dr. Wilson is <u>very</u> low. I went out there Monday night to inquire about him— they seem pretty hopeless. All of his family have come from N. Carolina.

Marg went up here to a dancing class last night (at 50 cents per lesson!) and was so thrilled with it. But can you imagine a dancing class of eight girls & <u>only four</u> boys? Johnnie Hinde is one of the boys— also Chucky Bundschu and Trusten Kirby's boy. The boys are more desirable than the girls— as some of those are Mormons—

Marg said she & the Harbin child did the Military March "Country Gardens" alright at the Methodist Church. <u>I hope so</u>.

The air filter fell off my car Monday— Had to be welded on— but it didn't cost but 60¢.

I'm going to have to fly to make connections.

Lots of love
Bess

Washington D.C.
November 19, 1937

Dear Bess:—

Well I don't have any hearings today, but I have a date with Mr. James A. Farley. We'll see just what they have in mind. Had dinner with Paul Nachtman and Mr. Pratt of the labor relations board last night and found out all the low down on the Ford, Montgomery Ward and Nell Donnelly situations. There is a lot more behind the scenes in all those troubles than publicly appears. I believe though that it will work out all right in the end. Our City Manager has had a finger in most of those things and sometimes a sledge hammer.

I told you last night that some of us are going deer hunting Dec. 1 with Guffey. We leave here Nov 30th and go up to a resort in the Penn. Mountains. Guffey said we would not do much walking, that we'd sit in a valley and the deer would be driven out for our bullets. I am not going to shoot any because it's too much like killing a person. I'll go along though and perhaps have other entertainment besides shooting.

Hope your hand is well or better. Wish you'd do something about it. Kiss Margey. Love to you.

Harry.

[Independence, Mo.]
[November 19, 1937]
Friday—

Dear Harry—

I am going to a book review with Natalie & <u>should</u> be on my way—
I don't know where the morning has gone— I can't see that I have done
<u>anything</u> but I haven't stopped a minute.

It surely is cold today & Hamrick says down to 12 tonight. I had
alcohol put in my boat Tuesday night when it first started down.

Have Elsie & the baby gone home? Have you seen them again?

I have just talked to Mrs. Wilson & she said the Dr. is a little bit better to-day. I guess they are clutching at straws.

Ethel is better but has <u>noises</u> in <u>her</u> <u>head</u>, which bother her a lot.

I hope you won't have too lonesome a Sunday. Also hope you are
<u>through</u> with that committee.

Lots of love
Bess

Washington D.C.
20-Nov-37

Dear Bess:—

The mail was all right this morning. <u>The</u> letter was there. I'm sure
sorry to hear about Dr. Wilson. Hope he can come out of it. I'm glad
you sent flowers to Henry Chiles. It is certainly too bad that those boys
have to lose a good mother. Whatever you get for Mrs. Gardelli will be
all right. You know more about how these things ought to be done than
I'll ever learn. I'm glad that Margaret enjoyed her dancing school. I guess
the reason boys are so scarce is that boys haven't changed much. A team
of horses couldn't have gotten me pulled into one when I was the age of
those boys and I was considered rather below par by most of my associates at that.

Eddie Jacobson came in yesterday and I took him to lunch. We
organized a 1/10 of a cent poker game last night and robbed him of .50
cents and Vic of .54 cents. If it hadn't been 10% settlement you can see
where that decimal point would have been. Every body had a good time,
went home sober at eleven o'clock and Eddie and I are waiting for breakfast at the office now. The lunch room doesn't open until 8:30.

I'm going to Baltimore today to get my picture made for the movies
in the Martin Bomber that's going to Russia. They are not going to fly it.
Hope you haven't frozen. I see it is 16 out there today. Kiss Margie.

Love to you

Harry.

It's a passenger plane not a bomber the *W. Post* says.

[Independence, Mo.]
[November 20, 1937]
Saturday—

Dear Harry—

Was glad to hear from you good & early this morning— and am getting your clothes off— express— at once. They told me if I could get them
to the office by noon, you would get them Monday— so I am going up
right away. I hope I put everything you want— & I hope you get off on the
trip— it will do you a lot of good.

It's colder than the dickens this morning— I waked up about five
o'clock half frozen, & missed my "heater."

Marg is practicing again this morning. It's funny how much more I
miss her on Saturday than on school days.

What about the Sedgwick apt? I judge Vic didn't have any luck—

Lots of love
Bess

WESTERN UNION
Independence, MO
November 20
TOLD JIM COUNT US OUT THANKSGIVING IS THAT ALL RIGHT=
BESS.

Washington D.C.
21-Nov.-37

Dear Bess:—

Well this is a beautiful cold Sunday morning. If you and Margey
were present it would be perfect. For some reason which I can't explain I
slept until 9:15 although I went to bed at ten. Maybe it was because I was
out in the air most of yesterday.

We were supposed to leave here at 9 o'clock but for some reason—
really a headache from the night before I think Al Holland didn't show
up until ten thirty. We got to the Glen Martin plant at noon and the
picture men were just on the point of leaving because they were afraid we
weren't coming. I went through the factory with the general manager and
saw a lot of planes under construction for the Dutch East India Company

and the Govt of the Argentine.

The one we went to see was out in the back yard. Its wing spread is 157 ft. body 91 feet long and its 20 ft high has four 1000 Hp. motors and will go 225 mi per hour. It can go five thousand miles on one fill up and will carry 26 people and several thousand pounds of freight & mail. Russia owns it and it cost them $750,000.<u>00</u>. It weighs 63000 pounds. We had a grand time ended up with lunch at the Belvedere in Baltimore. Got back here at 6 and called you at seven. Glad I didn't miss you. Here's Mrs. Black['s] letter. Thought it was an invitation so I opened it. Here's a wedding invitation. I don't know him very well but he was on my campaign committee from Ruby Ganett's office.

Kiss Margey Love to you

Harry

[upside down on top of page one] I'm going to Henderson's for dinner. Thanks for the Special. Glad Wilson is better.

[Independence, Mo.]
[November 21, 1937]
<u>Sunday</u>.

Dear Harry—

I was mighty glad to get your Special while I was at breakfast this morning— and gladder still to talk to you last night. That was making close connections— wasn't it? I didn't think about you <u>calling</u>— I fully expected to find a telegram when I got back.

I called Roylynn this a.m. & she was most <u>regretful</u>— said they would like to make an engagement with us for the holidays. We <u>must</u> have the Wrights & the Taylors to dinner while you are here.

I am going in town to mail this— as Fred just said— you might just as well throw a letter out the window as mail it in Indep. on Sunday.

What sort of a <u>heavy</u> coat are you wearing hunting? I looked your sheep-lined coat over but it was too disgraceful to send— Maybe one of the boys has a lined coat— Harry's would fit you.

Is Betty Gardelli's party still not "on?"

Lots of love
Bess

Washington D.C.
November 22, 1937

Dear Bess:—

Glad to get your letter in the first mail today. Had one from Mary too and she said they were nearly frozen. Hope you don't get any colds.

Maybe it will keep you from it. I suppose Margaret is having the time of her life in the play. Wish I could slip in and see it. I've done nothing more on apartments. Both were rented when I got back. Maybe 2929 will have a vacancy. Let's hope so.

The *St. Louis Star Times* had three pictures in a row showing your old man presiding over a hearing. I didn't know they took 'em— and the *Post Dispatch* had another good editorial. I'm not sure I'm doing right after that.

Had a fine dinner with Mr. & Mrs. Henderson and the twins. The boys were all somewhere else. The Col. & I had a fine visit and settled all the ills of the country. I came back to the office and studied the farm and reorganization bill and went to bed at ten o'clock.

I missed a call from Shannon by being away from the hotel. He's going home Wednesday. Jim P. said he hoped I'd keep him here but I'm glad he's going home. He says Stark will run against Clark and not against me. Well we'll see. Farley told me they were not going to help the Gov. against us on any count. I hope he was speaking for the White House, but you never can tell. I'm to see F.D.R when he gets back from Warm Springs.

Take good care of yourself. Don't take cold. Kiss Margey & tell her I want my two letters this week.

The clothes just came. All OK. Love to you.

Harry

[Independence, Mo.]
[November 22, 1937]
Monday—

Dear Harry—

I am about to get off to K.C. with Natalie to do Xmas shopping for Mother— I am hoping to get a lot done today. I spent most of the day looking— the other time I went for her.

I talked to Mary this a.m. and she said your mother wants some hose— so I am going to get her two pairs of the kind she wants for us to give her & Marg will give her the *Post*. M. said they are postponing the birthday dinner 'til the holidays. Marg & I will try to go out Thurs. morning for a while.

More snow is predicted for today & it looks very possible.

We went in to see *The Barrier* with Frank & Natalie yesterday. Can you imagine Frank going to a picture show on Sunday!! It wasn't much good.

Lots of love
Bess

Tell Catherine we enjoyed her letter immensely.

Washington D.C.
November 23, 1937

Dear Bess:—

Your Sunday letter just came. I'd made up my mind to wait and see if I received one on the last mail. I told Mildred she'd better get one for me if she valued her job. Fred Canfil called me this morning and talked for ten minutes. It's a good thing the County pays the bill. He's coming to Washington on Saturday and will go to the football game with me at Philadelphia. I had four tickets this year because I'm on Military Appropriations. Had to pay 45 cents tax on each one. Could have sold them for $25.00 each. Maybe I'd have been safer to sell 'em. I gave Vic two and kept the others. It would be a perfect day if you and Margey were with me at the Kickoff.

Well the filibuster is over. We took up the farm bill today and spent all afternoon listening to the reading clerk. There are 97 pages and it took him two hours to read it.

I presided yesterday for about 15 minutes and got into the *N.Y. Times.* Connally started a row and I squelched him.* The Senate upheld me. Afterwards I sat by him and he wanted to know what chance a Texan had when two Missourians were on him. The fracas was between him and Clark. You'll find it after the second quorum call in yesterday's record.

I've ended the Clark-Stark hook up. It is rumored that Farley and the Pres. are at outs which won't help me any. So far however I'm on top.

Kiss Margey and tell her I want those two letters. Love to you.

Harry

[Independence, Mo.]
[November 23, 1937]
Tuesday—

Dear Harry—

No letter this morning— Guess you were dashing around too much Sunday— Eddie J. called Sunday night— said he had told you he would— said, too, he had enjoyed being with you.

I am wondering what you are going to do on Thanksgiving Day. Most of the family are going to the game if the weather is decent, so we are waiting 'til Sunday to eat our turkey. So Thursday will be just another day.

Saw Mattie down town yesterday— & she said to tell you your

---

* Grandpa was presiding in the Senate in Vice President Garner's stead. Tom Connally of Texas was in the middle of a filibuster against a Roosevelt bill when Bennett Clark tried to interrupt him. Connally turned on Clark and was about to let him have it when Grandpa ruled Connally out of order, sparing Clark possible humiliation. Not only did this help Grandpa's relationship with Clark, but Connally apparently didn't mind.

"introduction" was perfect. I've been hearing nice things all around about it— even one of Marg's teachers said it wasn't* the finest she had ever heard.

Edna is having the bridge club way out at West-Avery (near Overland Park) today. May asked her why she didn't go on to Colorado while she was doing it. May & Nat. are ready to go so must hurry—

Lots of love
Bess

Washington D.C.
24-Nov-37

Dear Bess:—

I had a nice letter from Margey today and none from her mamma. I waited until 9:15 this evening hoping I'd still get one and I thought once I'd go on to bed and not write. I was so lonesome I took a fool notion to go to a picture show— the first one I've been to since we went to the Midland and sat up in the heaven [balcony]. It was Leslie Howard & Bette Davis in *It's Love I'm After* and it is a scream. Well after I'd laughed my blue spell off I just came back to the office and here's your letter.

We've been on the farm bill all day— Pope taking up all the time explaining its constitutionality etc. I presided part of the time and no rows took place. Burke, Minton, Halsey and several more are all going to the foot ball game Saturday. We're going on the train. Canfil called and said he'd come and go with me. Ten to one he doesn't show up. I gave Vic two of my tickets. I get four now being on the military appropriations. Vic asked me out to eat turkey tomorrow— so did Elsie but I'd already promised Vic. She said the boy is doing very well and growing to beat the band. Mrs. Gardelli is still in the anticipation stage.

Found a tailor today who agreed to press my clothes correctly so I guess I can begin to look decent again soon. I took him three suits today. He's an old Dane down here on Pa. Ave and I believe he'll do a good job. Hope I get two letters tomorrow. Kiss Margie. Love to you

Harry.

[Independence, Mo.]
[November 24, 1937]
Wednesday—

Dear Harry—

Your Sunday & Monday letters arrived this morning— & I was most glad to get them. Was wondering what had happened to you on

---

* ED: I hope she meant "was."

Sunday— Am glad you were with the Hendersons as I know you enjoy being <u>there</u> and it was nice of them to ask you.

I forgot to tell you Ed Kirby was killed in an automobile wreck Sat. night— I sent flowers for you. He & a neighbor were driving an unlighted truck & ran head on into another unlighted truck. Mr. K. was the only one killed.

No doubt you have seen Frank Lee's headline! I suppose he thought he should offset Cannon's boom for Bennett. Where did Jo. B. get his information about Mr. Stark running in '38? Guess Mr. Stark isn't feeling <u>quite</u> so cocky since the Supreme Court sat on him.* It's a wonder the *Star* didn't say they were hand picked men.

We had a nice time at Edna's party but it was a long jaunt for a bridge game— but the food was grand.

I do hope somebody asks you to dinner tomorrow.

Ethel is <u>very</u> much better & is planning to be in school next Monday.

Frank had the Dr. last night. Am afraid he is going to find a kidney infection— he has had a back ache for weeks.

Lunch time—

Lots of love
Bess

Washington D.C.
November 25, 1937

Dear Bess:

Well this is Thanksgiving and Mamma's 85th birthday and here I am sitting at 240 Senate office bldg. with the radio turned on to hear the news and there isn't any. Perry and I are going out to Vic's at 1:45 to eat a turkey Mrs. Messall has cooked. I received a good letter in the first mail but none yesterday. I'm glad you and Margey are going out to see Mamma. It will please her immensely and she may not have another one.

I've had all kinds of invitations to dinner and Mrs. Clark just called me up and asked me to come out for dinner Sunday. Barney Dickman and Mrs. Allen are to be there.

It is a perfect day— one of the kind you read about but seldom see. I'm going out looking at houses after dinner. Won't find any but it's too nice a day to work and we have to meet at eleven o'clock tomorrow so as to have an excuse to lay off Saturday and go to the football game. Wheeler

---

*The Missouri Supreme Court blocked an attempt by Governor Stark to declare invalid a ruling by a previous state insurance commissioner who had been a Pendergast appointee.

came in yesterday and seemed exceedingly glad to see me. I'm going to have to take on the Milwaukee & St. Paul Dec. 6. He's still giving lectures on the Court. I guess I might as well face the music and do the best job I can. Hope I don't miss any more letters. You and Margey mustn't take day about. Kiss her for me. Love to you.

Harry

[Independence, Mo.]
[November 25, 1937]
Thanksgiving Day
10 a.m.

Dear Harry—

Marg & I are just about to get off to go see your mother. It's a grand day— but plenty windy— but the football fans won't get <u>cold</u> anyway. Chris & Fred left early & May & George have just driven out. Frank is too sick to go— Marg wanted to go at the last minute— but I convinced her she wouldn't get $2.25's worth of fun out of it & that amount of money would see us to four and a half shows & as there are three in town right now she wants to see there wasn't any further argument.

I've been very selfishly wishing that the P.O. didn't have a holiday, to-day.

This morning's paper says that Gov. S. is going to Wash. to have a conference with the Pres. & to the Gridiron Dinner. Also that the Pres. is interested in Mo. having a new prison farm.

Hope to get two fat letters tomorrow.

This surely doesn't seem like a holiday of <u>any</u> sort— just "another day."

Lots of love
Bess

Washington D.C.
November 26, 1937

Dear Bess:—

I almost called last night but decided I'd wait until Saturday or Sunday. Probably Sunday because I won't be back from the football game in time Saturday. Just had a wire from Canfil saying he'd be here so I guessed wrong.

Mrs. Messall had a very fine dinner. Mrs. Roby and her two boys were there as were Stewart & Betty Perry and Mrs. Hunt and her daughter. She had a buffet style setup with bridge tables to eat from. Then we got the Mo and Kans game and I sent 'em a telegram. Mo. sure ought to have won. Just one foot from goal. They certainly should have gone over. Wish we'd been there to give 'em the necessary push.

I wish that you were here to see the Army-Navy game tomorrow. I'm almost getting to be a football fan although I'd still rather sit by a radio, unless I'm with you, to get the result.

I notice you are complaining of no letter Tuesday but I haven't missed a day. Some of 'em weren't mailed on time but I wrote one every day so you ought not to have missed. Maybe some of yours and some of mine got lost.

I'm glad the introduction was all right. I was afraid I'd been too short. Will call Sunday.

Kiss Margey. Love to you.

Harry

[Independence, Mo.]
[November 26, 1937]
Friday—

Dear Harry—

I was glad to get your Tuesday letter this morning after the <u>vacancy</u> yesterday— I immediately read the *Record* which came at the same time. It certainly is <u>something</u> to squelch one of those old timers who have been at that game for twenty years or so— Connally probably thinks <u>more of you</u> for doing it.

Surely am glad you are going to the game Sat. I'd give my store teeth to see that game. Maybe we can some day.

It was nice of the Messalls to ask you to dinner yesterday & I know you enjoyed being there. You probably felt it was the next best thing to being in Mo.

Tell Mr. Messall I will write him as soon as I get some information about Ben Murray.

I am dying to know how you broke up the Clark-Stark combination. The Pres. isn't very smart if he thinks he can get along without James A. Farley. But he is just about that "cocky"—

Did you ask to be put on the Military Comm? Which one did you have to give up to make the change?

Hope you have a grand time tomorrow & that C. doesn't quite talk you down.

Lots of love
Bess

Your mother looked better yesterday than I have seen her in a long long time.

[Independence, Mo.]
[November 27, 1937]
Saturday—

Dear Harry—

I don't know what happened to my Monday letter for I surely wrote one— It went the same route your Tuesday letter of last week did— I think I mailed it in K.C. as I spent the first part of the week in K.C.

It's simply pouring & I am <u>almost</u> hoping it will quit for a minute or two so I can get to the P.O. & to the bank for Mother. Hamrick says snow tonight!

Marg and I saw *The Firefly*[*] yesterday and it is simply great! <u>Be sure to go</u>. It made me think of little [opera singer Emma] Trentini more than once but J. McD. is so much more beautiful & her voice is lovelier too, I think.

No doubt you are on your way to Phil. & I do hope the weather is decent.

Hope the Danish tailor was OK.

Am glad you are going to Clarks' to-morrow. Is Mrs. Allen a political power?

Are you really interested in <u>houses</u> or did you <u>mean apt—s</u> when you said you were going to look at "houses"— I don't want to spend the <u>whole</u> winter working— and I don't want to <u>have</u> to have a maid— and I <u>don't want an extra bedroom</u>— so do look for an apt if you aren't set on a house.

It's sleeting so I'll have to get off at once or my back tires will be sliding all over Jackson Co.

Lots of love
Bess

Sunday A.M.
Washington D.C.
November 28, 1937

Dear Bess:

Well I had a grand wet day yesterday. It started off right by bringing me a good letter. Canfil was on the train and as pleased as a ten year old boy to go to the game. He had a blanket, hunting jacket, muffler, raincoat, overcoat and overshoes. It was a spring day with April showers and fog so the raincoat was all that was needed. Took him around and introduced him to the V.P. who made his usual hit. Sens. Duffy & daughter, Burke &

---

[*] A 1937 musical film starring Jeanette MacDonald and Allan Jones.

wife, Swellenback [*sic*] & wife, and Chavez & wife were on our car along with a lot of Senate employees. Minton was with his Sec. as I was. Vic & Perry used my other two tickets. I am on the Military Appropriations Sub-Committee not the Military Affairs Committee but I get the same sort of recognition. You remember when I ceased being an alderman for D.C. and got Sen. Glass to change me over.

Connally was happy over his squelching. He was just using [filibustering] tactics. Sorry I forgot to put a special on my Tuesday letter. I've given the girls orders to put one on the Friday letters.

Glad you saw Mamma and also that she's looking so well. I missed writing you yesterday— that's no. 1. I was so wet and tired when I got back to Washington I just took a hot bath and went to bed. When your special came this A.M. I felt very badly about not sitting up and getting one off.

The game was a soggy affair. Too wet for the parade and show. The Army out played the Navy though. The Navy's mascot is a goat & the Army's a mule. They have two mules one a regular mule & the other a South American donkey given them by the Peruvian Ambassador whose son is at the Point. They dressed the donkey up like a goat and unloaded him from an ambulance in front of the Navy stands, mounted an army man in an admiral's uniform on him and had a fellow on the mule in army uniform chase him around the arena and shoot him. The "Admiral" & the donkey both fell in front of the Naval contingent much to the pleasure of the Army boys. It probably wouldn't have been so funny if they hadn't won afterwards. Canfil yelled himself hoarse. When the Army was about to score and failed he shouted "More Brutality Army— what are you being trained for anyway." He entertained the spectators for acres around. Mr. & Mrs. Cochrane sat a couple of rows behind us. They left however at the end of the first quarter on account of the rain.

I hope you can see one of those games some day but I hope it won't be in the rain. I want to see one when they have all the trimmings. We'll do it some day.

I am going out to Clarks for dinner today. The Mayor of St. L. will be there as will his fianc[ée] Mrs. Allen and I don't know who else. I have, successfully I think, convinced Clark that the Gov. is after his scalp as well as mine. He apparently thinks there's something in it. The Gov. & the Pres. would like to be heroes and boss busters and Clark has definitely lined up with the Boss you see. He and Maurice Milligan almost came to blows the last time they met and now the Pres. & Stark are thinking of running him for Senator against Clark. I'm not sure it won't happen if the *Post Dispatch,* the *Star* and the Springfield & St. Joe papers can bring it about. My position gets better all the time. Kiss Margey, love to you.

Harry

<u>Wish you were here</u>.

✺1938

Washington was in a bad mood. President Roosevelt was fuming because his court-packing scheme hadn't succeeded. Republicans and conservative Democrats were fuming because he'd tried it in the first place. Both parties were knocking down as much New Deal legislation as they could, and unemployment had hit 19 percent.

Internationally, the Germans and the Japanese were annexing or invading their neighbors as a prelude to World War II, and President Roosevelt was urging a strong national defense to meet the threat. Isolationist congressmen, hoping to avoid the threat altogether, tightened the neutrality laws and nearly passed an amendment to the Constitution calling for a referendum before Congress could vote the nation into a war.

In Missouri, U.S. Attorney Maurice Milligan, with Governor Lloyd Stark's backing, was jailing hundreds of Pendergast loyalists for padding the voting rolls. Tom Pendergast himself was under investigation for accepting a bribe of $750,000 from an insurance company in exchange for favorable rulings from the state insurance commissioner, a Pendergast appointee.

With Pendergast in trouble and his machine falling apart, Roosevelt had begun to treat Stark as Missouri's official spokesman. They even began exchanging "Dear Lloyd" and "Dear Franklin" letters. This did nothing for my grandmother's already dim view of the President. Grandpa could, and did, deplore the way Roosevelt played politics while still praising his policies. My grandmother never could.

Stark, Milligan, and the newspapers were also happily reminding voters, at every turn, of Grandpa's ties to Pendergast, making my grandmother exceedingly wary. On July 7, she reported to Grandpa that a man had called in the middle of the night, wondering why Grandpa had not attended a funeral for the wife of someone named John Maloney. When my grandmother explained that Grandpa was away and couldn't have known, the man insisted she send Maloney a telegram, explaining. The caller was so plastered that my grandmother was sure it was some sort of trap.

Still, my grandmother had time for fun, actually trying to teach my mother to play tennis. In true Bess Truman competitive fashion, she did this by serving the ball with such a spin on it that it was impossible to return. In short order, my mother gave up, despite my grandmother's assertions that she had the makings of a good player. To me, the idea that Mom had the makings of a good tennis player is hilarious. I have never met anyone who, by her own admission, was more averse to sports, exercise, or health in general. In a restaurant once, she ordered a baked Brie appetizer and filet mignon. When told the Brie came with fruit and the filet with vegetables, she said, "Oh, leave that stuff off and just bring the cheese and the meat."

Continuing her policy of helping friends in need, Gammy entertained Emma Griggs and her son, John, who had lost his job at a cheese factory. They wanted Grandpa to help John get a job in Washington, but they were so wrapped up in their own problems and so inclined to bad-mouth everyone else that they wound up annoying my grandmother, who passed on their request not to Grandpa, but to his secretary, Vic Messall.

On the other hand, my grandmother was delighted to report that Senator Bennett Clark had gotten himself in trouble with the press for charging his employees 2.5 percent of their salaries to fund his reelection campaign. "The receipts had B's picture on them!" she wrote.

John Snyder was a Kansas City banker and old friend of my grandparents, who eventually became Grandpa's treasury secretary. His daughter, Drucie, was one of my mother's best friends and my godmother. Harry

Truman secretary Vic Messall
in 1938 (TL 58-161).

Vaughan was an old friend from World War I who eventually attained the rank of general and became Grandpa's military aide in the White House. One of his main duties was telling jokes and thereby helping maintain the presidential equilibrium.

Ft. Riley, Kans.
July 4, 1938

Dear Bess:—

This is what you might call corresponding under some difficulty. My pen is dry, the wind is blowing a gale, and the flies are about to eat my legs up. I have a tent about twenty yards from the shower and I expect to be in that shower in about half an hour. Arrived at about eight o'clock this morning and have seen everyone. There are some two hundred reservists here and most of them are old timers whom I've known for some time. Marvin Casteel of the Highway Patrol is here along with Jozak, Snyder, Vaughan, Ed Moore, the PM [postmaster] at Clinton, and a lot of others. They have a very pleasant schedule fixed up and I believe we'll have an enjoyable ten days. They are giving me a horse and have agreed to cut out the social affairs so I guess I'll be all right. Sorry this ink is so blurry but I can't get any more until tomorrow— everything on the post is closed.

Kiss my baby and <u>keep cool</u>.

Love to you,
Harry

It was nice to talk to you last night.

[Independence, Mo.]
[July 5, 1938]
Tuesday—

Dear Harry —

I was hoping for some sort of news this a.m. that you had reached camp alright— but am very sure I <u>would</u> have heard if you had <u>not</u> gotten there OK.

Marg had your Topeka card & was delighted.

Lucy called her early this morning & asked her to go to KC with her to meet Kath. Mize's daughter who is on her way to Denver. Kath always "farms out" her children in the summer time so she can have a real vacation. L. & the girls are having lunch in town & a picture show.

M. & I went to a show & to the station for supper yesterday with F. & Natalie & Fred & Chris— & that was the extent of our Glorious Fourth. We didn't have a firecracker on the place.

F. & C. took M. & David to Mission Hills to see the fireworks last night.

It's hotter'n Hades but I guess you know it.

Love from both of us—

Bess

I don't know whether I should have sent these letters on to Vic or not.

Ft. Riley, Kans.
July 5, 1938

Dear Bess:—

Harry Vaughan had some ink so you will get an ink letter today. I called on Gen. Henry as Colonel of F. A. this morning on my way over to the canteen to get a strap for Margaret's watch. He was pleased as punch and said he was just starting out to see me. He is one of the real B. G.'s in the army— name is Henry. I thought McCoy was in command. They offered me the Post Hqs for my use and a stenographer too. I told 'em I'm not dictating any letters for a few days.

Went to the hospital this morning and had my heart and blood pressure tested. Heart perfect blood pressure 110. He said I'd probably live to be 110 years old. It is rather hot out here but I had to have a blanket over me last night. Have been teaching the boys angles and line of sight and angle of site [sic]. Some of 'em are pretty good. Snyder and I were listening to a young West Point second lieut. explain a new instrument for laying the guns this morning and Snyder said "Harry, to realize that boy was a babe in arms when you and I were shooting in France?" We are now the Gen. Berrys of our time I guess. I'm getting as brown as an Indian, sleeping and eating much and feeling fine. Kiss Margie. Hope for a letter tomorrow. Much love.

Harry.

How do you like my paper?

[Independence, Mo.]
[July 6, 1938]
Wednesday—

Dear Harry—

Just have about two minutes before the P.O. closes— went to KC early & sent those wedding presents out— sent the "Royster-Brady"— two small Italian bowls or ash trays or what have you. Sent [illegible]-Gates a combination of four small cocktail shakers in a frame etc. It had been $20 but there were no takers so it was reduced to $10. It really was a snappy piece & an Army hostess will have much use for it. It was made of silver & some dark wood for a tray.

Was glad to have your letter this morning— glad you are enjoying it as usual.

Forgot to tell you I went to Mary G's party this afternoon— so the day was full.

Love & take care of yourself—

Bess

Ft. Riley, Kans.
July 6, 1938

Dear Bess:—

[…] Spent the morning with the outfit on the Trainor range. They
do a very good job on practice firing. Col. Peek and I have gotten rid of
the tea drinkers and have really made a regiment of it. There are sixty-
seven officers here and thirty of them are new R.O.T.C. university gradu-
ates and fine young men. They know more about firing than I did on
November 11, '18. So you see they are pretty good.

Kiss Margie & keep writing. I've made some notes on letters you can
send to Vic.

Love to you
Harry

[Independence, Mo.]
[July 7, 1938]
Thursday—

Dear Harry—

Was glad to get your Tues. letter this morning but I don't more than
half believe your story about the blanket. Am glad to say it has rained a
little & so far is somewhat cooler.

Some man who was decidedly "tight" called up about two o'clock
night before last & said John Maloney's wife had died & he had just come
from the "wake" & the said J. Maloney was quite distressed because he
hadn't heard from you etc. & I explained that there was no possible way
for you to know it— & then he insisted that I send a telegram to him— &
I told him I would but he was so drunk— I was afraid maybe there was
a "catch" somewhere so I just didn't do it. If you know the said John
Maloney maybe you had better write him a note— his address is 411
Westwood Webster Groves.

Your Aunt Ella is much better this a.m. I am enclosing two touching
editorials from Willie's paper— I know you would hate to miss them.*

---

* Colonel William Southern, publisher of the Independence *Examiner,* had a complicated
relationship with my grandparents. He was a member of the family (sort of) as father of
Aunt May, but he was also a Roosevelt detractor; hence my grandmother's sarcasm when
mentioning his editorials endorsing Senator Bennett Clark and Missouri Supreme Court
Justice James M. Douglas, a favorite of Lloyd Stark.

M. is going to mail this as she goes to the picture show. Natalie [*illegible*] is here & they are taking in *Robin Hood.*˙

Love—
Bess

Are you getting good food?

Ft. Riley, Kans.
July 7, 1938

Dear Bess:—

It was a very great pleasure to get your good letter today enclosing two from Vic and one from Dan Willard and one from Nat'l. Chamber of Commerce about my ten minute railroad speech on the last day of the session. I had thought it was a dud but it evidently hit in some places. When the Nat'l. Chamber wants copies and Mr. Willard writes a four page letter it must have had some meat. We are having a very good camp. It rained all morning but we went to one of the riding halls and held our scheduled instruction. The Gen's visit got results. They've mowed all the weeds and given us all extra space in front of our tents in the form of a fly and a platform. The gang all give me credit for it, but I didn't say a word or do a thing about it except to let the Gen. sit in the sun when he came to see me. It looks as if we'll have a badger fight. That'll make everyone happy. You don't have to use stamps on those envelopes when you are enclosing official letters. ~~Use 'em only~~ (I'm being talked to) when you just have a personal stamp on it. I had to go to the P.O. for the one today. It lacked 3 cents. I'm as brown as an Indian & feeling fine.

Kiss Margie. Love to you.

Harry

[Independence, Mo.]
[July 8, 1938]
Friday—

Dear Harry—

Was glad to get your letter this a.m. & am sending the enclosed letters right on to Vic.

I meant to tell you yesterday your Chinese dinner coat has arrived & is very good looking but is not white— more of an ivory. H. sent me a beautiful luncheon set & I sent her sister's box right on down to her.

Marg is starting her music lessons again this morning.

˙A 1938 film starring Errol Flynn.

Jo Waters is going to marry Ernie Roberts to-morrow! He apparently has recovered from T.B. but they will have to live in Denver.

Mrs. Palmer has just been here & brought a book for <u>us</u> to read— she wants to see you as soon as you get home!

It is considerably cooler & last night was grand— even slept inside. Marg had a "bad dream" & came in with me about two o'clock.

Must get M. to Mrs. Story's.* Take care of yourself & don't try to keep up with those infants—

Love—

Bess

[Independence, Mo.]

[July 9, 1938]

Saturday—

10 a.m.

Dear Harry—

I sent off a "Special" to you early this a.m. but was sure you wouldn't get it any sooner under another Special stamp— so if it doesn't get there in time for you to do anything about it— I can't help it. You probably won't want to do anything about it anyway.

I have just had Marg & Jeanne Rogers out on the city courts— & it was plenty warm! I tried to show M. how to serve but it was a washout— I am convinced the courts are about a mile longer now than they were when we played. I believe M. has the makings of a good player.

I had <u>two letters</u>! from you yesterday— but it wasn't so nice when none came this a.m.

I hope you have plenty of <u>new</u> recruits so the Badger Fight will "go over."

A "Tony Gilmore" of Jeff. City is applying for Fred T's [Truman's] job in Wash. & he had a flock of recommendations— I sent them on to Vic. Hope that was alright.

I have two million things to do— cleaning washing etc.

Love—

Bess

---

* Mrs. Story, the church organist, gave Mom her first formal music lessons. Prior to that, her teachers had been Grandpa and Mamma Truman. Mom hated to practice and found so many ways to avoid it that my grandmother suggested she give up lessons. Mom loved music enough that the threat straightened her out. I, too, hated to practice, but Mom knew better than to offer me a way out.

Ft. Riley, Kans.
July 11, 1938

Dear Bess:—

This is a sorrowful evening— no letter. But it will probably mean two for tomorrow so I'll try to stand it. This has been the hottest day and I got a real sunburn so Jozak says. It was good to talk with you yesterday. Snyder, Vaughan, Kirby & I were all in the hotel at once. The first two & I went to a polo game over on the west end of the reservation at nine o'clock. It wasn't very good because everyone on the team, on both teams, in fact were at a party at the same polo club given in my honor. I had to leave at ten o'clock so the Gen. and his wife could go home. […] We came out to camp at four o'clock and started a W.P.R [?] poker [game] and I quit at seven thirty, took a bath and went to bed at 8 o'clock.

The mess gets better everyday and it was excellent to start with. (I'm getting undeserved credit for that too).

I've got to go watch a shrapnel problem at 7:30 and it is nearly that time. Kiss Margie. Love to you.

Wish you'd call Mamma.

Harry.

[Independence, Mo.]
[July 11, 1938]
Monday—

Dear Harry

It was nice to talk to you yesterday & nice to get two letters this morning. Am glad, too, you are feeling fine in spite of the heat. We are in for another blistering day— but at present I am sitting in a grand cool breeze.

I've had a swell toothache for two days— & am going up to old Berry & have it out this morning. It's too hot to go to KC to have it done.

Katherine left yesterday for good— & it takes all of us to corral these two imps. Christine doesn't have a glimmer of an idea where she can get anyone. She expected Pauline to come but she has a torn ligament in her ankle so it will be a long time before she can do any work.

Marg went over to see your Aunt Ella Friday & she said she was much better.

Must get dressed— & go to the slaughter.

Love—

Bess

Mildred came in just long enough to say "hello" yesterday—

[Independence, Mo.]
[July 12, 1938]
Tuesday—

Dear Harry—

I was glad to get your Mon. letter this afternoon & am glad you are having such a good time. It can't be so <u>terribly</u> warm or you wouldn't feel like dashing around so much.

It's plenty warm here today but I don't mind it quite so much since getting rid of those aching teeth.

John & Emma [Griggs] were here last night. The cheese factory has closed of course and he is jobless. He says he really doesn't want to go back to Washington if he can just get something else to do— I assured him I thought his job had been promised to someone. I am enclosing his letter which came this a.m. <u>I</u> told him last night it would go right on to Wash. and he was so upset about it that I weakened this morning & wrote him a card saying I had gotten all of the mail this a.m. & would send it to you [at Fort Riley, Kans.]— They're down on everybody on earth except the <u>Griggses</u>— were laying out the Salisburys because they had managed to scrape enough together to buy another house & were driving a decent looking car. By the time they left I was really boiling and that was when I told J. his letter would go on to Vic— then he hit the ceiling—

Have just talked to Mary & she said your mother is fine but not enjoying the heat.

Lucy told me Vivian was right sick so I called Luella yesterday to ask about him— but he had gone to the office & was alright.

Am hoping the end of the week will hurry up & come.

Love—
Bess

[Independence, Mo.]
[July 13, 1938]
Wednesday—

Dear Harry,

I am in the basement waiting for the iron to heat so I can get Marg a <u>costume</u> ready to play tennis in— I have an idea I will make one trip to town <u>only</u> today & that <u>one</u> will be <u>early</u>— so that I'd better get this ready to go.

This is another stinger but we had a good night for sleeping & that helps—

Betty Ogden is back in town so Marg is delighted. Lorene says they taxed all of them 2½% of their <u>year's</u> salary (apparently) for Bennett's campaign as the receipts had B's picture on them!

I got Mrs. K. on the phone alright Sunday. She was glad to hear from him as she said it was the first time in a week.

Iron is hot— & as usual I'm behind time—

Love—
Bess

[Independence, Mo.]
[July 14, 1938]
Thursday—

Dear Harry,

You may be on your way home before this arrives in Riley as I will not get it mailed very early.

Am going in with Chris to take the babies to see the Dr. They are not sick but M. [Marion] won't eat so Dr. Cowherd has to tell her <u>why</u>.

Was glad to get your letter early this mornin—. Am <u>relieved</u> that you finally acknowledged it was warm out there.

Today is somewhat cooler & I am hoping the promised rain will arrive.

Mr. and Mrs. Meyer left for Calif. Tuesday— C. [Christine] was glad to get them off— they were both so nervous & upset about everything.

Ethel was over with the two small boys last night— said her mother had had a miserable day. I hear James Allen is "stepping out" but I can't find out who the gal is. Won't the Nolands have a spell if he marries again very soon?

Lunch time— Take your time coming home! Am sorry your letter arrived too late to save the teeth.

Love—
Bess

Hotel Loraine, Madison, Wisc.
Saturday, August 27, 1938

Dear Bess:—

This is a very beautiful city. If you and Margey were here the visit would be perfect. I left Des Moines at 7:30 yesterday after breakfast and arrived here at 3:30. Would have been an hour sooner but had 40 miles of detours. The roads were good but very narrow and full of curves.

There are two lakes here, one north of town and one south. The capitol is an ismus [*sic*] between them and the town is built around the capitol square. I happened to stop at the right hotel. They are having a strike at the other big one. There are all sorts of cottages to rent on the lakes.

Will be home some time Monday. Will call you from [*illegible*] Sunday as soon as I get there. Kiss Margey.

Harry.

[Independence, Mo.]
August 27, 1938

Telegram
HARRY S TRUMAN
LORAINE HOTEL
   GLAD GET WIRE EVERYBODY FINE DICK DUNCAN ANXIOUS
TO TALK TO YOU THANKS FOR CANDY=
BESS.

[Independence, Mo.]
[December 7, 1938]
Wednesday—
11 a.m.

Dear Harry—
   Am hoping to have a telegram in an hour or so— saying you are safely in Wash. Surely hope you didn't run into any more snow.
   I am enclosing this Dem. Comm. letter. It came Special Airmail so I thought it surely was of some importance & opened it. Am entirely out of large envelopes for forwarding mail.
   Beck bought two more gallons of sorghum Monday— one for us and one for the President— He wants a letter from you to the boys— on your Senate letterhead to use as the subject of a civics lesson.
   Chris & the babies all have colds this morning— but no temperature yet.
   Let me hear often—
Love—
Bess

[Washington D.C.]
December 8, 1938

Dear Bess:
   It was a very lonesome evening. I could hardly keep my hands off the telephone, but thought I'd be all economical and wait until Saturday since I'd sent you a telegram. The girls were pleased to see me and I'm up to date on the mail. They both want to be remembered to you.
   My dinner party at Marshall was very fine. Bill Denham, the State Employment Director, Bill Kirby, the Kansas City Director, Jimmy Doarn,

the Asst State Director, Ted Marks, Vets Placement Officer, and the host, Wright Lloyd, Employment Director for Central Missouri, were all put to work, except Ted, by me back in 1934 in various minor positions and have all made good and been promoted. I hope you'll notice the absence of Bill Taylor who should have been there. I think they wanted to indicate that they are for me and not the Gov. [Lloyd Stark] so Bill wasn't asked. The papers say the Gov. and his staff will be the guests of Mo. Society on the 14th. Aren't you sorry you're not here? I'll be on the road to New Orleans, thank goodness, and I wouldn't go if I were here.

I've been interviewed by every newspaper man in Washington and they all acted like they were glad to see me.

Kiss Margey. Love to you. I'm looking for a letter.

The table cloth is a beauty. It's worth it.

> Harry.

> [Independence, Mo.]
> [December 10, 1938]

Dear Harry—

You will be a bit surprised to find <u>this</u> waiting for you no doubt. I don't know whether you meant you were <u>starting</u> for N.O. [New Orleans] on Sunday or would <u>arrive</u>— so am getting it off in time. Thanks for the stamps— I judged you wanted them <u>used</u>.

Wasn't that a tricky Christmas card from the Shields— Was it in with the table-cloth? Am mighty anxious to see the cloth— am glad you didn't feel too badly stung on the duty.

Marg & I went to K.C. yesterday & bought her evening dress. She is wild about it but I'm afraid it will hurt your eyes.

Bud called up last night— He & Sharon are in K.C. on their way west— B. to Denver & S. to Dodge City— They are coming out tomorrow for a short visit.

Hope it's nice & warm in N.O.— It's chilly here but more pleasant than that warm weather was—

I got some nice cologne in attractive bottles at Wooly's [Woolworth's] for the girls & will send them to Vic & ask him to "distribute" them. (Writing on a soft magazine has its difficulties.)*

Have a good time and hurry home—

> Love—

> Bess

---

* The handwriting in this letter is less neat than usual, especially the last words here.

🏵1939

On May 22, Tom Pendergast pleaded guilty to accepting the $750,000 insurance company bribe ... and to altering the books of the companies he owned to avoid paying $1 million in taxes, all to support a gambling habit that had swelled to as much as $100,000 a day. He was sentenced to fifteen months in federal prison. His city manager, Henry F. McElroy, avoided a similar fate by dying before the feds could incarcerate him. He had apparently hidden a $20 million city budget deficit.

Tom Pendergast and nephew Jim, the two guys who got Grandpa into politics in the first place, ca. 1939 (TL 2009-1535).

Needless to say, this was bad for Grandpa's prospects for reelection. The *Kansas City Star* referred to him as the last survivor of the Pendergast machine to hold high office; the *St. Louis Post-Dispatch* declared that this association automatically disqualified him from serving another term. Happily, President Roosevelt would eventually sour on Lloyd Stark, telling my grandfather that Stark had a huge ego and no sense of humor. Worse, the president didn't think the governor was a real liberal.

My grandfather backed Roosevelt on the neutrality issue, working to change laws that forbade the president from selling arms to either side in a war. His support of FDR could have jeopardized the Wheeler-Truman Transportation Bill, designed to reorganize and regulate the nation's railroads. As a senator approaching the end of his term, my grandfather needed a significant accomplishment to show the voters he was doing his job.

1939 inspection trip (TL 59-873).

My grandmother, by her own admission below, would have preferred he skip the whole thing and come home. She, meanwhile, was baking hams for his office parties, giving and attending teas with the other congressional wives, and hobnobbing with the King and Queen of England, who arrived in June to drum up some help for the looming war with Germany.

Only one of my grandmother's letters survives from 1939. Wherever the others went, they may be keeping company my grandfather's letters from June of that year, because we don't have any of those either. They may simply have been lost or they may have accidentally gone up in flames with most of my grandmother's other letters around Christmas 1955.

Of course, the one surviving letter from this year *would* contain the raciest line in the whole collection, that of the "thin negligee." Grandchildren never want to think about these things, but it must be said that my grandparents obviously had very healthy marital relations. As David McCullough pointed out in *Truman,* in the early 1950s, when they would have been in their mid-60s, they broke one of the bed slats in the master bedroom at Blair House.

[Independence, Mo.]
[July? 1939]
Tuesday—

Dear Harry,
I never did get around to a letter yesterday but M. is sending one by

The family on a boat in 1939 (TL 86-76).

airmail to-day— so you <u>will</u> get one tomorrow.

I am wondering if you are leaving Thurs. for Ft. Riley or just what— I can't stand the thought of you driving back again right away— but I guess you <u>will do it if you want to.</u>

M. & I went to KC yesterday— & bought her a large straw hat at $1.69 and a thin negligee for me.

I am unpacking the <u>last</u> of the boxes this a.m. I put your clothes in the cedar closets in the attic— & they <u>should</u> be safe there— however to make doubly sure I have put some of those deadly moth crystals in the closets.

Am going to wash all my blankets in Chris' electric washer— and "do" poor old Mrs. Lyle out of $2.50.

These bills came the morning we left & I packed them [in] a bag and forgot to give them to you.

Is there any chance of skipping the neutrality legislation this session so you can adjourn soon?

Marg talked to your mother this morning & she said she was fine.

It's getting warm again I'm sorry to say—

Let me know what you are going to do about coming out this week-end— I should think you'd feel as if you are commuting—

Love
Bess

⊛1940

I think of the campaign of 1940 as a dry run for the campaign of 1948. Both times, Grandpa was the underdog. In 1948, he crossed the country by train, giving speeches at every whistle-stop along the way. Eight years earlier, he had campaigned by car, crisscrossing the state of Missouri, speaking at every town hall and courthouse rally that would have him. In both campaigns, he occasionally ran out of money and gas and had to call for a contribution to get things running again.

In 1940, Lloyd Stark unintentionally helped my grandfather by being so much of an ass that he alienated potential supporters like Bennett Clark and President Roosevelt. U.S. Attorney Maurice Milligan, who had almost ruined Grandpa by going after Tom Pendergast, now pitched in to help by running against him, siphoning votes from Stark—and thoroughly confusing the anti-Truman editorial writers.

Bennett Clark, Grandpa's ally/nemesis in the Senate, in 1940 (TL 58-454).

My grandmother knew how much the Senate meant to Grandpa and had, herself, come to love her life as a senator's wife. She paid close attention to Grandpa's campaign, passing on possibly helpful contacts (e.g., Mr. Cullison, who turned out not to be so helpful), enjoying Stark's losing face with Roosevelt, and advising Grandpa not to travel with his unmarried secretary, Mildred Dryden, lest the St. Louis politicians try to use it against him.

She worked hard during the campaign, venturing out in public to an uncomfortable degree. When the early returns put Stark ahead by ten thousand votes, she went to bed crying. Grandpa, astoundingly, was already fast asleep.

Portrait of the
family from the
1940 Senate
campaign
(TL 71-4246).

When the votes were all counted, Grandpa had beaten his Republican opponent by forty thousand votes.

On his first day back, the Senate gave him a standing ovation.

Washington DC
[March 26, 1940]
Tuesday— 11 a.m.

Dear Harry—

We had a <u>very</u> comfortable trip and got in at 7:30 & Vic met us!— in spite of me telling you not to let him know. Am going for the bags after school & will go by the office.

I wired Mother this morning as soon as I got home. I didn't know

<u>where</u> to wire you but knew that if you were in KC you would call the house to find out if they had heard.

Have gotten the <u>top</u> dust out [of] the apt. and Millie has scrubbed the kitchen & bath so am about settled.

Marg had the thrill of her life in Cincinnati in the station— One of those <u>roving</u> broad-casters stopped her and got her life history in sixty-seconds.

Well I wish you were on your way— it will be right lonely for the next ten days—

It's plenty chilly here but the sun is shining— the snow flurries didn't get this far East— but we saw traces of it until it got too dark to see last night.

They gave us Comp. D. & it was fine.

Hope things are working out alright in St. Louis—

I'll try to call Col. Snyder this evening & see if Mrs. S. is here, too.

Lots of love — & let me hear from you often.

Bess

[Independence, Mo.]
[April 4, 1940]
Thursday

Dear Harry—

It surely was a relief to hear that telephone ring Tuesday night even tho. it was two o'clock in the morning. It looked so cloudy in the west as we came home, I was afraid you might run into bad weather by dark.

Am anxious to know about the St. Joe meeting. It was rotten luck about the KC election.

Have just talked to Millie & she said Sen. Stewart thought this a.m. there is some chance of his getting things "fixed up" so he can go tonight. Surely hope it works out alright.

We went down to see Ben's new place last night & had dinner with her. She has a much nicer room than she had on New Hamp. & there are just two women in the house besides B. & one of them owns the place & works for the gov't.

I am sending the Gunston check today— $46.88. Thank goodness there will be only one more of those.

The Cong. children are starting to practice today for their broadcast.

Let me hear from you when you can <u>conveniently</u>.

It sure was lonesome last night

Love
Bess

Washington DC (to Ft. Riley, Kans.)
[April 8, 1940]
Monday night—

Dear Harry—

I was delighted to get your air mails yesterday and today— According to Mildred it was most uncertain that you would be in K.C. today so I didn't try to get a letter off yesterday.

I didn't have time Sat. to tell you all about the seat covers so didn't even mention them. They had three prices— $9.50 $10.50 & $17.50— and I chose the middle one as they are reversible— straw for summer & some kind of hard twisted cotton [canvas] for winter— but material you can still slide on— The $9.50 were straw only— & the $17.50 were Chrysler-made— but that seemed pretty steep. These look very nice and fit nicely— & it's a joy to get into the car now & not have to fight your way across the front seat. I also had to have a new inner tube in that left front tire. The new valve didn't help a bit— & they couldn't put enough air in the tube to find the leak. Called it a "high pressure leak" in a "defective" tube.

Do you remember that Mr. Cullison (a friend of the Messalls from Enid)— who was a Gov't statistician? Well, he is living in N.Y. now & is in town & told M. to have me call him— & I did tonight. He gave Mil. a lot of messages for you but he told me confidentially to pass on to you that he is working for the Nat'l Board of Fire Underwriters which is the top of the 232 stock companies that ruined T. J. and O'M. [O'Malley]— & he had some information to pass on to you which might (or might not) be of some political value. He is coming back to see you the week-end of April-20–21— Also said he would do anything he could for you— go to Mo. & make speeches at his own expense etc. etc. Seemed very much in earnest about it.

Am glad things generally seem brighter—

Did Milligan get anything like the reception the *Star* said he got at the Young Dem. meeting in K.C.? I hope you are entirely satisfied about Senator Stewart going to Kirksville—

It's been raining every minute all day— It's too bad some of it couldn't go to Mo.

Ben came out & had dinner with us yesterday & we took a long drive.

Am glad you saw the family yesterday— hope they were all well— Hope too that Mary's throat is better.

Guess Mr. Stark didn't get to say very much to the Pres. in ten minutes. Did you see in the *Star* that you were in there for an hour or two at the Pres' invitation?

Surely hope things work out as you want them to next Monday—
Will B. C.* really try to keep the Gov. off the committee if he possibly can?

It's bed time— Will write to St. Louis. Don't give any of that St. L.
outfit a chance to talk about you & Vic being with the girls down there.
Nobody is going to miss seeing Mildred!

Love from both of us—

Bess

Washington D.C.
[April 11, 1940]
Thursday—

Dear Harry—

It was grand to talk to you last night, even tho. I was so sleepy, I
probably didn't make sense. Am glad, too, you had a fine meeting and
hope the one tonight will be just as enthusiastic. I don't see why the
telephone companies don't have a flat rate, say of 25 cents, to any place
at any time. Then we could talk more often— & I bet their increased business would make them a lot more money.

Just had a letter from Mother & she said you had dropped in for a
few minutes Mon. evening. I wish you had someone with you when you
are doing so much driving. I thought of course Vic was along.

Our Mo. bridge benefit at the club was a great success— Everybody
apparently had a good time and we cleared $58 for the building fund.

I know you are sick about Sen. Burke.** I hate to see Mrs. Burke and I
will undoubtedly have to see her at Mrs. Hatch's luncheon today.

The census gal was here this morning— & I surely was glad to be
able to tell her we already had a "slip"— but she had to be convinced— &
still had to know how much rent we paid and how many rooms—

Love—
Bess

Washington DC
[April 12, 1940]
Friday—

Dear Harry—

It's practically time to go for Marg— and as usual I'm behind time.
I've spent the entire morning on the telephone making arrangements for
our DAR tea and (on the side) making a chocolate cake for Marg. It's the

---

* Possibly Bennett Clark, Truman's fellow U.S. Senator from Missouri.
** Edward R. Burke, a senator for Nebraska, was not renominated for his seat in 1940.

first time she has asked for one for two months so I just got busy—

I guess you are on your way to Kahoka [Missouri] today. Hope you are having better weather than we are. It's pouring and getting <u>cold</u>.

Mrs. Hatch's luncheon was <u>very nice</u>— Then Miss Kerr asked me to pour at a tea she was having.

Later, Marg & I went down to the Point & had a round of golf. It was a gorgeous day— & too nice to stay in.

We are going to the office after school to get the inevitable bread & papers.

Good luck for Monday!—

Lots of love—
Bess

✸1941

In the spring of 1941, with the Germans and Japanese gobbling up Europe and Asia, respectively, both interventionists and isolationists agreed on the need for a strong national defense and voted $25 billion to expand the navy, build training camps, and boost defense industries like steel and aluminum.

Early in 1941, Grandpa discovered, to his consternation, that 90 percent of the money allotted for the construction of Fort Leonard Wood in Missouri was going to giant corporations from the Northeast. Shortly after, he proposed creating a committee to investigate these expenditures. President Roosevelt praised the idea but immediately worked behind the scenes to stifle it in ways such as having the Senate Audit and Control Committee vote to budget the fledgling Truman Committee a measly $15,000. Grandpa sidestepped the president's attempts by paying his staff through other government agencies. He also made sure he had no Roosevelt yes-men on the committee.

He and his crew went after the new training camp building program and in short order discovered that architects and contractors were earning up to 1,669 percent over their usual annual profits. Much to my grand-mother's delight, these revelations brought respect and recognition from the very papers that had vilified Grandpa the year before.

As Grandpa flew around the country investigating, my grandmother, the fearful flyer, worried about him. "It was a tremendous relief to get your phone call last night," she wrote when he had landed safely. "I kept watch-ing the clouds toward the south and southwest and they didn't look so cheerful." She preferred trains, unless "some goof" was hogging the writing table in the lounge car.

Actually, she spent a lot of time in the front seat of her automobile, parked out front of voice teacher Margaret Strickler's house while Mom took her voice lesson. At this point, it was beginning to look like Mom had the makings of a pro.

My grandmother also mentions visiting Mamma and Mary Truman, which was especially important at this time since a vindictive, anti-Pendergast county court judge, in an attempt to embarrass Grandpa, had foreclosed on the Grandview farm, forcing Mamma Truman and Great-Aunt Mary into a small house in town.

My grandmother had a maternal attitude not only toward her own family but toward the families of friends and staff members as well. More than once, she prodded Grandpa to do something for somebody—write a note, pay a visit, or intercede if he could.

The National Limited, B&O [letterhead]*
[August 15, 1941]
Friday.

Dear Harry—

It is now 9:30 and I'm about to turn in am writing in my room—Some goof has been attached to the desk in the lounge for a solid hour so I finally gave up— Luckily I brought your pen along— you surely were right, it's an awful job to fill it.

Had a good dinner— but also had a gabby woman across the table. Her husband came in with her but didn't stay long. She said he was ill— he looked to me as if he was just getting over the DT's.

Hope you and Mr. Vaughan found a good place to eat— & that you are now at home, in bed.

We ran into a big rain just north of Silver Spgs.— lots of lightning etc. Hope to goodness it gets all the storm out of its system before tomorrow— either that, or that you are grounded.

Am glad to see there is a heavy blanket on my bed. This train is really chilly— but at least the air seems fresh.

Will be anxious to hear from you tomorrow—
Love
Bess

* The train on the Baltimore & Ohio Railroad route between New York and St. Louis, which also stopped in Washington, DC.

[Independence, Mo.]
[August 17, 1941]
Sunday—

Dear Harry—

Nine o'clock & I guess you are out in the middle of the wide open spaces & here I am just up & had my bath.

It was a tremendous relief to get your phone call last night. I kept watching the clouds toward the south & southwest and they didn't look so cheerful.

I had a most comfortable trip— even slept like a log— the steward knew who I was and asked about you and was very attentive.

Ethel & Nellie have gone to Mexico City— the rumor is that Jack went too— but I will have to get that confirmed as long as it came from the Whaley ménage.

Ardis & Herb are staying with your Aunt Ella.

Marg called Mary right after she stopped talking to you & your mother was fine.

Everybody seems alright except Frank— he is as tired as ever— but not going away.

There is a wonderful breeze this morning but it's going to be a warmish day— Everything looks nice & green. I was so afraid I'd find things burned up.

Will surely be listening for the phone late this afternoon. If you have time you might call Miss Jessie in San Marina & don't forget that Ben Bee died about two months ago. And Harriett's address is Picardo Arms Apt. 2491 Ellsworth— Berkeley.

Love from both of us

Bess

[Independence, Mo.]
[August 18, 1941]
Monday—

Dear Harry—

Marg and I were delighted to get your Dallas letters yesterday just after I had finished writing to you— and I was especially glad to have your very nice Wash. Air Spec. this morning— I was secretly glad that things worked out as they did on Friday— I was rather dreading going to the train without you— & felt I got a "break" & you were not delayed after all.

It's raining this morning & is much cooler after a torrid yesterday— As I told you M. & I went out to see your mother & Mary & take them the Fannie May [candy] I bought & they were both well & your mother didn't seem to be minding the heat a bit. I called Mary right after I hung up from your call last night & they were relieved to know you were there safely.

Hope you get lots of helpful information from the L.A. hearings & don't have to work too hard to get it.

I told Mr. Vaughan I wanted him to come out to dinner one night when he is in K.C. & he said he would be mighty glad to.

Fred said they are pounding Mize again— this time on his hand-writing! Pres. Moss told <u>him</u> he would have to <u>write better</u> or get out— so M. is taking <u>writing lessons</u>— & they rescinded his vacation so Fred thinks that he's probably still on probation. Lucy is awfully sunk about <u>some-thing</u>— I talked to her this a.m.

Hope to have some other mail on apt. delivery—

Love—
Bess

[Independence, Mo.]
[August 19, 1941]
Tuesday—

Dear Harry—

Was mighty glad to get two air mails this morning— a belated one from Dallas and the first one from L.A.

I am now sitting out in front of Maj. Strickler's [husband of Mom's voice teacher]. Needless to say Marg is taking her lesson. Have I told you Maj. had a relapse & has been pretty sick again? They are staying at the lake & I think <u>today</u> is the first time he has been at the office for weeks & the Dr. is allowing him just <u>two hours</u> today. Margaret (S.) says he is awfully jittery—

I hope the "Mrs. Paul" who called was Nelle Rugg—

When you get to that camp or post near San Francisco you had bet-ter call the Meyers at Carmel— "Sundial Court Apts." Maybe Monterey is the nearest post to them— I can't remember what Chris said—

Enjoyed reading the clippings— & will save them. Ed Karnes had a <u>very nice</u> editorial in the *Exam.* last night about your committee & you. Imagine that! "Willie" is in Manitou.

I wouldn't trade weather with you— it's simply great— but I would like to be in Calif.

M. & I are going out to Souters this evening and spend the evening raving over their "Scott" I guess. Eugene got a Brahms concerto yester-day— that he thinks is marvelous— & he wants Marg to hear it— Guess he really has some lovely records. Wish you were going, too.

I read your speech etc. in the *Record* yesterday. Sounded OK.
Have a little fun on the side if you can—
Love
Bess

[Independence, Mo.]
[August 20, 1941]
Wednesday—

Dear Harry—

I was greatly disappointed when I didn't find a letter this morning—
but am hoping for much better luck this afternoon. I <u>did</u> have a letter
from Harriette & she said she had talked to you and was delighted to hear
from you etc. at much length.

Marg & I spent most of yesterday in KC and I talked her out of a fur
coat by telling her she could have a lot more clothes for the fall & winter
if a fur coat didn't have to be part of her wardrobe— She apparently is
completely happy over not having the coat— and we got a three piece suit
(with a long coat she can wear separately) and a pair of shoes and will fill
in the <u>gaps</u> some day soon.

It is delightfully chilly this morning.

Marg & Natalie Henkes are going to KC to see Mickey Rooney— N.
is going home the last of the week—

The musicale at Souters last night was really lovely— It's amazing to
me the type of records Eugene is buying—

How do you like living in such a swanky hotel?

Marg is going to mail this for me— so goodbye 'til tomorrow—
Love
Bess

[Independence, Mo.]
[August 20, 1941]
Wed. afternoon

Dear Harry—

This is #2 today and I didn't <u>get</u> a single one!

Julia Rice Latimer called me few minutes ago & said her son Billie
is in the Station Hospital at San Luis Obispo— & is most anxious just
to speak to you. He left here in March with other draftees & has been in
the hospital several weeks with a bad knee which was not taken care of
at the right time. If there is any chance of you getting out there to see the
boy she would like to know just how serious the trouble is— etc. Is terribly worried of course. She didn't want to be any bother— she thought

you hadn't gone yet— The boy had written you were going to inspect
the hospital & he was afraid he wouldn't be allowed to speak to you or
something. So I offered to write to you—

If I don't hear early tomorrow you'll be getting a reversed call—

Lou Holland is on your trail— also a Mr. McCord who wants you
to go to Neosho for something or other— I imagine the dedication of the
new Camp.

Love
Bess

This is Maurice Latimer's boy.

[Independence, Mo.]
[August 21, 1941]
Thursday—

Dear Harry—

You just saved your neck by getting a letter here on this afternoon's
delivery. I know you are plenty busy so I'll forgive you not getting one
here yesterday (as long as I can't do anything about it).

I took Natalie & Julia to lunch at the Westport Room today— I had
let two summers go by without doing anything for J. so I decided I'd better not let another.

It is a perfectly marvelous day— would be a grand day for a trip or a
picnic— but have neither in sight.

We are going down to the Lake for Marg's lesson tomorrow and
Margaret [Strickler] asked us to stay for dinner & said we'd have a boat
ride before dinner— I could do without the boat ride.

Hope you get the letter about Billie Latimer in time to see him—
Julia seemed so distressed about him.

Did you talk to Nelle Paul? Was she in LA?

I probably told you how delighted Harriette was, that you called
her.

Have enjoyed the clippings—

Mr. Shannon [the Head Democratic Rabbit] was eating lunch in the
Westport Room all by himself— He didn't see me so I didn't dash over to
speak to him—

Take it as easy as you can.

Love
Bess

[Independence, Mo.]
[August 22, 1941]
Friday— 2 p.m.

Dear Harry—

Was glad to get a letter just now. Was afraid you might have been too busy yesterday to write. I didn't know you were going back to LA. Thought you would go right to SF from San Diego—

It looks to me as if you are really getting some valuable information.

I hope you had a chance to talk to Miss Jessie—

Guess you think the best (largest) part of Missouri has moved out to Calif. Had no idea Jim Taylor & Dr. Woolley were out there.

Margaret Ott [Natalie Ott Wallace's mother] is sick again— they aren't putting out anything about her but Mrs. Bundschu's nurse told Natalie that her arm is badly swollen— It's perfectly evident all of those lumps they've taken out in the past year were malignant in spite of what they said. They hadn't even told Natalie that she was sick so N. doesn't know what to do about going out etc. They are so queer about illness in the family— you'd think they were all [Christian] Scientists—

Went over to see your Aunt Ella yesterday— she was worrying herself half sick because she hasn't heard from E. & N. [Ethel and Nellie] when she thought she should. I think Ardis is having quite a job— Jack did go with them.

Your friend Mr. Short from Spgfld [Springfield] dropped in Wed. for a few minutes. He's as breezy and loud as ever. He thought you were here.

M. & I are going to Lotawana in a little while if it doesn't pour cats and dogs—

Will put a Special on this as it won't get there before Sunday I'm sure & I have no idea whether they deliver mail at big hotels on Sunday or not.

Love
Bess

[Independence, Mo.]
[August 25, 1941]
Monday—

Dear Harry—

Again, I am perched out in front of M. Strickler's while Marg has a lesson.

It was a tremendous relief when you called last night— I felt a little anxious most of the day for some reason or other. I stayed home most of the day and evening thinking a wire might come & Mother would not get it straight.

I talked to your mother this morning early & she was glad to know you had landed safely <u>once more</u>. I'll be glad when you get on the ground again for <u>some time</u>.

Mother has a cousin, Mrs. Isaac (or Flora) (Kenwood 0470) Nichols in Seattle & if you <u>have time</u> you might try to call her & tell her that Mother wanted you to— Her son-in-law is a big banker in S. but for the life of me I can't remember his name & I forgot to ask Mother. She keeps up with Cousin Flora to a certain extent.

There were <u>three</u> telephone calls for H. Vaughan before I left home. They evidently have not reached KC as there was no one at your office. Am planning to have him to dinner tomorrow night.

Marg has another date with Tom tomorrow— Adelaide said he was quite "impressed" with M. Am glad it is one-sided— Adelaide was thoroughly delighted, I think, at the way they had mended her cup—

It's hotter'n Hades out here today. Am going to meet Chris down town. Marg is going to meet Harriett Allen & go to lunch with her & her guest.

Said she would write to you tonight.

Take care of yourself.

Love—
Bess

[Independence, Mo.]
[August 26, 1941]
Tuesday—

Dear Harry—

I have just talked to H. Vaughan & he is coming out to dinner tomorrow— I didn't take the time to ask him how things were coming but he said he had just sent you an Air Mail to Seattle so you will know everything about it as soon as you get this anyway— & perhaps sooner.

Marg & I are most anxious to see our gifts from Chinatown— they sound <u>very interesting</u>.

Do you have any definite date for starting back to Wash? Have you decided to stop off here and drive back with us? I think Mother has decided to go for a little visit— and I thot [*sic*] we had better be <u>ready</u> by the <u>third,</u> in case you come right on from Salt Lake. If you have any brighter ideas on that subject, let me know so we won't delay things. I feel as if I am sort of working in the dark— but I guess it's not a matter of any importance whether it's the third or tenth— <u>but</u> if M. & I are going to do the driving, I'm going to get ready & get off and get it over with.

We really had a storm last night— M. & I had gone out to Mrs. Graves' and were stuck there. Wind, rain & lightning— it blew KMBC down & smashed a house and KCKN is wrecked too. Plenty of trees etc. are down here.

Am so glad you got to see Mr. Thatcher— that was worth the whole trip—

Have to take Mother to the dress makers—

Love—
Bess

[Independence, Mo.]
[August 28, 1941]
Thursday—

Dear Harry—

Was glad to have a letter before I left home this morning— Am now sitting in front of 630 – W. 69th for a change. I don't know what has become of my letters— (maybe they <u>did</u> arrive after all). I didn't write yesterday for I had no Spokane address & up to that time you had said you were leaving Seattle on <u>Wed</u>. I called HV [Harry Vaughan] & he said he had no address there either. He had dinner with us last night & seemed to enjoy it & the family all enjoyed him. He stayed until eleven o'clock so I took it for granted he had a good time. He is "doing" Lake City & the Fairfax Bombing Plant today & starts home tomorrow stopping off at Glasgow for his family.

Why not let M. and me start on to Wash. & then if you want to meet us at Wheeling or Wash, PA that last night out, it won't be so much of a trip for you. We can be ready to leave by Thursday or Friday of next week & be in Wash. by the time you'd get out here & Col. Vaughan says they're just like a bunch of vultures waiting for you. Some man called this morning & asked when you were coming and I told him I didn't think you were coming at all & he had the nerve to say, "Well, I'll call again in a day or two & see!"

It's cloudy and cool and <u>very</u> pleasant.

M. Strickler says Marg is making remarkable progress and she wants her to sing for that tall hat teacher of hers, in N.Y. around Easter when she will be there!

Mary called yesterday and said Stanley had just told them your mother's eyes are <u>greatly</u> improved!

Am enjoying the clippings & keeping them.

You got a paragraph in the *Church of England News*— on MRA.*

Everybody is fine. Take care of yourself. Am surely glad you didn't go to Alaska.

Love

Bess

[Independence, Mo.]

[August 29, 1941]

Friday—

Dear Harry—

Geo. Marquis has called & said he had had a letter from Dr. Mather saying that you wanted him (Geo. M.) to write your biographical sketch for Grand Lodge— Mr. M. wants to know <u>at once please</u> if that is so. He says he most certainly does not want to "horn in" but he felt he should follow up Dr. M.'s letter— as he had to write Harry Chiles' on ten hours' notice & he didn't want to do <u>that</u> again. He will be in town the first of next week and will get the data etc. then <u>if</u> you want him to do it.

This insurance notice I found in the car today— some of Marg's carelessness in not mailing it—

The wonderful box of candy arrived in perfect order & M. & I are surely enjoying it. Thanks a million for sending it— it really is delicious—

No letter this morning, but I guess you are moving around too much to get one in.

I am going to take Mother to the city this morning. She wants to get a hat & coat & dress— I sure dread the trip— she won't find anything at the prices she will want to pay, I'm afraid.

The pup bit Marian [Wallace, Fred's daughter] yesterday and now we have that to worry about for ten days more. Have to keep him [the dog] [locked] up to see if anything develops. It seems the Pasteur treatment is quite an ordeal in itself so they don't give it unless it is absolutely necessary.

Mrs. George Collins called & said Maj. Collins wants to see you five minutes— (or she does— can't remember which she said) about a "high-way"— (or am I nuts?). He is back in a hospital— not doing well at all.

Hate to think of you flying again tomorrow & again next week—

Must hurry along—

Love

Bess

---

* Possibly Moral Re-Armament, a popular movement in which Truman was interested.

[Independence, Mo.]
[August 30, 1941]
Saturday—

Dear Harry—

We are really having a <u>concert</u> this morning— M. Strickler came
here to give Marg her lesson and we have surely enjoyed it. Am anxious to
have you hear Marg after all these lessons this summer. Hope you see the
same amount of improvement I do.

Was glad to have the letter from Spokane this a.m. & am so glad you
could see the Schwellenbachs & have dinner with them.

Afternoon

M. Strickler stayed to lunch & we had lots of fun, but she left soon
after as Maj. is having twenty of his supervisors to a picnic dinner tonight
& as she said, she had a <u>few</u> things to do.

We went to see your mother last night & took her the gas heater we
had in the attic for her to use in the fireplace— Mary thought her local
gas man could fix it up so it would do the job. She said she felt fine &
certainly looked that way—

It's hotter'n the hinges of H today— and more promised for tomorrow and Monday—

Well, I guess they put too much heat on Chief Reed— he just quit
under fire. Imagine most of them would wilt under some investigation.

Have to go to town—

Love
Bess

🌀1942 and 1943

Grandpa was now making headlines with the Truman Committee's investigation of waste and fraud in military spending… and my grandmother was gleefully cheering him on. Grandpa also made headlines at home by sending her twenty-three red roses on June 28, their twenty-third anniversary. With the flowers came the kind of sentimental, romantic letter that he'd been sending her since 1910.

Despite the enormous good he was doing with the Truman Committee, there was nothing Grandpa could do about the course of the war itself. Despite the victory at Midway, things were not going well for the Allies. "Looks as if we had better send some smart Americans over there to run the war for them," my grandmother said of the British. "Not that we have done too well ourselves." In 1940, Grandpa, still a colonel in the National Guard, approached General George Marshall about serving as an artillery officer. "You're too damn old," Marshall told him. "You're three years older than I am," Grandpa said. "I know," Marshall replied, "but I'm already a general."

The Truman Committee at work, 1942 (TL 66-2143).

237

Many of my grandparents' friends and family were in harm's way. Grandpa's aide, Harry Vaughan, was an Army colonel stationed in Australia, which the Japanese seemed poised to invade. Paxton "Pax" Keeley, the only son of my grandmother's oldest friend, Mary Paxton Keeley, had enlisted in the infantry. And Brigadier General Charles Drake, husband of my grandmother's cousin Maud Gates, was trapped on Bataan in the Philippines.

In the spring of 1943, when Grandpa had again worked himself into a frazzle and checked into an Army hospital, my grandmother was on the job as usual, worrying about his health and deeply suspicious that he wasn't telling her everything. But as usual, she could ignore her own woes. As they had twenty years earlier, painful teeth again plagued her, but that didn't stop her from taking Mom to voice lessons or getting Mom to try to learn to swim.

And just to remind Grandpa that being a senator and making headlines should not give him too swelled a head, she frequently gave him shopping lists. In 1942, she asked him to fetch her talcum powder, Mom's pink box of body powder, and a white slip from the closet. "That's all I can think of to bother you with," she concluded, "but I guess Marg gave you another list."

Still, he was accustomed to, and capable of, domesticity. "The rug cleaned up fine," he wrote. "Had to iron some tonight. The d—d laundry sent some wet clothes back, two pajamas, underwear, and some handkerchiefs."

One letter mentions Roger Sermon, the mayor of Independence who blew into office on an anti-Pendergast, and therefore anti-Truman, ticket. Obviously, he was not one of my grandmother's favorites.

Washington D.C.
June 15, 1942

Dear Bess:

Just got in from the speech, and got your telegram over the phone. I'm so glad you could listen in. If I'd been sure I'd have said hello to you. It's been quite hectic getting ready. The one speech I found when I returned was no good so we went to work on a new one. After we got it outlined, Bill & Malletts worked all night Monday night on it and got it ready by seven fifteen when I went down. Then it had to be mimeographed, distributed and read three or four times, and on top of that I had to make another statement on the oil situation on the West Coast to the Senate, decide on the conversion report, make a date to hear Nelson and see the King of Greece. Some day I'd say.

Fulton had me out to his apartment for dinner last night and I went with John Snyder, Nat Brown, President of the 1st National Bank of Chicago, and Mr. Fairchild from the Boatman's Bank in St. Louis & Tom K. Smith, Stark's treasurer & President of the Boatman's. I asked him how his double crossing Gov. was getting along and he changed the subject. John then went to the broadcasting station with me— and then to the office where we read three letters from Harry Vaughan which came today and one which came a day or two ago.

Then we discussed Mo. politics, John's future and the war. I took him home at ten o'clock after we had a drink of water. By the way, Bennett told me today that he'd heard about me & Neal— and that he'd gone on the wagon! Hope it's so but it's hard to believe.

Tomorrow's another day too. Suggest you read the record of today and you'll see what's transpired about the Standard of Calif. It's a real one too.

It was cold as the dickens here last night. Had to shut the window. Today has been an ideal one. Clear & cool wind northwest but it warmed up tonight.

No letters yet— but the telegram helped.

Kiss Margie— Love to you. Say hello to the family.

Harry.

[Independence, Mo.]
[June 16, 1942]
Tuesday—

Dear Harry—

Your speech last night was really "somethin'"— I think it was the best radio speech I have heard you make. Ethel & Lucy called up & of course said many nice things. Your radio "technique" really has improved immensely— Ethel said your consonants were all pronounced just as her speech teacher had taught her. In your "spare time" it really would be a good idea to take a few speech lessons if you are going to be on the radio from now on— But if you keep on doing as well as you did last night you won't need any.

It's still cold and cloudy and I'm about to take off for Biloxi or somewhere else— just so there is a little sunshine.

Was the apartment very dusty? Did they start the milk on time & did you get some bread on the way home? Mr. Dayberry is here fixing the bathroom door— you will agree it surely needed fixing.

Natalie & Marg are going to K.C. to get a settlement on that record that was broken.

Let me know if the keys get there alright— The *Post* generally gets there on Wed. & your *Life* on Thurs.

Did you hear [columnist Drew] Pearson & Allen Sunday? Am anxious to know if the report is made today etc. One of the news broadcasters at ten last night mentioned you in connection with the rubber drive.

Is there any further word of H. H. V. [Harry H. Vaughan]?

Last night's paper said 685 were leaving Shanghai on June 23rd for Port. E. Africa* so maybe Leighton will get there after all—

Frank seems better— he took quite a long trip up into Platte County yesterday. Hoping for a letter today. We don't get any mail until after eleven—

Love

Bess

Washington D.C.

June 17, 1942

Dear Bess:

Your extremely lovely letter came today. I guess I am making progress sure enough. That was the most important radio speech I have made because it was more widely broadcast and because it was on the most vital subject affecting the war effort. Lots of work was put in on it and I was most anxious for it to be believed as founded on actual facts. If you say it sounded convincing it must have been. Thank Ethel & Lucy. Of course I need instruction, but I've been too busy to get it— and too timid I guess.

No the apartment was not dirty at all. The milk started on time and I got some bread— eventually— and the keys came OK.

I didn't hear Pearson & Allen Sunday but someone told me they were needling me. I postponed the date of release out of courtesy to Nelson expecting him to come and talk to me— but he talked to Tom Connally and Tom called him to see me. He came down at 9:30. Tom came and Sen. Burton happened in. Nelson really told me how I'd ruin his setup and stop the war if I made the report. He'd sent me a nasty letter and when he got all through I told [him] just what I thought and what I expected to do. I told him what I thought of his help and what would happen to him if he continued with some of his most outstanding SOB's, that the report would be made as agreed on by the whole Committee

---

* Portuguese East Africa, today Mozambique.

and that I wasn't running the Committee for the W.P.B. [War Production Board] but for the Senate & in the Public interest as the Committee & I saw it. Then I called the Committee together at 2:30 told 'em what had happened and to a man— except Tom and he said he wouldn't oppose me— they backed me up and suggested I make it tougher. Mead, Herring, Kilgore, Brewster, Ball, Burton and Connally were there. Hatch was out of town but I had his vote and Walgren [Wallgren] was in Washington State & I had his vote. How's that for handling Prima Donnas? Wheeler says we all are so I guess it's no insult. So she goes in tomorrow and I'll be skinned by the "kept press" but it's right. Kiss my baby. Love to you. We're having an all-night black out & I'm in the hall.

Harry.

Millie had a nice dinner with Frank Erhart, John Snyder, Bill & the office girls. It was buffet style. Fried chicken, beans green, potatoe [sic] salad, hot biscuits, two kinds of cake, ice tea & coffee. Everybody had to leave at 9 o'clock because the all-night black out started at ten. What I mean it's black, too. The buses I came home on were jammed. I got here just twenty minutes to ten, watered the flowers, got ready for bed, read my speech for tomorrow & wrote to you.

I didn't enjoy Millie's dinner much because I had one of my usual fits* just before I left the office— caused by all the fuss I'd had I guess but I'm ok now & will be in bed pretty soon.

[Independence, Mo.]
[June 23, 1942]
Tuesday—

Dear Harry—

Your Friday letter arrived yesterday— good service— but I was glad to get it anyway. All of the Air Mails are the second day getting here.

I read the *Record* for the 18th yesterday— & enjoyed it hugely— hope the 19th will come today— What's the matter with Scott Lucas? It's somebody else getting the headlines that's bothering Tom C. [Connally]

I hope you can do something for Bill Nix—

Marg & I are quite excited about the new piano— What make did they send out? Is it the same size? [*Illegible*] is supposed to come this morning to tune this one— but I've waited a whole week for him.

Did Mrs. Ricketts let the piano people in or how did you arrange about that? It's too bad you had to bother with it on top of everything else.

* Probably referring to the gall bladder attacks he had been suffering since the spring of 1941.

I wish while you were feeling so "cranky" you had clamped down on Mrs. R. & told her we had to have some painting & papering done this fall.

M. & I are going to K.C. today to get Natalie's birthday present and Sen. Connally's wedding present.

It is still very chilly but thank goodness the sun is shining.

Did your belt fit alright?

Maybe Dave B. won't be pestering you quite so much from now on— Bet Schonberg wishes he had the money back he spent on M's graduating present!

Aren't you supposed to help break ground for Pratt & Whitney on July 4th?

Mr. Hodge told Fred yesterday he was sure he had gotten a good job for Frank Meyer with P & W so at last maybe Frank got a job.

Did Erhart go to England? Looks as if we had better send some smart Americans over there to run the war for them— not that we have done too well ourselves.

Love
Bess—

Washington D.C.
June 23, 1942

Dear Bess:

Two letters from you today, one from Margie and one from Mary— a pretty good haul I'd say, even Capt. Kidd should be satisfied with one that rich.

One more busy day. Met Fred C. & Boyle at the office early this morning and discussed everything under the sun. Have come to the conclusion that the Republican lobbyist is really doing business. Gave Dick Nacy's letter to Brewster— the one in which he mentioned that he'd had dinner at the Monroe's house at 2101 R Street with Austin, Bridges, Gurney, and Brewster from the Senate and a couple of Colonels from the army procurement section and some naval officers. You'd have enjoyed Brewster's look of surprise. I said "Well it looks like Tommy the [*illegible*] is a piker." He left the committee meeting right away and I ran into him about seven thirty tonight when I was going into the Mayflower dining room with Neal Helm and John Snyder.

He introduced me to some Army Brigade General and a Colonel & said he wanted to talk with me tomorrow. Saw Dick and Mrs. Duncan in the lobby too. She said she is going home in a day or two. Neal is still on the wagon 100% and he sure looks fine. Said his wife is the happiest old lady in southeast Mo. and that she'd hug & kiss me at the first opportunity. You'd better protect me. I'm not sorry I got him to quit though and neither do I think it would hurt me for a while. Went to three committee meetings. One of my own on gasoline transportation one of the Agricultural subcommittee where Norris presided for Gillette and O'Mahoney testified on steel & iron and threw the ball to me and I caught it.

Had lunch with [James] Forestal, under Sec. of the Navy. He wanted me to take up Naval Investigation in earnest. [Fred] Vinson's attorney for the House Naval Committee died and Vinson is about to quit investigating. Forrestal paid me high compliments. I don't know what's on the fire. Had a meeting of Appropriations and another knock down & drag out with [Kenneth] McKeller. He or I, one, is getting balmy. Same thing over tomorrow.

The rug cleaned up fine. Had to iron some tonight— The d—d laundry sent some wet clothes back, two pajamas underwear and some handkerchiefs. Will do what I can for Mrs. King. There may be a recess. If so I'll wait. Kiss Margie. Love to you.

Harry.

Washington D.C.
June 28, 1942

Dear Bess:

Well this is *the day*. Lots of water has gone over the dam. There've been some terrible days and many more nice ones. When my store went flooy and cost my friends and Frank money, when Margie came, don't think I ever spent such a day, although the pains were yours. And to name one more, when we thought Stark had won and when I lost actually for eastern judge. But the wins have far outweighed 'em. June 28, 1919, was the happiest day of my life, for I had been looking forward to it for a lifetime nearly or so it seemed. When a man gets the right kind of a wife, his career is made— and I got just that.

The greatest thing we have is a real young lady who hasn't an equal anywhere. That's all the excuse we need for living and not much else matters.

It was grand to say hello last night. I was so tired I could hardly sit up. Went to bed right away after playing Margie's song record and the Minuet (in G) and Chopin waltzes. It's pretty lonesome around there without you...

Kiss Margie, lots and lots of love and happy returns,

Harry

[Independence, Mo.]
Sunday—
June 28—

Dear Harry—

Thank you very much for the lovely roses— all twenty three of them— and for the lovelier letter, which really arrived when it should have. It always amazes me that you can write a so called love letter when you have had so little practice— Anyway it was very nice— especially so, coming on one's <u>twenty-third</u> anniversary. It doesn't seem at all possible it had been that long but I'm pretty sure it has—

Why didn't you have Canfil stay all the time with you— did you prefer a little breathing spell? I hope you found another sheet & clean pillow cases for him. I didn't tell you where they are— (top shelf in bathroom & the narrower sheets are in the center pile).

If you have room in your new bags you might bring my Yardley talc powder in [the] bathrm. & Marg's pink box of body powder on [the] window sill in [the] bathroom. If you think Marg's won't come thru without breaking just bring mine. I can get her some for 50¢. Also look just on the first hook at the right in our closet & see if there is a <u>short</u> white slip there. That's all I can think of to bother you with— but I guess Marg gave you another list.

This is one warm day— and I am staying right at home. Did a huge ironing early this morning—

I hope you & Canfil have nice weather for your trip— & please take it easy— you'll get a sort of rest by spending the time on the road— You are supposed to help dedicate the new amphitheater here on the first with the Hon.(?) Mr. Sermon. If half of what Wills told me yesterday about Rog is true he ought to be "<u>impeached</u>." You might set one of your investigators on him— (preferably Canfil!).

Dinner is ready— wish you were here to eat it with us.

Would like to see Ms. Kerr's letter.

I hope you are not working <u>all</u> day.

Frank said he wired you yesterday about the grain man coming— I think he is on the verge of losing his mind over the mill's situation.

Am glad you will be by <u>next</u> Tuesday.

Love & many thanks again for the grand remembrances—

Bess

I'll be ready to go any day <u>you</u> are.

Washington D.C.
June 29, 1942

Dear Bess:—

Well here I am back in the office again after a real day of rest. I went home about 3 o'clock and read the papers and then went to bed about six o'clock and didn't get up until six this morning. The milk didn't come yesterday, but I guess I'll get two today. I'm going to stop it and the papers, too, before I leave so we won't have anything on hand to worry about. I am enclosing you the letter from Miss Kerr and a couple of other communications. Tell Margie I forgot to enclose her movie magazine with the Sunday papers, but I'll send it today. I'll just put all the communications in one envelope and send them together so as not to delay your air mail letter.

I have a terrible day in front of me. A conference on the Relief Bill, an interview at the White House with the Housing Administration, Edsel Ford and McIntyre.* Anyway they've found I'm here, but they still kick me in the nose when it comes the other way. Just vetoed a bill that is absolutely essential to straighten out Platte County for Duncan. The Army Engineers caused a flood up there in an off year and now they don't want to accept the responsibility and the Pres. backs 'em up.

If everything works out I should leave here at noon on Wednesday. But I've scads of things to do.

Hope everyone is well. Love to you. Momma had a fine day and enjoyed it immensely. Made a note of it specially. It was a lonesome anniversary. Hope we can spend one together sometime.

Harry.

[Independence, Mo.]
[June 29, 1942]
Monday— 8:15 a.m.

Dear Harry—

The roses are still beautiful this morning in spite of a very warm yesterday. Today is not quite so bad & there is a black cloud in the northwest.

Marg is taking her voice lesson this a.m. so I hope it postpones raining until about one o'clock. She went to a show with Tom last night but I don't think she enjoyed it an awful lot. He leaves for Leavenworth on the 15th.

---

* Edsel Ford (1893–1943) was the son of Henry Ford and president of Ford Motor Company from 1919 until his death in 1943. McIntyre may refer to Marvin McIntyre, who was FDR's correspondence secretary from 1941 until his death in 1943.

I surely hope your clothes come back all ironed tomorrow. If you didn't leave word for Annie May not to come next Sat. etc. tell Ralph to get word to her— an aunt of hers works for somebody in the building. In case you are rushed, don't forget to pay the rent the day you leave. If the other bills have come, bring them along so I can check them. Maybe we had better have the apt. mail sent on here— <u>not to the office</u>.

Don't bother about leaving the apt. all <u>cleaned </u>up— you will have plenty to do just to get off.

I am anxious to see your new luggage— did you think of asking them at Becker's if you could have the Guatamala [*sic*] bag fitted up inside with a rack etc.?

Fred has been in Excelsior since Friday going to a W.P.B. [War Production Board] "school." They are finishing up today. He was offered a $4,600 job in Denver with [*illegible*] but he is staying with W.P.B. as he thinks he will get that, by fall, here.

I hope you didn't work too hard yesterday— I had a very lazy day & felt very guilty.

Love

Bess

Washington D.C.

June 30, 1942

Dear Bess:—

I didn't get any letter yesterday. I suppose your letter was a half interest in Margaret's or maybe I'll get two today. I am sending her pictures and magazines by mail. Forgot to tell her that. Will you tell her?

The committee
on the road,
1942
(TL 2006-78).

I have it from the State Dept. that Leighton Shields will leave China today and go to Porto Laurenco [Lourenco] in Portuguese East Africa and be home in a couple of months. Breck Long told me at lunch day before yesterday. I was afraid to write Mrs. S. for fear there might be a slip up. I'll call [illegible] today and try to get confirmation and then wire her.*

Arthur Wilson is back. He called me last night and I'm to see him at seven thirty this morning. I have a date with Gen. Marshall at 9:15 and I should hear all the low down on the War Dept. Canfil and I will leave at noon tomorrow and in all probability land home Friday night. I hope so anyway. My spade job at the engine plant starts at 9 a.m. But I may be late. It is with much dread that I face the Jackson County situation. But it has to be done. It looks as if Roger has completely balled the Jack and that it can't be unballed. We'll see. Harry Easley will be offered over the good-for-nothing Hatton man because I'm going to support Donnelly. Roger switched Noels on me and agreed to old Montgomery. Now I think I'll start from taw** and organize a ticket that some of the ward leaders and all the county can support and then leave for Hot Springs. Hope I get two letters today. Going out to Bill's for dinner. How do you like my new stationary [sic]?

Kiss Margie. Love to you.

Harry.

[Independence, Mo.]
[July 22, 1942]
Wednesday

Dear Harry—

Just time for a brief one. Our friend M. Woodson asked Marg & me to have lunch with her at the Muehlbach today. She has a young guest & besides she wants to write a Pi Phi letter for M. & I guess she wants to look her over.***

It was a grand surprise to hear your voice early this morning when I expected to hear some nut ask, "Is Sen. T. there?" Am so glad you had a prolonged nap yesterday—

---

* Leighton Shields, the lawyer whom my grandmother had prodded Grandpa to help (which he did by sending him to Shanghai), had been interned by the Japanese during the invasion of China. His wife implored Grandpa to intervene, but Leighton managed to get out on his own. He later practically camped in Grandpa's office, demanding a new job. Grandpa finally got him a job in the Attorney General's office.

** The line from which players shoot in a game of marbles.

*** Margaret Truman joined the Pi Beta Phi sorority while attending George Washington University.

I called your mother about eight o'clock & found Mary at home (her day off).

Will have time tomorrow to write a longer letter—

Love

Bess

Washington D.C.
July 22, 1942

Dear Bess:—

This day really started off right— there was a <u>letter</u> in the first mail. I'd no more than put the phone down until the boy came in all full of grins and handed me the letter. It made the day start right.

Fulton came in and talked for 30 minutes much to Millie's disgust, then Bill took a turn at me and then each of the girls wanted some special instructions, and then came the Committee on Detroit Housing and then the Senate.

The photographer who took Margie's picture at the Pearson & Allen show at Keith's gave me a copy which I'm sending you. It's a grand picture of both Margie and the old guy who is with her.

I'm having a committee meeting in my office in fifteen minutes with the War Dept. on policy. Hope it works out. Will have dinner with Nelson at the Sulgrave Club tonight and all the Committee was invited to discuss the rubber situation. That's one way to hold a hearing anyway.

I've had one heck of a day— and it isn't over yet. I was awake when we went through Indp. and I wanted to get off but too much is at stake. I've set the wheels in motion for some terrific things to come. Steel, ships, housing and some ordinance contracts.

Hope you find my discharge button. It sure was nice to talk to you.

Kiss Margie. Love to you. My best to everybody.

Harry.

[Independence, Mo.]
[July 23, 1942]
Thursday—

Dear Harry—

Surely was glad to have your letter this morning. I guess you are <u>really</u> busy again. The *Star* had a column on you & the Higgins mess, so I judge you won't have any spare time.

This enclosed card [missing] is some more of the Jenkins broken record, so if you have any time you might stop & sign up for Marg. There was just <u>one</u> record broken out of an album of 3 or 4.

We really had a <u>very</u> nice time with the Woodsons yesterday. Their young guest is very attractive & Marg liked her a lot and asked her to luncheon tomorrow. I am taking the Minons & Louise McCoy to lunch at the Westport Room tomorrow— am greatly indebted to the Minons and never have done anything for Louise in all the many visits she has made at home.

It's the most gorgeous weather— had to have blankets the last two nights.

Marg's hay fever is pretty bad today— she couldn't go for a voice lesson.

Finally got my hair washed yesterday & does it feel good!

Tom T. Jr. was turned down at Jefferson Barracks— haven't heard what for— but he is at home again.

Hope the apartment was not <u>too</u> dirty. Have you started the milk again? (Mich 1011)

Was the mail piled high?

Love—
Bess

[Independence, Mo.]
[July 24, 1942]
Friday—

Dear Harry—

I am afraid you won't get a letter today— After writing yesterday, I waited for Marg to go to see Stanley & mail it on the way & I waited so long it was dinner time— and I don't think any mail ever gets out of here after five o'clock. But you will just get two tomorrow— I enjoyed getting two yesterday— so I hope you will do the same tomorrow. It is getting cloudy & looks muchly like more rain. Still coolish—

Your letter sounded as if there was <u>plenty</u> to do the minute you arrived. Guess <u>everybody</u> wanted to shift a bit of responsibility.

Marg's hay fever was really bad yesterday & she spent most of the day in bed— but is better today.

What have you decided to do about having Annie May come back to clean? I surely hate to think of you living there in a more or less dusty place.

Do you know whether the Irvines have left or not?

I have just called again about your button & the girl in the office says the presser says it was in the lapel when he pressed it— so now she is checking on the girl who put the suit in the sack. The button-hole does not look as if there had been anything in it during the pressing process— but he may have taken it out & forgotten to put it back. I told the girl I'd be glad to pay some sort of a reward for its return. I wish to goodness I had taken the time to go thru that suit before it left— I most certainly would have seen it— but I just grabbed it up off the floor & took it downstairs as I started to the city Mon. morning.

I have a pile of ironing to do before going to K.C. so had better start on it.

Clarence Swenson died yesterday— I am ordering flowers from Sands. Looking for a letter soon—

Love—
Bess

Washington D.C.
July 25, 1942

Dear Bess:—

Well it's a better day, two letters from you and one from Margaret. Have a telegram from Brewster this a.m. wanting us to come to Maine on Aug. 14th to help launch tea merchant ships on the 15th. He wants you to sponsor one of them. I will send you the telegram as soon as Millie gets the answer off. I rather think we should go. Brewster has been one of my wheel horses on the Committee.

It has been raining since yesterday evening about nine o'clock. I rode the bus out to Nebraska last night and ate at the chicken place— not chicken, but roast beef— started to walk home and almost got caught in the rain and it's been going good ever since. Went to bed and right to sleep and didn't wake up until 7:30. Guess I was pretty tired.

I canceled my date with Mrs. Atwell. Had Millie tell her I was going out of town. Also told Mrs. McLean I'd be away the night of her dinner. Too much society to suit me. Maybe I'm nutty but I can't see anything to those people but a bunch of drunks and parasites, most of whom would be better off in some institution. And they are not conferring any favor on me by asking me out as one of the animals for display purposes. I've got a job to do and I'm going to work my head off to do it and maybe it'll help save the country for our grandchildren— if we have any and that's all I care about.

Tell Margie I'd sent her a letter on the same day she mailed me one. Also tell her the *Missouri* is still to be launched. So she'd better commence braking [*sic*] bottles on the corner of the barn so as to be in practice. So had you if you go to Maine. Love to you.

Harry

[Independence, Mo.]
[July 26, 1942]
Sunday

Dear Harry—

The one thing I have wanted to know about is whether your glasses have come and if so, what they are doing for you— and then I forgot to ask you Thurs. morning. Let me know—

Was surely hoping you <u>would</u> call this morning— but you sounded so tired.

What about the Snyders? Are Evelyn & Drucie not coming on at all this summer?

Another thing I've been wondering about is how C. Clark and Mallory (Melletts) or whatever his name is are staying out of the draft so long? You had better <u>tear up this</u>.

Had a letter from Harriette saying Mary Louise is engaged & is going to fly to Havana on August 18— to be married. She is just sick about her not waiting to see Leighton. I'll send her letter as soon as I answer it. I saw in the morning paper there are still 2,000–3,000 Americans in China. Do you think L. is <u>undoubtedly</u> on his way home?

Some of the family are going to town so will get this off. M. & I are just starting to your mother's.

Love—
Bess

Washington D.C.
July 26, 1942

Dear Bess:—

[…] If you have any turnip seed they should be sown today— I forgot to tell you over the phone. This also is Nellie Noland's birthday. She must be sixty two or thereabouts but I guess she won't tell you.

I came on home to get the special but it failed to come through— too much rain I suppose. I've been listening to the newscasters and reading the editorial and columnist comment on the war and it gives me the dumps sure enough. The country would be better off if all the column writers were in jail and all the broadcasters were shot but I guess we can't do it.

There ought to be a smart government man who could give out facts in a series of one paragraph for each fact and the papers should use that instead of the columnist comment. The Pres. told Lister Hill and me that's what he intended to do— but you know the Pres.

Kiss my daughter. Love to you.
Harry.

[Independence, Mo.]
[July 27, 1942]
Monday—

Dear Harry—

I am sitting in front of Maj. Strickler's while Marg takes her lesson and it's a hot spot. Your <u>Friday</u> letter arrived just as I left home & am hoping for another one when I get back.

You really had a strenuous morning on Friday & I'm not surprised you lost your lunch <u>as usual</u>. Are you not having breakfast at home? I think you eat more at the Hot Shops etc. so I hope you are going out.

We had a nice visit with your mother & Mary yesterday and they went to The Granada to see "Ten Gentlemen from West Point."* It was <u>very</u> good— Historical as well as entertaining as it centered around the time Clay saved it from "oblivion."

Well, I am terribly afraid your button is gone. I called again this a.m. and also jumped the driver about it but <u>nobody</u> can find it. Sure am sorry. Isn't there any place at all you can get another one?

Have you heard anything more from H. Vaughan? Have you any idea <u>where</u> his new address is? Today's news sounds as if Aus. [Australia] may be in the thick of it again soon.

Lucy asked me down to supper last night but I couldn't stand a whole evening with the Dukes & K. Bostian & the Petersons— Mary was the only bright spot.

Helen has gone to Minn. to stay with Margaret Louise for ten days.

Hope the Higgins investigation doesn't prove too tough & keep you there. The *Star* suggested yesterday you might have a month's <u>informal</u> leave— how about it?

Love—
Bess

Washington D.C.
July 27, 1942

Dear Bess:—

The letter came just as I got back from Bill's dinner. Mrs. Boyle had a good roast beef dinner and Lou and I enjoyed it. Then she & Lou went to look at a couple of houses in the neighborhood which were for rent furnished. Thinks maybe he'll take one for a couple of months and then let Mrs. H. spend time looking.

I hope the dental work gets [*illegible*] out. I have been worried about

* 1942 movie starring George Montgomery and Maureen O'Hara.

the condition of those teeth. Please get the whole job done while you are at it.

Just let the shirts and bathrobe stay there. I'll leave here Friday night and get home Saturday night, too late to make a speech, Vote Tuesday and start back. I have a steel hearing on Thursday Aug. 6. Will have Higgins tomorrow. Kaiser and Land Wednesday and probably Douglas, Martin and the chairman of the Air Committee of the WPB on Thursday. Clean up my desk and the apartment Friday and start for home. The Washington papers are still giving the Congress the dickens and without justification. That psychological sabotage sheet the *Herald* had a nasty editorial by Waldrup yesterday and so did the *Washington Post.* Of course they want an anti Congress. They'd rather lose the war if that would discredit the President. Eugene Meyer owns the *Post* and the McCormack-Patterson outfit own the Chicago *Tribune,* the New York *Daily News,* and the Washington *Herald.* How they all hate the New Deal.

Kiss Margie. love to you.

Harry.

[Independence, Mo.]
[July 28, 1942]
Tuesday—

Dear Harry—

Your Sunday letter arrived this morning & Marg's letter & paper and money & we were glad to hear from you— Hope Monday's letter may arrive this afternoon—

It surely was nice of the Boyles to have you and Lou to dinner Sunday and I know you enjoyed it a lot more than anywhere else you might have had it.

Am going in to see Dr. Ollson this aft. He was the one who pulled my tooth for Dr. Hull. Hull is sick & this place is staying sore too long so O. said to come & let him treat it.

It's red hot again & I hate to think about going to K.C.

Nellie & Ethel & Jack started to the Ozarks early this morning— Mrs. R. is staying with your Aunt Ella.

We are having all the Platte Co. contingent over tomorrow for our annual luncheon.

I saw your friend Heinie on the square yesterday (for the first time) and he was a little coolish and I was no warmer. Did you tell him how keenly I appreciated <u>that letter</u>?

I quite agree with you about the columnists and commentators. I asked Fred what about the news at 10:30 last night— & he said it just depended upon which commentator I wanted to hear from— There were two entirely different stories at 9:30 & 10. So I chose the pleasant one— but the morning paper looks as if the other one was more correct. I can't see any hope except thru a second front— the psychological effect would be tremendous even if they can't wade all the way thru to Berlin in 15 or 20 minutes.

Lunch time & I must get off.

Love
Bess

Won't you be able to stay longer than you thought? The House seems to have folded up— Why can't the Senate?

Washington D.C.
July 28, 1942

Dear Bess:—

Well this day is a lot better than yesterday— two letters, Sunday's & Monday's. Yes the specks [*sic*] came. And they bother me much. Good to read with but I don't know whether I'm going to make out on the seeing part or not. You know I'm as bad on spectickles [*sic*] as George is on teeth. And I don't suppose I'll ever again get a fit like [*illegible*] gave me. I was tired Sunday but not now.

I am having dinner with John Snyder tonight and I'll find out about Mrs. S. and Drucie. They are not here now. Can't tell you anything about the Shields situation except what Breck Long told me. He said positively he was on the boat. I have been drinking tomato juice at home and eating at the Hot Shop & Senate lunch rooms. Had dinner at the Continental last night. Will eat somewhere with Snyder tonight and somewhere else with someone else tomorrow night. I did not start the milk or the paper because I'd just have to stop it again Friday. [...]

Glad you saw Mamma & Mary. There will be no month's vacation for me. My hearings start again on Aug 6, so you see what I get for getting in all the papers. My meals are staying down the last two days.

Love to you.
Harry.

[Independence, Mo.]
[July 29, 1942]
Wednesday—

Dear Harry—

As usual it's going to be a red hot day for the Platte City people to come to lunch— but I guess if we can stand it, they can, too.

I just saw the mail wagon man put our mail in the box across the street & it will be hours now before we get it. Here's hoping I get <u>two</u> letters this morning as your Monday letter didn't get here yesterday—

The *Star* gave you a column & a headline on steel yesterday. No doubt some over-zealous (including McHuselton) person will send it to you and you will also read it in the paper.

Am actually getting Marg off to take her piano lesson without too much of an argument this morning.

Dr. Olsson said my tooth operation is coming along normally but it sure is uncomfortable.

I hope you are all packed and ready to leave when this arrives— & we will be meeting you Friday evening at 6:30.

Have at least two million things to do—

Love—

Bess

Surely hope your laundry got back on time.

Washington D.C.
August 5, 1942

Dear Bess:—

Just twenty-five years ago today I was inducted into the service of the Federal Gov't as a 1st Lieut. of field artillery, N. G. [National Guard] In the opinion of the regular army, N. G. stood for no good. But it turned out differently. I was lucky, got to France fired some three-inch bullets at the Boch [*sic*], got home, got my sweetheart, went broke, became a politician and to some extent am putting a small finger into the next war. What will another 25 years bring? You answer, I can't.

It was nice to talk with you this A.M. Had an airmail from Mary after the doctor was there yesterday and things seemed to be in much better shape with Mamma. Hope you called her. I didn't think to remind you to but I'm sure you did. [...]

Hope your mother is still on the mend. She seemed much better Tuesday morning.

It is cool and cloudy here. Been sprinkling rain nearly all day. The girls have been out trying to see the Queen of Holland but have had no luck so far. She's late or lost or something. My desk wasn't piled quite so high as usual. Been dictating all afternoon and will be up to date tomorrow.

Kiss my baby. Love to you.

Harry.

[Independence, Mo.]
[August 5, 1942]
Wednesday—

Dear Harry—

You are just about pulling into Wash. right now if you are on time. I hope you had a comfortable trip.

I have just talked to Mary & she says your mother is better and ate a little more yesterday & Dr. G. is giving her a tonic but wants her to have mostly liquids for a while yet.

It looks as if we got a good trouncing in the county yesterday. I guess Mr. Sermon will direct the Court for two years anyway— I hear Roger T. was called Monday & is leaving for Leavenworth. I suppose they will send him back tho. on account of his ears.

Natalie & I are going to K.C. today— she is buying a coat (she hopes).

I hope things aren't piled up too deep in the office.

M. & I will probably go out to see your mother this evening if it doesn't rain— it's very gloomy this morning. Marg is going in town to have lunch with some prospective & ex-Gunston girls.*

Am sending that letter from Dr. Graham that I <u>put</u> <u>in</u> <u>my</u> <u>bag</u> Monday night & found it there yesterday afternoon—

Try to take care of yourself. I hate to think of you at home alone.

Love
Bess

Washington D.C.
August 6, 1942

Dear Bess:—

Was rather a hectic day. Had the steel hearing and it is a mess. A call came from old man Baruch saying he'd been appointed by the President to go into the rubber situation and that he wanted my help to get the facts. He was very complimentary to my way of doing things and told me he also might make a steel investigation along with mine. The *American Magazine*** wants to interview me on the situation. I told 'em I'd take it under advisement. The Columbia Broadcasting Company wants me to open a roundtable for them tomorrow on the situation. I may not do it and then again I may. Jimmy Byrnes was over at the Senate today and told

---

* Gunston Hall School in Washington, DC, a private girls' school from which my mother graduated in 1942.
** A monthly magazine published from 1906 to 1956.

me I'd better make the broadcast. I think that's what he came over for
because he said the husband of his only and favorite niece was the man
who is putting on the broadcast.

The Queen of Holland was a nice old lady. She made a good speech
and was very gracious to all the people around her. She spoke rather bro-
kenly but it was understandable. Maybe you heard her because all the net-
works carried it. My steel hearings will continue all through the next week.
Hope a solution can be found but I doubt it. We are surely balled up.

Was most happy to hear Mamma is better. I've had a hunch all
along she'd get over this attack. Sometime however one will get her.

Kiss Margie. Love to you.

Harry.

[Independence, Mo.]
[August 6, 1942]
Thursday—

Dear Harry—

Mary called up early this morning & said she thought your mother
is very much better today— She ate a good breakfast & seemed to enjoy it.
She is sitting up just for a few minutes while M. makes the bed etc.

It is raining c + d [cats and dogs] today— Marg was supposed to go
to the lake for her lesson but it was raining so hard we put it off and are
waiting now until three to see what it is going to do—

Tell Millie I wouldn't object to some Air Mails.

You were mentioned twice over the radio last night— in connection
with the Higgins matter of course. But maybe you heard it.

How do you feel by this time? Hope the first hearing went off
alright— and that the others won't be as much of a job as you think they
will be.

That's interesting news that Mr. Baruch may be drafted for Rubber.

This is ready to go— so must get this off.

Love
Bess

[Independence, Mo.]
[August 7, 1942]
Friday—

Dear Harry—

I am sitting on the Strickler Terrace— and for a change, it's raining—

I talked to Mary just before I left home and she said Dr. G. [Gra-
ham] was out last night and thought your mother so much better he

wouldn't come back for a week, unless they called. Mary said she is enjoying her meals and is eating much better.

There was some editorial in this morning's *Times* about you. I had to read it twice to be sure I wasn't "seeing things"— I will try to get home in time to put it in this letter— It was about that Higgins matter.

Will try to write more of a letter tomorrow— the rain is about to get us.

Love
Bess

Washington D.C.
August 8, 1942

Dear Bess:—

Well the letter of the 6th was in the first mail. Sure glad to hear that Mamma is able to sit up. Had a letter from Mary but she didn't tell me about her sitting up. Hope you & Margie made it to the Lake all right. It is pouring down rain here this morning and has been ever since I got up.

Bill Boyle and I went to the radio station last night and made the steel broadcast. We seem to have made quite a stir with that statement and with the whole steel investigation.* Bill said some of the boys were in this morning and told him that dozens of people down the street thought what I said over the radio should have been said but that no one had the nerve to say it. They were newspaper boys. The *Saturday Evening Post* canceled the story they were to print about me by Nye's Secretary after the steel investigation started. Now the *American Magazine* is preparing an article on me and the committee for publication on October 6th. Perhaps they won't use it either.

Thanks for the election returns. Old Monty still makes me angry. I suppose we'll have to be nice to the new political boss of Jackson County but we don't have to vote for Montgomery. It goes to show just what an old [*illegible*] can become a saint when he does the *Star*'s bidding. Please check the enclosed & mail it.

Kiss Margie. Love to you.

Harry.

---

* The steel investigations concerned allegations that Carnegie Steel was turning out defective steel for use on American battleships.

[Independence, Mo.]
[August 8, 1942]
Saturday—

Dear Harry—

Your talk last night was very good— what we heard of it. KMBC
didn't carry it at 6:30 but after fishing, we found you at 580— & heard
about five minutes of it. Then at 7:15 Mary called & said you were on
KMBC so we heard a few minutes of that. Wasn't it <u>quite</u> a compliment
that you were asked to be on that program? Fred said he couldn't remember but one other person making a talk on *March of Time.*[*] He said your
introduction was wonderful— they were in K.C. & heard it there.

I didn't get a letter yesterday but I know you were mighty busy on
Thurs!

I didn't get back to town until too late to get this clipping in the mail
yesterday— We had lunch at the lake— Maj was home all day— and we
took a long boat ride in the afternoon— & didn't get home until almost six.
We had a nice day & the sun came out halfway around noon.

Do you think you can finish up the steel hearings next week?

I have just talked to Mary & she said your mother sat up to eat
breakfast & had some bacon added this morning. Said she felt just fine—

Mother seems a lot better and is getting around the same as usual.

Just had a note from Harriette & she is so distressed about M. L.
[Mary Louise] leaving. Guess it would be right upsetting to see your only
daughter flying off to marry a boy who is not even an American citizen—
especially in these times.

Hoping for <u>two</u> letters today.

Love—
Bess

[Independence, Mo.]
[August 10, 1942]
Monday—

Dear Harry—

Had a big thrill this morning— two letters!

I am all dressed— ready to go to Mr. Dudley's funeral— <u>for you</u>— I
called Geo. & he is going with me— I sent flowers of course— Surely am
glad you took those few minutes to go see him in July.

Talked to Mary about noon & she said your mother was having
lunch in the kitchen! And that she sat up quite awhile yesterday & was

---

[*] *March of Time* was a weekly radio broadcast produced by *Time* magazine that used actors,
sound effects, and music to reenact news events.

not tired.

Surely was glad you called yesterday— it makes the Sundays a little shorter.

Just got back from the funeral & found your Sunday letter here. Am glad it cooled off over the weekend— I had just had a note from Mrs. Halstead & she was howling about the heat earlier in the week.

There was a pretty good turnout at the services— but it would have been a mess without the Masonic end of it— The preacher was such a dumb bunny. I saw Alex Sachs there.

Shall I write checks for Bundschu $17.13— Cairns $4.08— Hazfelt $1.38— & White Rose $5.45— & Jaccard's $31.67 (that's for those five wedding presents we had to send <u>last month</u>) or shall I send the bills on to you?

Starting to rain for a little change— & a really chilly breeze has started up. Am glad you knew where the blankets were.

Geo. says a lot of Republicans voted in the Dem. primary— so that explains some of Boss Sermon's success. Don't you think Mother can quit trading with the skunk <u>after</u> we leave?* She & C. [Christine] would like to do most of their trading at a Chain Store. It is surely <u>much</u> cheaper. Why, now, should he get $100 a month out of our family?

Geo. & May are having their house painted— Is Geo. apt to lose his job in Jan'y? I wish to [Hades] we <u>could</u> elect H. Sturges— He would be more agreeable than that wretch Montgomery.

Have I told you Lorene Gans married on June 27? She had been going with Mr. Martin <u>fifteen years</u>. She did about as well as we did— wouldn't you say?

Time to get this in the P.O.—

Love—
Bess

Washington D.C.
August 11, 1942

Dear Bess:—

Well tomorrow is Mary's birthday. I wrote her a letter & I am sure you and Margie sent her something. I know how you all feel about Roger. I was pretty much put out myself. But— and there is a but I still have some political use for him. You remember when Shannon almost pulverized me in 1924 when the young lady was very young? Well times came when Shannon was very useful on occasion and Rog hasn't done

---

* Mayor Roger Sermon, a political enemy of Truman's, also ran the local grocery store.

me half so badly. Of course George won't get fired nor anyone else in that office. We'll keep all our people in the Clerk's office and I'll manage to keep most of the court boys too you'll see. If old Marty should accidentally happen to get beaten it might make things somewhat easier— and that may happen but it's too early now to talk of it. I can't tell your folks where to trade and they've quit him before. They should use their best judgment. Right now Mr. Sermon has the best house but those things wear out you know. You pay the bills including Taylor's which I sent you and send me a list so I can keep the bank account level on my book. Went to Bill's for dinner last night. Had fried chicken. Had a black out at eleven o'clock just as I got into bed. Took my suits to Longs and sent the laundry this a.m. Fred Canfil is in town and we are going to see Fred Whitaker graduate Friday. Then I'll go to Maine. Been going like a house on fire.

 Kiss Margie. Love to you.

Harry.

[Independence, Mo.]
[August 11, 1942]
Tuesday—

Dear Harry—

 I thought I was going to have those last three teeth out today but Dr. Olsson had something else come up so it is postponed until Thursday— That's a "break" for me as the Stricklers asked us to stay to dinner tomorrow night— fried chicken dinner at the yacht club down the lake— & wouldn't that have been tragedy for me with three front teeth missing?

 It is <u>really</u> chilly this morning— blankets were muchly in demand last night. Some of your "cold snap" must have moved westward.

 There is talk of a contest in the county— for Fleming & Phillips.

 Your steel hearing must have been <u>something</u> to get on the front pages of all <u>those</u> papers. Am glad you have decided to go to Maine— I think you will enjoy it and it will get you away from the grind for awhile anyway.

 Mary just called and said the Dr. had just left & said your mother is <u>fine</u> and can dress in another day or two. Am glad he is keeping a watch on her as he promised you he would.

 M. is going to town & I want to send this by her.

Love—
Bess

Grandpa in a plane, right
where my grandmother
always wished he wasn't, in
1943 (TL 59-408).

Washington D.C.
August 12, 1942

Dear Bess:—Your ghost walked again last night. I was very sure I heard
you come in from the hallway. But it was only a delusion. It's a mighty
lonesome place out there I'll tell you. Bill Boyle's twin brother's wife is on
the point of death at Ft. Riley and he is going out there today. That's going
to leave me short-handed sure enough. Catherine is off for the week, but I
guess we'll make out. When I leave for Maine we'll be in it sure enough.

I'm sure sorry to hear of Ed Dudley's death but we expected it. I'm
glad I went out there and I'm glad you went to the funeral. From now on
I guess we'll spend a lot of time going to funerals of people we've known.

I adjourned the committee for a while. Will go to Maine and then
try to get caught up and come home to bring you all back. Hope those
teeth are getting fixed as they should.

There are a raft of Missourians here and they all want to see me.
And the things they want usually can't be had. Hope you and Margie
are enjoying as cool weather as we are. It was warmer yesterday but has
clouded up again this morning.

Keep writing. Love to you

Harry.

[Independence, Mo.]
[August 12, 1942]
Wednesday—

Dear Harry—

Just about to get off for Marg's lesson— so must make this brief— I

don't know <u>where</u> the morning went to— guess the washing & ironing I did took up most of it— and then did some marketing etc. (<u>at the
Safeway</u>).

Am hoping for a letter this afternoon— the three notes were in the
morning mail but no letter.

I haven't even had time to call Mary today but I <u>know</u> <u>she</u> would
have called had your mother not have been alright.

I answered this note of Miss Kerr's & told her to use her own judgment so I don't think you need to do anything further about it. That's OK
with you, isn't it?

The large desk for the study hall (which was done over last March)
might be a <u>very</u> good thing. So—

Everybody is fine here— Heard you mentioned over the radio again
yesterday— Don't you ever skip a day?

I forgot to tell you I got that note off to Sen. Brewster (Dexter). Are
you still leaving on Friday?— It seems to me it's a lot more important
to go there than to see F. W. get his commission— Am glad he got thru
alright.

Noticed by K.C. *Star* Hale Faris is getting married. She sure is
good-looking.

I wish you were not going to do all that <u>flying</u> in Maine. Can't you
skip the air fields?

Must get off—
Love—
Bess

[Independence, Mo.]
[August 13, 1942]
Thursday—

Dear Harry—

Am breaking my neck to get off to K.C. to have my teeth out—
(such a pleasant thing to look forward to) so this <u>will</u> be brief. You
probably will be on your way to Lee before it gets there anyway—

I am very sure I <u>should</u> be in W. [Washington] to help out in the
office if possible. Am so sorry about Bill's sister-in-law— Couldn't C. be
called back until Bill returns?

Am enclosing a note from Lelah Knox.

Hope you have a nice week-end—

Give my regrets all over again to Sen. Brewster—
Love
Bess

Washington D.C.
August 13, 1942

Dear Bess:—

Tom Vanzant [Van Zandt] is sitting here talking to me. I've threatened to fire all the girls because there is no letter. Guess the planes are held up.

I've had one hectic day. Fulton to start with on the steel program—then Jim Mead on a political speech he wanted to make to the Senate and which he wanted to help him in New York. Fulton and I sat beside him and kept him in line and he made a good speech.

Then they gave me the bad news about making a radio speech at Portland on next Sunday at noon that will be on a national hook up and be on a short wave to Great Britain for the extended period of 4 ½ minutes. Well I guess I'll have to do it.

Then at 2:30 I gave Mr. Batt the gun from a to izzard and he took it and begged for more and the interview was at his request.

Maybe we will get some results. He was talking for the whole War Production Board, Mr. Hopkins, Gen. Somerville et al. Some interview I'd say. Your old man is coming up in the world I'm afraid. Don't know if it will work.

Please send me two letters tomorrow. Fred and I are leaving for Richmond in a few minutes to see Fred Whitaker made a 2nd Louis [lieutenant] and will be back here at 1 p.m. tomorrow.

Bill's on the way to Ft. Riley & Fred C. is substituting for a few days. Kiss Margie. Love to you.

Harry.

Washington D.C.
[April 16, 1943]
Friday—

Dear Harry—

Am afraid this will be late getting in the mail today. I got busy putting things back in place after my new Senegambian [person from West Africa, around the Senegal and Gambia Rivers] cleaned yesterday. She did all the kitchen cabinets & I'll <u>never</u> get dishes & glasses back where they were. She does a pretty good job at cleaning tho. & Mrs. Ricketts says she is a good cook— so I hope I can hold onto her. She's the one who had lived with Mrs. Sasser (203) for twelve years & they fell out over the sugar coupons!

I am enclosing a note Mrs. V. sent— copy of some of H's letters about whether you & John should attempt to get him home— in answer to the one she sent him asking what <u>he</u> thought about the idea.

It's cold and windy— I do hope you will find lots of sunshine in Hot Spgs.

Leighton took Marg & me to the Statler Tues. night to dinner— We had a very fine time & M. got to dance <u>once</u> anyway.

Hugh Fulton sent a huge shipbuilding report out & wanted me to read it. Just why, I couldn't say—

Marg <u>floated</u> the width of the Y.W.[C.A.] pool yesterday with her head under water— so I believe at least there is some hope for her. She is going back today, voluntarily, to practice!

Hope you get the best of news from the clinic report.

Had lunch at Mrs. Boyles' yesterday & played bridge— Mrs. Holland & Garrett's wife & Don Lathrom's wife were there. Lou & she are going back to K.C. on the 28th. Garrett is in the Army at Camp Meade.

Take care of yourself—

Love
Bess

Washington D.C.
[April 17, 1943]
Saturday—

Dear Harry—

I want to get this in the morning mail— otherwise it won't go until 7:30— so this will be brief.

I've spent most of the early morning <u>getting</u> <u>ready</u> for a nig to clean the bedrooms & now at 9:45 she hasn't turned up— Guess the showers we are having were too much for her.

It sure was fine to talk to you last night— but I was so dead asleep I probably sounded groggy.

Marg & two other girls are going downtown to lunch & a show this afternoon and I'm going to P.E.O. and <u>going in the car</u> if this rain keeps up.

Marg is going to a show tomorrow with that McConike boy who was out here last week—

Mrs. Ricketts brought me some potatoes! from the country yesterday— There isn't an Irish potato in any store in town &, the paper said yesterday, none in town until the last of May.

Now, whatever you do, go to the Hospital & have a checkup— and <u>get plenty of sunshine</u>. I wish John could have gone down with you— but maybe you will get more rest <u>alone</u>.

Time for p.m.

Love
Bess—

Washington D.C.
[April 19, 1943]
Monday—

Dear Harry—

I didn't get a letter off yesterday— didn't get up in time to get it in the morning mail & knew it would do no good to get it in the later one.

Was glad to hear your voice & to get your special later on.

Hope to goodness you can <u>really</u> get a rest.

Millie sent the *Globe Dem* article & it <u>really</u> is <u>fine</u>.

Fred Whitaker tried to call you last night— but I didn't know who it was until after he had canceled the call. I think I would have told him where to get you— I didn't find out where he was— we had [a] very poor connection & I could scarcely hear the operator at all. Thought maybe he was at some port of embarkation. He may try it again tonight.

It is simply pouring. I wanted to go downtown but don't think I'll try it.

Marg & Jane had a nice afternoon & evening with their Sigma Nus. Marg's date & another boy came home with her around ten & stayed until midnight. She was plenty sleepy this morning.

Mrs. Ricketts bought me some potatoes from down near Warrenton! I probably could sell them for their weight in platinum.

The candy hasn't arrived yet— but will get a hearty welcome when it <u>does</u> get here.

I'm going downtown to send your mother & mine some Fannie May for Easter.

Time for pickup—

Love—
Bess

Washington D.C.
[April 20, 1943]
Tuesday—

Dear Harry—

The sun is shining this morning (at least halfway) after a horrible yesterday, so I am going downtown to buy my Easter bonnet. I <u>hope</u>.

Your candy came late yesterday & we surely feasted last night. It's unusually good & we are really enjoying it. John S. [Snyder] called yesterday— & said a Mr. Turley (?) of St. L. was having a dinner last night & wanted me— but it was <u>Monday night</u> so of course I couldn't go— not that I wanted to much anyway.

Eddie and Harry Jobes called too. Eddie will be here all week but

H. J. is leaving Wednesday.

I opened H. V.'s [Harry Vaughan's] letter so I could tell Mrs. V. what he had to say— She was in bed with a cold but came down to hear the letter.

There doesn't seem to be any news so I'll get off before the crowds pile into the stores downtown.

Love—

Bess

The morning *Post* says Cong. probably will adjourn from July 4 to September 1st!!

Washington D.C.

[April 21, 1943]

Wednesday—

Dear Harry—

Was glad to get your <u>Sunday</u> letter this morning— Your <u>Monday</u> letter came yesterday— It looks as if they have the same sort of mail service there that we have here. Or perhaps it all happened here— who knows.

What did the heart man say about you? I notice you skipped <u>that</u> report.

It's chilly today after a big hail storm at bed time last night.

Mrs. Ritter asked me to lunch today at Pierre's. She may <u>think</u> she is going to get me actively interested in MRA but if she only knew!

I have the candy ready to go— I put Mary's name on your mother's package, too.

I thought maybe this clipping might not be in the Ark. papers—

Bill called yesterday— said to tell you there was nothing of importance on deck & wanted to know if there was anything he could do for Marg & me. Said Hugh was leaving for the West Coast— he thought Wallgren was going too— but I guess you know what that's all about.

Hope you are really resting—

The candy is still being enjoyed!

Love

Bess

[Independence, Mo.]

[June 14, 1943]

Monday afternoon—

Dear Harry—

Mother & Marg & I have spent most of this hot day in K.C. Mother got some of the things she needed before going to D[enver]. I picked up the tickets etc. They were all ready for me and we should have a <u>very</u> comfortable trip. I wish you were going along, tho. <u>You</u> are the one who <u>needs</u> that sort of trip.

I surely hope you are having a more pleasant day in OK than we are here. It must be a hundred in the shade. Frank insisted upon us using his car so it could have been worse if we had had to use the bus.

We had a nice little ride last night. Went down to see the flood— It is still pretty high—

An invitation to "Polly" Compton's daughter's wedding came this morning so that means a present for us as well as for Marg.

Mize & Ann brought the baby up yesterday evening for Mother to see her. She's a cute little thing & has red hair. I found out that Chas. Mize died of pneumonia after an operation.

Could you send me one of the clocks without hurting it? Also my white shoes. I don't know how I forgot the shoes— They need working on & I think I can have them fixed up & save my good ones.

Had a letter from Harriette & she is returning the book to you at the office. I think the Koos have gone back to London so I don't know how you will get it to her. Maybe L. knows.

Hope to hear from you tonight.

Love
Bess

Afterword

When I was young, I viewed my parents and grandparents as peas in a pod. They seemed to agree on everything. They backed each other up. It never occurred to me that they might tease or annoy one another or otherwise misbehave, especially since we were talking about a radio and television personality, the managing editor of *The New York Times*, and a former U.S. president and first lady.

I should have known they were human the day in 1969 that my forty-five-year-old mother climbed up on the roof of the house in Independence, with my brother and myself in tow, and completely discombobulated my grandmother and the U.S. Secret Service. But it didn't sink in for another twenty years, when I came into possession of one of my grandmother's letters, the first one I'd ever seen that didn't have my name and "Merry Christmas" or "Happy Birthday" on it.

In 1974, when I was seventeen, two years after my grandfather died, my grandmother came to visit us in Washington, DC, for Christmas. The morning after she arrived, I came downstairs to find her in the breakfast nook and my mother at the stove, making bacon and eggs. I poured a bowl of cereal and milk and sat down.

At that point, my hair was long enough that I could tuck it in my shirt pocket. My grandfather had been horrified by this. He hated long hair on men. In the 1960s, when a man with long hair approached him on one of his walks and said, "Good morning, Mr. President," Grandpa immediately came back with, "Young man, you'd look a lot better if you saw a barber." When he saw me with long hair at age fifteen, he could barely bring himself to speak to me.

That morning in the breakfast nook, however, my grandmother looked at me and said, "My goodness, you have beautiful hair." Across the room, my mother dropped the spatula and roared, "Mother! For God's sake, don't tell him something like that! Now he'll never get it cut!"

True. The next time my mother suggested a trim, I said, "Nope. Bess Truman likes my hair."

Years later, after I had bored scores of people with that story, the Truman Library gave me one of my grandmother's letters. It was mailed on April 17, 1972, to Mrs. Kenneth Bostian of 907 South Main in Independence, Missouri.

In it, my grandmother thanked Mrs. Bostian for a box of oranges and grapefruit she'd sent from Miami and lamented that Grandpa hadn't felt up to visiting Key West the previous month. She appreciated Mrs. Bostian's letter ("the longer the better") and some clippings that were included. She apologized for not mentioning earlier that a mutual friend had died, then.... "I am really sorry Nellie Post has to contend with all those hippies," she wrote. "It does seem time something was done about them. When I saw my two big grandsons with long hair at Christmas time, I almost expired. But they were clean and had on decent clothing."

God knows what the hippies did to bother Nellie, but it turned out that my grandmother hated long hair on men every bit as much as Grandpa did. But she was willing to overlook it just long enough to annoy my mother.